SECRETS
SHE
HOLDS

SECRETS

EXPOSING

SHE

THE TRUTH

HOLDS

ABOUT MARRIAGE

SALOMÉ M. CRIDDLE

A catalogue record for this book is available from the British Library.

ISBN: 978-1-9196496-0-3 (paperback)
ISBN: 978-1-9196496-1-0 (e-book)

Grandma Edwards, thank you for sowing into me throughout some of the most difficult parts of my life – you are such an inspiration.

DOES HE KNOW?

§

Every wife has a secret. Behind the masks that we wear and the façade of our perfect marriages lies the painful truth of all the sacrifices that we have had to make for love. What is yours?

This book will unveil it all… including yours. The vision is to bring your secret into your awareness, give you the tools to resolve it and step into a life free from repression. So, whether you have lost yourself, fallen out of love, struggle with finances or resentment, your secret is written here, in black and white. This book will inspire you to grow, laugh and cry while taking you on a journey of self-discovery that will free you of your secrets. Be prepared to expose those hidden places in your heart that have gathered dust for so long. Embrace your life-changing transition to unearth the Queen within.

I have come that they may have life,
and that they may have it more abundantly.
— John 10:10 (NKJV)

CONTENTS

Acknowledgements   x

Introduction   xii

1   Secrets… Does He Know?   1

2   Reaching Breaking Point   32

3   Who Am I… Again?   46

4   Drowning in Emotional Waves   86

5   It's the Thought That Counts   108

6   I Had a Dream… Once   132

7   What's Your Fantasy?   158

8   I Don't Love My Husband   186

9   Strained Relationships and Family Feuds   206

10 Money Matters   246

11 Cheated and Broken   268

12 When Marriage Is Killing You   296

13 Life After Marriage   324

14 Secrets That Save   342

    Conclusion   348

    About the Author   350

ACKNOWLEDGEMENTS

§

I have to honour the true visionary behind this book, who has used me as a vessel to run with the vision: thank you, Jesus, for it all. My life, the lessons, this book would be nothing without you taking the driving seat. I am honoured to be along for the ride and look forward to the rest of our adventures.

Paul, our bond's depth is immeasurable, so I will just say that it's such a blessing to be your wife. Thank you for dreaming with me, covering me, inspiring me, filling in the gaps for all the other responsibilities and making sure that this book looks really pretty! You have championed me and fuelled my journey. You believed in me when I wanted to give up. It all makes sense now. Thank you for loving me the way you do and being patient when this book was all-consuming. I love you deep.

Ezra and Boaz, thank you for being my greatest inspirations and one of the underlying reasons that I had to finish this book. I know one day you will see this, and it will be an example of what is possible when you step into everything that God calls you to be. You are my joy. I love you both so much. I can't wait to see the wonders that God unpacks in your life as you continue to grow!

Mum, thank you for the lessons that you taught me. You are a true woman of valour. I love and appreciate you. Thank you for your unwavering support and investment in this project. I am honoured to be the daughter of someone who has such a beautiful heart and love for others. I want to be like you when I grow up! Haha!

Special thanks to Sue, Julie, Sandy, Natalie, Esther, Lindsay and all my lovely friends who have been bold enough to give this baby a test drive! Thank yooooooooou! This book would not be what it is without you.

All my love,

INTRODUCTION

FINDING YOUR SECRETS

§

Every wife has a secret. It may not be detrimental to your marriage or relationship, but it needs tending. Allowing your secrets to fester stops you from living in complete truth and ultimately giving your best to your marriage and family. Some secrets can even cripple the best aspects of our lives. There are many ways that secrets come about. I want to address the secrets that occur due to perpetuated cycles, surrounding circumstances, disconnect from God and not being able to foresee the consequences of the decisions that we make. We all find ourselves having to course-correct from time to time. It's the nature of growing and learning. When we receive the life lessons that God teaches us, face our fears, secrets and hindrances, we can't be held ransom or hide in the shadows – always nursing and protecting our secrets instead of letting them go. We have a choice, and we can choose to live a lifestyle that relinquishes shame, regret and façades in exchange for freedom, clarity and direction. There's nothing more liberating than knowing what you want and knowing where you are going. I write to provide the tools that will give you that clarity – that strength to take what is rightfully yours.

I have been a wife for over seven years, and I speak honestly when I say I have found aspects of this journey quite difficult. I wrote this book because it is something I would have loved to have received at the beginning of my marital journey. I wrote from a candid and open space, knowing that there are many other wives out there who find the journey through marriage turbulent. If you're determined to be in it for the rest of your life, then it's going to take countless moments of soul searching to ensure that you don't lose connection with yourself. This book has been written to help you nurture yourself throughout this life-changing experience that we call marriage.

I am a Christian, and many of the practices and the philosophy I'll be sharing are based on the principles of my unwavering faith in God. Whatever your walk, perspective or spiritual journey, I'm sure you'll agree that marriage challenges us all. We all have to find the strength to face ourselves, and no one can make the journey for us. This book has been written to be a great source of enlightenment and direction to owning our greatness, liberating ourselves and living life at its best. Please don't allow your personal beliefs and experiences to hinder you from discovering the impactful principles you will receive from this book.

It may not be something you are deliberately withholding, but it is definitely something that you don't actively share with your husband.[1] Whether it is fulfilling your dreams, creating more happiness or focusing

---

[1] All references made to wife/husband and/or spouse refer to any person in a long-term relationship in which there is commitment and/or children.

on your wellbeing, there is something in this book for every woman who is a wife, has been a wife or is expecting to become a wife.

The contents of this book may be challenging at times, albeit incredibly rewarding. You will need to be brave enough to coach yourself to get through the reflective and challenging aspects in the most honest way possible. Remind yourself that you are reading this book because you deserve to live a better life, one without regrets and free from shame, secrets and hiding. This book is your invitation and aid to your own personal victory, and it could be the catalyst for your marriage's success. I would encourage you to go and spoil yourself at the end of each chapter. Buy yourself some chocolates, flowers or even a piece of jewellery for doing the work. Show yourself the appreciation that you deserve. We are all born to be loved and to love others in return. However, if you're not loved by the one that you want to love you back, then be (to yourself) what he is not able to be. Know that you are never alone and that, with God on your side, you have everything you need. Build your confidence and strength. Tell yourself the words that you wanted him to say. Feed yourself only good things, because that is where your strength will come from.

Above all, remember to tap into your innate God-given strength as you journey through this book. You can do "all things through Christ who strengthens"[2] you.

---

[2] Philippians 4:13 (NKJV)

How to Use This Book

In the following chapters, we'll explore:

Secrets... Does He Know? (Chapter 1): The nature of secrets, their impact on your marriage and what constitutes a loving relationship.

Reaching Breaking Point (Chapter 2): The reasons marriages reach breaking point; the part you have to play in it and how to navigate a way forward.

Who Am I... Again? (Chapter 3): What happens when you have an identity crisis, how it affects your marriage and family life, and how to take ownership of your life.

Drowning in Emotional Waves (Chapter 4): The impact of fluctuating emotions; the ties between depression and emotional turbulence; and how to identify and find emotional healing.

It's the Thought That Counts (Chapter 5): Identifying how your thoughts and mindset play a part in your marriage and how to develop mental wellbeing.

I Had a Dream... Once (Chapter 6): How to rekindle old passions and unearth new ones, so they work in harmony with marital and family life.

What's Your Fantasy? (Chapter 7): How to identify and heal any painful or dark urges – whether they are festering, lingering or intensifying.

I Don't Love My Husband (Chapter 8): Falling out of love with your husband. How your feelings have impacted your marriage over time and whether you could fall in love with your husband again.

Strained Relationships and Family Feuds (Chapter 9): How to deal with fallouts, alienated friends, breached boundaries and uncontrollable conflict.

Money Matters (Chapter 10): Why money, and your financial personality, can harm your marriage; discover how to find a healthy perspective and improve your money management.

Cheated and Broken (Chapter 11): How to find healing and move into new growth levels after feeling cheated and being cheated on.

When Marriage Is Killing You (Chapter 12): How do you heal from abuse? When do you walk away? Relinquishing your fear of the future and forging a path forward if your marriage ends.

Life After Marriage (Chapter 13): Finding healing after a marriage ends, having a healthy mental approach to the future, overcoming the stigma and shame that comes with separation and divorce.

Secrets That Save (Chapter 14): Knowing when to shush, the power of your tongue and the secrets that you should keep; learning to influence by the words you use.

So, what is your secret?

When you find it, go directly to that chapter or, if you prefer, read from the first page to the last. Either way, every gift imparted to you is designed to challenge, inspire and liberate you. Embrace your growth fearlessly and boldly. This book focuses on *wife life*, but you may find that the principles will guide you through life's mazes outside of marriage. Just prayerfully journey through this book and be revitalised by the nuggets of truth and inspiration that are liberally shared.

You can also read this book (and be enlightened about wifehood complexities) if you are engaged. However, if you are engaged, please don't view this book from the perspective of taking thousands of notes to dodge the invisible bullets that may come your way. Every relationship is unique, and yours may not experience all the secrets explored in this book. Just extract all the wisdom that has been written to enlighten and encourage you on your journey to a lifelong, enriching marriage.

You may find it useful to keep a journal by your side as you read. I've created journal sections throughout each chapter to give you support during your times of reflection. You will see the following box:

JOURNAL

- A list of questions will appear here.

At the end of each chapter, you will see this mirror:

The purpose of the mirror is to remind you that you will only grow through self-reflection, by looking at those areas of yourself, your life, that are ripe for growth and development.

Within this mirror, you will also find the prayers relevant to the chapter topic. Use these prayers as a guide to inspire a deeper connection to God, to grow and reflect – just as you do when looking at your reflection in a mirror.

REFLECTION

ONE

SECRETS… DOES HE KNOW?

§

She stood a few steps from her new future.

Hopeful and dazed.

Love drunk.

All her hopes and dreams summed up in two words: "I do."

She proclaimed in response to the vows spoken by the Officiant.

The days, hours and minutes she waited to stand before the man that she would now call her "husband". The plans that she had for them both.

How happy they were going to be…

Well, at least that's what she once thought…

Days, weeks and years passed after the vows were spoken, and even she knew… something was wrong. So very wrong. She thought marriage would be a fairy tale. A *happily ever after*, she thought, that would save her from the pain that ate away at her soul. She was wrong.

This wife may be you to a lesser or greater degree – the woman behind the false smiles, façades and immaculate makeup, posing on social media with her beautiful husband and family. The one that so many people wish they could be. Yet, you might wish that you were not. Weighed down with secrets that paralyse your soul. Muzzled by rouge lipstick and the perfect dress (or not). Trapped in a narrative that you didn't create. Stuck on a train taking you to a destination that you didn't choose. Afraid to call for help yet afraid to stay silent. Afraid to stay in this state but afraid of being judged. Your family and friends probably told you that this was the right thing to do: get married, honour God and have a beautiful family. Or, maybe he said that if you left, he would *break you*, or is it what he doesn't say that frightens you? You might feel that you literally can't survive without him. And what about the children? How could you leave him and cause them so much pain and confusion?

Marriage looks so beautiful from the outside, but it is a maze for so many. A honeytrap. A glorious mistake. How it builds and how it breaks. A simple choice? Definitely a life-changing one.

I can almost hear the voices of the women trapped in the pain of their secrets. They call to me, saying, "Write the book, Salomé. Write my pain. Let my freedom be birthed from the healing words that you bring to my silent struggles. Speak my truth and ignite my journey to healing. Help me heal from the pain of the decisions made a long time before I took my vows. To find healing and to love completely without walls."

The only thing I ask is that you open up. Let your walls down. Cry. Weep. Let your makeup run and mirror the imperfection of your soul. Look at your pain without deflection. Don't recoil or retreat. Your healing is in your ability to face yourself. You have to journey through the darkness of the pain to break through to the light of your healing.

It's time to stop hiding the wounds within your soul and expose them. Whatever secrets you have been hiding must come to the surface so that you can begin the process of breaking free of them.

Does he know?

Does he know… you smile during the day, but when he's asleep, you cry?

Does he know… you don't love him anymore?

Does he know… you fantasise about things that would terrify him?

Does he know… you don't want to live anymore?

Does he know… he's never been enough for you?

Does he know… you no longer wish to be married?

Does he know… your faith has changed?

Does he know… you miss your single life?

Does he know… your sexuality has changed?

Does he know… you married him for all the wrong reasons?

Does he know… you hate his friends or family?

Does he know… your desires, hopes and dreams have changed?

Does he know… you wish you had another life?

Does he know… you wish that you never got married?

Does he know… you are no longer physically attracted to him?

Does he know… you still haven't forgiven him?

Does he know… you feel unfulfilled and misunderstood within your marriage?

Does he know… marriage stole your dreams, and you resent him for it?

Does he know… your greatest fear is living the same way for the rest of your life?

Does he know… you are terrified of him?

Does he know… you previously had greater loves and feel like you're settling with him?

Does he know… you've never gotten over your ex?

Does he know… you're not the same woman he married?

Does he know… every time he touches you, you can feel the hands of your abuser?

Does he know… those soul-crushing voices are still inside your head?

Does he know… he is the reason that you are insecure?

Does he know… you're still grieving the loss of a loved one that he has never accepted?

Does he know… you blame him for the finances or business going wrong?

Does he know… you've cheated once or have been cheating on him?

Does he know… you're struggling with an addiction that is crippling you?

Does he know… you're spiritually engaged in something that has damaged you?

Does he know… you don't trust him?

Does he know your secret?

Does he even know that although you're married, you're still incredibly alone? Isolated by overwhelming pain? Or is he living obliviously in a lie that your marriage is something different to the truth of your situation? He seems weightless, but your heart is heavy. He seems to float on high while you crumble below. Or maybe you're both smiling but broken inside: *this is the way our marriage will always be*, or *I can handle it.* Is this the lie you tell yourself? You may feel like you can handle it right now, but the truth is that you were not built to carry such heavy matters of the heart. The truth is that you have complicated something that you can make simple.

Choose the Mask or the Mirror

In life, you will always be challenged to make one of two choices: hiding behind a mask (or multiple masks); or embracing the mirror – the truth of who you are. You can hide your shame, flaws, unhappiness and discontentment behind the mask of *a great life*, but over time, it may choke out every ounce of your identity, leaving you hollow and unfulfilled. If you choose to face yourself, to expose the wounds, then you can heal.

> *When the cool evening breezes were blowing, the man and his wife heard the Lord God walking about in the garden. So they hid from the Lord God among the trees. Then the Lord God called to the man, "Where are you?"*
>
> *He replied, "I heard you walking in the garden, so I hid. I was afraid because I was naked."*
>
> *"Who told you that you were naked?" the Lord God asked. "Have you eaten from the tree whose fruit I commanded you not to eat?"*
>
> **—Genesis 3:8-11 (NLT)**

This account from the Garden of Eden reveals that our human, natural instinct is to hide when we feel vulnerable or exposed. There can be great fear in revealing the nakedness of our pain and secrets. Sometimes we apply a mask when we feel exposed to the expectations of others. Sometimes we don a mask to conform to a particular social, traditional or religious system. Maybe there's a sense of hoping that it will save us from judgement, rejection, or it makes us feel *safe* to hide. But there is a point at which the mask becomes suffocating and hiding becomes a curse. Hiding can save and rob you at the same time. How do you know what your true face looks like if you never look at it? How do you know your true identity when you spend your life in the shadows? Eventually, something's got to give.

Healing comes when you ditch the mask(s) and face the mirror. Face your flaws, your shortcomings, your reality, your identity and your secrets. Could there be a chance that *they* may fall in love with the version of you that you're trying to hide? As we journey through this book, I want you to think about the masks you wear and relinquish them in exchange for the mirror. Instead of making it a habit to hide, make it a habit to reflect and to improve the areas of your life that require tending. Let's start with the truth.

> **JOURNAL**
>
> ◆ What is your mask?
> ◆ What triggers my impulse to hide behind my mask?
> ◆ What truths do I need to acknowledge about myself?

First Steps into Awareness

The first step to becoming free is to admit that you don't have the answers and that you are flawed. The beauty of our flaws is that they give us some of our greatest lessons if we are willing to learn from them. We are all flawed, but while on our growth journey, it's important to recognise that our failures are not the whole story. Maybe there are many factors that you were unable to control, but true wisdom is making the right decisions to thrive. From this very moment, make a promise to yourself that you will do what it takes to grow. No more hiding, fear or worry – just boldness and a determination to move forward with a desire to heal. What secrets are holding you down? It could be something simple, like sharing a budget, or something more complicated, like the statements written above. It could even be a secret so heavy that your relationship may change once you share it. One way or another, that secret overwhelms you, and the reality is that you can no longer carry it. You were made to thrive, my friend.

As you continue to read, you'll find "good secrets" and "bad secrets". The good secrets lead to the most fulfilled marriage that you could ever experience. The bad secrets could damage everyone and anyone in connection with your marriage.

They say that in marriage, two become one, and it's a space where everything is shared: homes, cars, families, children, bodies, secrets. In a fallen world, fear rages – that Adamic instinct to be naked and ashamed; to be naked and rejected. In a world overflowing with masks and deception, the truth seems costly. Expensive. Unsafe. The shadows hide the pain, or so it seems. Really, it's a wound that festers and infects and spreads to the core of your being, paralysing everything that you hold dear, operating in silence. As you nurse your secret from a seed, it can become an uncontrollable monstrosity that threatens to strip away all the potential beauty in your marriage and life.

I have to share with you the brutal truth: marriage should not look like this. It has never been God's intention for your marriage to disintegrate into this level of dysfunction. Marriage isn't something that you should struggle to maintain or keep up with. It's not something that you should have to shuffle through in the hope that if you settle on the side lines, things will magically sort themselves out. Marriage takes time, truth, work and dedication. It takes determination to win *together*, to look back over your life and say that you're glad that you stayed.

Even though it was hard, you didn't give up but waited for better days to come. You may have to go through some of the darkest nights before you see the dawn. In some seasons, it may feel like you're not going to make it. Rest assured, the dawn will come, but you will have to push for it.

Maybe your marriage will end because you shared your struggles, and he couldn't handle them. Maybe you both have already let it completely die. Maybe he doesn't want to make it work, and you are unable to convince him otherwise. That's not within your control. What is in your control is your releasing yourself from the pain that you've been carrying. You may have to unshackle yourself from the fear and shame of being exposed and trust that it will work out. The truth isn't always pretty, and that's why some call it "the ugly truth". However, the truth is *necessary* for your life, healing and sanity. You've been suffocating for so long, and now it's time to breathe. It's time to experience a freedom that you have never known before. Share the truth of your pain, whether your husband is willing to work it through with you or not.

You commit to your own growth and progression. Share your truth and be free to fully embrace your healing. Face your pain by allowing yourself to be immersed in it. It is only then that you can fully embrace absolute freedom and be transformed by and impervious to the darkness that once consumed you. You are a super conqueror in the making. You just haven't realised that you are about to fight, and win, the greatest battle of your life – the battle for your heart, mind, soul and joy. It's going to be the fight of your life because your life depends on it.

Honey, it's going to be so worth it.

Some things are just too big to handle alone. We can't always work through them overnight. Sometimes it takes many years of grafting to realise that life just hasn't been what we had hoped that it would be.

Can we make it right? Can it get better? Can marriage be revolution-ised? Whatever you tell yourself is going to be your truth. If you believe that you will never live your best life, then what you believe will be-come your reality.

The good news is that your life can absolutely blossom. The not so good news is that it may be the hardest fight of your life. Your jour-ney's toughest aspect may be that your husband may not want to fight for the marriage anymore. That's the point where you have to start fighting for your own growth and healing. You deserve to be with someone who values your worth, and who would fight relentlessly for you. The brutal truth is that you can't make him do it. If his heart doesn't belong to you, then don't try to use the tools in this book to make your marriage something that it will never be. Instead, use the tools to build a stronger, flourishing and better version of yourself. A woman who isn't fighting for someone who doesn't recognise her value, who loves fiercely regardless of rejection, who lives a Christ-centred life, who doesn't seek revenge and isn't bitter. You're so much better than that. You are GOLD.

I'm sure you already recognise that a healthy marriage isn't one weighed down with secrets. It's seeing the person for *the truth of who they are* regardless of whether you like it or not. It's saying, *I see your "ugly side", and I love you anyway.* It's bringing out the King and Queen in each other. It's being a team and not competing against one another.

Relationships take a lot of work, graft and nurture to thrive. It's possible to love being married but simultaneously dislike elements of marriage. You can even want to make your marriage work and be frustrated with it at the same time. It's also possible to be in love with someone but not like them. The sex could be phenomenal, but when you get out of that bed, you could literally be living separate lives. That's the greatest robbery and will stop you from living your personal and marital life in abundance. That's absolutely dysfunctional and goes against the purpose of marriage. The words "separate" and "marriage" are not even compatible in the same sentence. Marriage is about loving one another and LIKING one another. Do you have a friend in your husband? Can you share your deepest pains, secrets, hopes and dreams? Marriage is all these things. Marriage is about believing that if you win, we all win. It's not *yours* or *mine*; it's *ours*. It's comforting your partner through the loss of a loved one. It is being their rock at their darkest days and moments. It's always acting with good intentions, even if you make mistakes. Please be careful; this statement should not be used to manipulate anyone. For example, a partner with an abusive, manipulative or narcissistic personality can use the above perspective of everything being shared to emotionally manipulate you for their benefit. Pay attention to red flags: tendencies to control or situations where you give more than you receive. These are great indicators that the above perspective has been taken out of context.

What Does a Failing Marriage Look Like?

Have you ever looked at a painting in a museum and thought, *that picture is stunning*, only to find a plethora of cracks and imperfections when you looked up-close? I can imagine that the feeling of awe and amazement swiftly disappears, with a strong sense of disappointment immediately taking its place. Not quite the perfect picture that you once thought it was, right?

We all can see an obvious breakdown in a marriage when the couple no longer wants to even be in the same room. There are, however, failed marriages that can be just as deceptive as the museum analogy that I have just shared. A marriage can still look like it is thriving but be as empty as a hollow tree. Divorce is not always the conclusion of a failed marriage. Marriages die all the time, and the couple remains married. Sometimes both individuals know the marriage is no longer working. Other times, being left or presented with divorce papers can come as a surprise. Marriages can fail anywhere and everywhere. Some are obvious failures, and others burn slowly. A lot of marriages fail in a variety of ways and for a variety of reasons. Some failures are abrupt and swift; other failures happen over a prolonged period. It's so important not to compare your marriage or judge based on what a couple *looks like*. I'm sure you've heard comments like, "They look so good together" or "They look so in love!" You never know what is happening behind closed doors and what that couple that you admire, is going through.

There are so many marriages that are like a lofty oak tree with dead roots. They look great to the beholder and even dependable. Sometimes the parties of that marriage have no idea that the roots are dying. Lack of attentiveness, the busyness of life, time and other distractions can cause couples to drift apart and eventually lead to a breakup. However, if the foundation is stable, then the marriage can last a lifetime and impact generations.

> *For God so loved the world that He* **gave** *His only begotten Son.*
> **—John 3:16 (KJV)**

When you love, you give. One of the most popular scriptures in the Bible provides us with a powerful truth about what is required for a marriage to have a long-lasting impact. It also describes what is absent from a failing marriage. A failed marriage is a selfish one. That's *yours*, and this is *mine*. My house, my money, my car, my children. Why marry someone whom you aren't willing to share everything with? The popular wedding vow "All that I have I give to you…" further emphasises the purpose and nature of what it means to be married. The gospel of John[3] reveals the vision of what perfect love should look like. Although these are not the words that have been written into the vows of some lovestruck couple, they have been the proven successful formula of the greatest love that we can ever encounter.

A major part of marriage is serving and giving to your spouse. You give the best that you have as an expression of that love. It tells your beloved, *I trust you. I am dedicated to this union. It's the price of love.* If you didn't want to pay that price, then the single life should've been your first and only port of call. It takes graft to make marriage a success – two people giving to each other, supporting each other and, yes, serving each other. It's falling and trusting that the other person will catch you. To have this kind of love and trust, you've got to pay attention to who you're marrying before you say those vows. If you said those vows ahead of making the necessary observations, you might have to work through the overlooked areas with your husband. That is, of course, if your husband is willing to do the work with you. There is a price to pay for making decisions in haste and without truly weighing up the cost. Marriage changes you forever, for better or for worse. Although it may be difficult to work through, I do believe that it is possible to make positive strides and to see change. It doesn't necessarily have to be a lost cause if you are both willing to move forward together. If this is the case, push through, do the work, persevere and be patient with one another as you grow.

Pay close attention. Listen to your husband's heart and mindset. Selfishness should not be a prominent aspect of their character. Love

---

[3] John 3:16 (KJV)

is selfless. It's putting the other person's needs before yours every single day. It takes understanding and knowing who you're married to.

That being said, I believe that there should be a healthy balance between selflessness and showing up for yourself. Otherwise, how can you give to others from an empty cup? The cup has to be filled first before it can be dispensed. Make the time to build yourself up so that you can be a blessing to others.

Many marriages fail because they were neglected from the beginning. In contrast, some marriages start out healthy but eventually, like a plant that goes unnurtured, wilt and die over time. In a failed marriage, no one pays attention to the foundation and the details, like how your partner treats his family, how he spends his money or how he responds when you ask about the pain of his past.

Inevitably, we will change and develop throughout our marriage. External factors, such as the death of a loved one, weight gain or loss, or change of income can affect your marriage. The change could even be of a spiritual nature, like the connection with God or spiritual disconnect. We all need spiritual nurture and stability. Our spiritual foundation is a fundamental compass to meaningful and intentional living. I believe that if our spiritual foundation is the roots, then God is the rain. Dynamite happens when the two connect. When our spirits connect to God, we become fully functional, which has such a powerful impact on our marriages. Without God, our spiritual lives can easily be directionless and unfulfilling. When you're grounded spiritually and drawing strength from your Source (God), you will then have the strength to build on your relationship's weaker facets. Listening to your partner's heart will give great indicators of whether or not your marriage can be preserved.

How do you hear your husband's heart? You pay close attention to what he has to say. Whatever comes out of his mouth is what will tell you who he is. If you know me, you know that I am a complete chatterbox, but my husband, Paul, is not. So, I have learnt to listen without intending to reply. To hear what he is saying and not what I *think* that he is saying asking questions without making assumptions.

Men are typically less talkative than women, but I have learnt that if you create opportunities for dialogue, then you're more likely to make progress. It takes time and deliberate focus to nurture every facet of your marriage. Our job before marriage is to look at the roots and ask ourselves questions, such as, can I trust this man with *everything*? If the horse has left the cart, then damage control is necessary, but it's crucial to take ownership of your part in the failure or strain of your marriage. You may ask, *why are you talking about what happened before I got married? Does that really matter?*

Yes. Self-evaluation is important so that you can make sure that you are not perpetuating cycles. In the past, you may have failed to observe closely enough. Maybe you failed to observe your weaknesses or his. Maybe you didn't take the time to get to know him, or you didn't truly understand what it takes to be married. It could be that you didn't take the time to make God the centre, or your spiritual connection to God wasn't strong when you said your vows. You will eventually see very clearly where your marriage has failed and whether it can be strengthened if you take the time to be brutally honest with yourself. It is possible to revive your marriage *if* your husband is willing to contribute to your marriage's healing. Even if he is not, it is possible to build on your own healing and have a fulfilling *life after marriage* (see Chapter 13, *Life After Marriage*).

The Vision of a Healthy Marriage

So, what makes a healthy marriage? Is it a façade or perfection? Manipulation? Being aggressive, violent or beaten up? Is it belittling, shaming or character assassination? Is it exploiting the shame or pain of your partner? Is it leaving your partner financially crippled?

Absolutely not! None of these things constitutes a healthy and happy marriage. If your marriage looks like any one of these, then you have to assert your worth, seek help and alienate yourself from anything that is going to jeopardise your mental, physical and emotional health. That being said, we live in a time when people don't even bother to work things out. If it's broken, we don't fix it – we just throw it away! This generation lives in what I call a "fast-food mentality" or "get everything quickly". But when we focus on get rich quick, get married quick, get divorced quick, we miss the beauty and richness of the rewards that come with long-lasting marriage. I find that when you get anything quickly, without working on that thing, it's usually too good to be true.

I am attracted to the succulent slow roast of a lifelong marriage. Grounded and deeper than anything that lies on the surface. I really don't know what the rush is all about. I've learnt that crucial decisions are best made very slowly, reflectively and strategically. I want to grow old with one man (namely Paul), leave strong foundations and a legacy for my children and descendants. I don't mind being challenged by the flaws that marriage may flag up. I like that my marriage holds me accountable for my actions and challenges me to grow. It means that I have to be self-aware, assessing the consequences of my actions and decisions. I am mindful that my choices have an impact on everything that surrounds me. Most importantly, I believe that my marriage is divinely orchestrated to make a positive difference to those around my husband and me.

A successful marriage will always have two imperfect people working together. They're not better than the couples that got divorced because they made their marriage work. They are just as imperfect.

There's just the absence of a façade and the complete acceptance of who the other person *is* and not who they think the person *should be*. It is dangerous to try to mould another person into who you think that they should be or to overlook who they have always been all along. It's easy to walk into a marriage with both eyes completely shut, only to find that they are abruptly forced wide open in the future. Especially with husbands, they tend to be deep wells and usually less overt about their emotions. It takes a wise wife to listen closely to hear what isn't being said. It takes a loving and attentive husband to show his wife that he is without fear when she searches his soul. It obviously goes both ways. It takes tremendous strength to be vulnerable and lay your soul bare.

Marriage isn't for the faint-hearted, and it actually isn't for *everyone*. Marriage takes selflessness and sacrifice – so much so that if everyone is thinking about each other, then no one gets left out. It's about being united as a team. Marriage can sometimes mean that you are considered last. It's about servanthood over being served. It can mean pressure and perseverance over pleasure. It goes beyond euphoria and erotic acts. It's about seeking to know and be known. Marriage takes grit and shaking off your pride. It's more about developing character than ticking off a to-do list.

If you're unwilling to build your character within the role of being a wife, then your inability to grow may suffocate your relationship. I could say that it takes so many more characteristics to be in a successful marriage, but I want to emphasise that it is more about capturing the essence of being a wife than following a bunch of rules. It's a mentality shift. It's taking out *me* and replacing it with *us*. It's growing in the nature of Christ, who is the author and creator of marriage and who marriages need to imitate. Like Christ, we love when our husband seems unlovable (and vice versa), we intercede and carry weight, we *give.*

Don't get me wrong, marriage to the right person will bring so much joy, fun, pleasure, happiness and the like, but without selflessness, which creates strong foundations, the marriage may not stand the test of time. We all know that couple that has been married for 40, 50 or even 60 years. If the marriage is strong and vibrant, then you will find *selflessness* there. They grow together and understand each other. Their focus isn't their own selfish needs, but their life partner's interests. They don't run when it gets hot. In fact, the heat brings them closer together. When that family member died, they were holding hands. When they lost everything, they remained united. They were resolute in their character, in their faith and in their marriage. *Nothing worth getting comes easy.* When it comes to a great marriage, the principle remains the same.

It's so important to understand that the principle, the idea and the vision of marriage came from our Heavenly Creator Himself. It wasn't something that the government made up, and there can be no variations of the innovative concept of union in marriage, no matter how much the world tries to rewrite the script. There is a mystery to marriage; its oneness creates worlds and lives. Marriage is the backbone of communities, societies and creates stable environments if it is successful. When marriage is unsuccessful, it brings hopelessness, pain and confusion. Commitment to marriage brings structure and balance. In children, it helps them to understand the value of structure, authority and unity. A healthy marriage is physical proof of the phrase "we are stronger together". Not only are we stronger together, but we can all flourish as a result of the healthy marriages that surround us. Marriage should never be trivialised or taken lightly. It is an invaluable gift and a beautiful mystery that God has given to us – His reminder that we, the Church, are His Bride, and in the success of our marriage, we reflect this truth.

Self-forgiveness

Did you have a part to play? More importantly, can you forgive yourself for the wounds your mistakes have inflicted – the wrongdoings that have led you to the current situation, whether it is a result of not owning your truth or whether you just let life batter you from pillar to post? You may have made wrong decisions, or you may have just reacted to circumstances that were out of your control.

Whatever the case for you losing your "good fight", I am talking about that honourable and resilient stance to push through those hard places in your life and marriage with an assurance that you will come out with your *win*. Maybe you feel like you weren't paying attention or made an error in judgement regarding your marriage. Whatever the case may be, it's never too late to learn from our mistakes and course-correct. The benefit of experience is that we gain wisdom from the lessons that we learn. Amazingly, we have so many great opportunities to grow and allow our experience to contribute to the blessings that we have. I hope that this book is a catalyst for the change that you want to see. I pray that it guides you to a life free of the pain and the weight of your secrets. May you be inspired to venture into a whole new world pregnant with the possibility of abundant freedom. Allow yourself to feel the pain of regret that comes along with making the wrong choices. Let the pain of regret course through your soul. Take a deep breath. The purpose (of reckoning with your pain) is not to make you feel like you are trapped in guilt or shame but to feel the burn within your soul that compels you to progress.

Start by apologising to yourself. Acknowledge your self-neglect when you chose not to speak up for yourself. Make promises to yourself and dedicate yourself to fulfilling them. Be okay with saying "no" or "respect my boundaries" whenever you feel like you're being mistreated. Move from that place of regret and commit to the positive and fruitful lifestyle changes you make as a result of this book. You can even say out loud, "I apologise for not nurturing myself before entering this marriage. I apologise for continuing to mask my pain. From this day forward, I will take care of my mind, body and soul. I won't let anyone or anything near me that will damage or cause me harm."

Recognise that you let down the person who needed you the most, and that may be a part of the reason that this journey has been so difficult. The biggest person you let down is not your husband or your children, friends, foes or anyone in between but – *yourself*. It's honestly okay to weep about it. When you weep, you let all the pain and tension leave your body and your soul. God designed tears to speak up for you when you are lost for words. It feels so good to cry, doesn't it? Just let it all go. Especially if you haven't let yourself cry for so long, then the first step in being kind to yourself is letting yourself feel and weep. Grieve. Mourn the loss of the life that you could've had. Cry because of the choices that you made without considering the consequences. Your tears speak for you when words fail.

Our Heavenly Father understands every nuance of your pain. You are not weeping alone. It's okay to mourn the loss of **you** that never was but could have been. Acknowledge the pain, the flaws and the loss before you can move on into the person you are about to become. My Queen, this is the last time that you should cry for all the things that you have lost. From now on, shift your focus onto all the things that you are opening yourself up to receive. Focus only on your healing. Be determined to push past the pain, develop resilience that you never knew was in you and grind. Before you know it, you will be at the other end of this process and revealing all the treasures that lie dormant within you. I can't wait for you to shine like the Queen you are!

The Reinvention of You

When you nurture your soul, when you talk with God (I mean real dialogue, which means *listening* too), when you reflect on your own journey through life, you start to become a more formidable woman. Someone who thrives and is a force to be reckoned with. Someone who allowed her pain to shape her into an unbreakable woman. Someone who has flipped the script and is no longer bound by the pain or shame. Someone who is conquering life and not being conquered by it. No more apologising for your existence, because you know that you're here on this planet to make a difference. When people see you, they should see the light that exudes from your soul. You deserve to be here. Your laughter should be hearty and deep. Your shoulders should be squared, and you should be rich with goodness and the possibility that everything good flows to you. The truth is, you have to embrace the possibility of new growth. Believe in the embers of faith stirring deep within as you reflect on the fact that change is possible – because it absolutely is.

Some secrets scorch the soul. Some secrets are hard to bear. They weigh you down and cause you to become stuck in a spiritual state of paralysis, always worried about being found out or not being able to move forward or even going round and round in circles. You may consider the things (that you keep close to your heart about your marriage) too trivial to be categorised as "secrets". Ask yourself, why don't you want to share those trivial things with others? Are you concerned that others may look at your marriage and think that it is in trouble? What about that feeling of being exposed or found out? The fateful words "I knew it!" confessed from the mouths of your friends and family could immediately have you running in a cold sweat. So many people wish to have what you have, even if they don't realise the price that you had to pay for it every single day. On the outside, marriage looks so good. For instance, many singles seem to think that couples have sex all the time and that there is always someone to confide in. The reality is that every marriage is different (as we know). It's easy to be in a marriage and be alone. It's easy to look so close and be so far apart. The fact that you're reading this book shows that there are things that may be pushing you both further and further apart. You may be acutely aware of it, or it may have hit you like a brick in the face, but there is a great awareness within you that something in your marriage needs to change. Here's an opportunity to do some soul searching and have some very truthful conversations with God about the condition of your partnership and marriage.

JOURNAL

- What is the state of my relationship with God?
- Do I feel like improving my connection with God will make a difference in how I see myself?
- What improvements do I need to make to my self-awareness? How will the awareness of myself improve my identity?

Obviously, the aim is also to be a supportive, happy and fulfilled wife, but it all starts with you. You'll be surprised what discoveries you'll unearth about who you are and the nature of your marriage on this journey. We all need to take this walk from time to time. It starts with how you see yourself. What value are you adding to your marriage? What value does your marriage add to your life? You take the journey so that your life can be fulfilling and abundant. Enriched. So much so that when you come to the end of it, you can smile and know that your marriage was enriching for you both and had a great impact. You're building a marriage that will leave ripple effects on every generation after you and those close to you. Most importantly, you're in a marriage that makes you both happy. After all, I am sure that's why you got married in the first place.

No Is a Beautiful Word

Here is the hard part. Let's start with what you need to say no to. Is it living a lie, family traditions, or removing yourself from a particular social circle? Do you have triggers that make you slip back into negative states or addictions repeatedly? Is it a lack of discipline? Or just riding the waves of how you feel? Do you pull your husband along on a rollercoaster of negative and toxic behaviour? Be honest. Save your husband by saving yourself. What do you need to let go of? What do you need to change to be at your best? You can be your own worst enemy if you do not learn to win the war against your self-sabotaging impulses.

We must be determined to overcome the cycles that we perpetuate, toxic habits and the self-destructing mentality that has caused our lives to spiral out of control. We can be the cause of our own downfall when we build up fears and have a lack of faith. When we believe the lie that our previous experiences are the truth over God's word; when we believe that the pain of our past can happen over and over again; when those fears trigger defences and negative perceptions of the world around us, it prevents us from walking in the abundance that God has provided in every area of our lives. It is silent and violent. Every time that we try to claw ourselves from the ashes of our pain, there it appears again – the enemy within. It's the thing that prevents us from having enriching, deep and fulfilling relationships with everyone around us. It's the thing that creates a spiritual blockage from our connection with God – distraction, fear, pain, resentment, holding on to the pain of past experiences and lack of faith. Yes, that enemy has the potential to choke the life out of your marriage if you let it. The reality is that history will be blocked from repeating itself if you are able to identify and kill toxic patterns.

Every day is a fight for all of us, regardless of whether we declare it or not. Some are more victorious than others, and that's simply because they understand that they can't win if they fight alone. If we are going to win this war against this silent, deadly enemy (that is, ourselves), we will have to partner with God. It takes an incredible amount of self-control, but with God, nothing is impossible. Accountability is also incredibly powerful – to be able to confide in someone about your journey, struggles and pain. It lightens the load of our journey, and there is also the added bonus that we are supported in our pursuit of being better. The end goal is life: transformative and impenetrable life that enriches the very core of who you are. A life well-lived, reflective of a winning woman who has the prowess of a lioness – someone who doesn't let life push her around because *she* does the pushing. Become a woman who has found her fight and is relentless in pushing through to an enriching life.

It was Christ's mandate to act as your agent of change. He is the reason that we have a blueprint to abundant life. He said, "I have come that [you] may have life, and that [you] may have *it* more abundantly."[4] Or, as another great version puts it, "My purpose is to give

---

[4] John 10:10 (NKJV)

them a rich and satisfying life."[5] So, in essence, to live and not just exist must be the ultimate goal. A life where you don't just pretend to be fulfilled but truly are fulfilled. Does that mean that you have a weird smile on your face all the time? No, but it does mean that you genuinely don't wish that you were someone or somewhere else 24/7. It means that you are not physically worn down by family life or that weariness doesn't creep through every line or crack on your face. It means that you sleep better at night and that you cry less. *A lot* less. It means you live a life that is free of shame and hidden things.

It takes so much effort to hide the secrets that weigh on the soul, especially when you've been hiding for a long time. You deserve life at its fullest, and this truth must be something that you conceive within your heart before it becomes a reality. Whatever you tell yourself is your truth; whatever you allow to sink into your mind, heart and spirit and what comes out of your mouth –that statement that you repeat regularly – is your reality. Be intentional about the words that you make your reality. Glean your value from everything positive, uplifting and fruitful, especially the word of God. Allow it to strengthen your spiritual core so that you have support through those really difficult times. Don't make this a journey about what your husband is or is not doing but more about what you are doing to enrich your life and marital experience.

I understand that there are extreme instances where you may not be able to stay within the marriage. We can definitely talk about that later. Right now, I'm talking about your nature and approach to wifehood. That's not actually conditional upon whether or not you stay with your husband or not. That's a heart condition. Your heart's condition is what matters most. It matters most to you where you are

---

[5] John 10:10 (NLT)

heading and, most importantly, it matters to God. Can you pray for your husband even when he's broken you? Do you want to see him heal and heal yourself regardless of the outcome of the marriage? Can you work through the pain that you have caused and take ownership of the part that you have played in the unravelling of your marriage? Your approach and heart towards your husband will speak volumes about where you are headed. There's something so liberating about knowing that you gave your best to the situation and that you showed honour regardless of how hard things got.

The pain of your experiences, the bewilderment and confusion can be overwhelming, but like the process of making wine, the pressing and the breaking are bringing something from you that will be so beautiful that you will be unrecognisable. Working on all the pain, fears, weak facets of your marriage and unearthing all your secrets will build you. At the right time, you will look back at this version of yourself and realise that you are no longer that person. You have outgrown that space, and even though you had to go through some dark tunnels, you now have a new appreciation for the sun. Don't despise the process, because it will be the making of you. No hate, bitterness, tit-for-tat, fear. No more mess! I celebrate that resilient, bold, stronger version of you.

What's Love Got to Do with It?

Love is everything, but not in the stereotypical way that people think. Love doesn't look like our feelings. Love looks like the everyday sacrifices that we make for our marriage; some are painful, and some are fun! Some leave us feeling short-changed, and others replenish us. It's truly a rollercoaster. It's great when we feel in love, but when the feelings change or evolve, how committed are we? Can we be the catalyst for turning the tide? Can we be consistent in watering the roots of our marriage to become deep, sturdy and strong? Can we stay through the hard parts? Make no mistake, there are definitely hard parts. Love can be complicated, but it is also rich and deep. It's taking the ugly aspects as well as the beautiful aspects of marriage. Love is loyalty. Love is raw. Love is progressive even in the stillness. Love is silently overpowering. Love is friendship. Love is funny and serious at the same time. Love is AGREEMENT. Love needs time.

Regardless of how well you think you know your husband, you will always need time to *understand*, because, trust me, men and women speak different languages. We are all wildfires when our marriages begin. We are hot with passion and expectant. We burn bright, and the desire we feel oozes from our pores until we can no longer be in the same room as anyone else but each other. In fact, some of us were super annoying to our friends and family because all we thought or talked about was how amazing *he* is. Be honest. We had tunnel vision for our beloveds. He was perfect in every way.

However, as the years go by and your marriage moves forward, the passion dissipates, and eventually, the cracks start to show. Just so you're aware, every marriage will have a crack or two. Maybe even more than that: some of the things that we once loved become annoying. Little things. Big things. Lots of things. It's so easy for the things that you refuse to say to start to build and become the elephant in the room. They are the secrets that need to be unearthed. The elephant in the room is why you should make the time to have the necessary conversations with yourself, with God and with your husband. It's the hardest thing to speak the truth but, even more, it's the saddest thing to live a lie.

For the record, all marriages are tested. Even Mr and Mrs Jones, whose marriage is always "perfect". You know the couple that always looks head-over-heels in love, happy, smiling. Façades are deceptive.

Some couples allow the pressure of being perfect to be the reason that they hide the truth. Others feel that they need to protect their spouse, while others don't know whom to turn to. Every single one of us has to work on our marriages for them to thrive. The marriages that are at their best have been tested... and proven; then they will be tested again. Honestly, that's just life. When you're with someone who actively fights *for* you, not against you, then you will find a joint rhythm in riding those tides that are thrown at you both throughout your lives. I write this to help you to recognise that you are not alone. As you read through the various sections of this book, I need you to be aware that there is a section here for *every* wife. We're all watering the fruits of our relationships, marriages, collective and individual growth with diligence, but it is not by our strength that they will flourish. It is God that will give increase and allow our marriages to flourish boundlessly. Through this journey, God is revealing truths about you and your marriage. Take the time to reflect, pray and talk to God. Trust that He will orchestrate the change that you crave.

Love Without Boundaries

Is it even possible to love without conditions or boundaries? Is it unrealistic to love in the way that the Bible describes it? If we are talking about boundaries protecting the parameters of respect that every one of us deserves within marriage, I firmly assert that unconditional love thrives upon setting boundaries. Boundaries help us understand how to love better, especially within marriage. Marriage thrives when both parties recognise and appreciate one another's value. They are then able to respect one another's boundaries. That being said, is it possible to see the darkest side of your spouse and still embrace them? I believe that we all love to a degree. However, I don't believe that humans, in their own power, have the potential to love unconditionally. We are fortunate to have God on our side who does not love in the way we do. His love is so much fairer, richer and true. He does not give up on us at the first sign of our ugly. We learn from Christ's Divine nature that all things are possible, including boundless love, even though we (in the natural sense) have limitations on how far the scope of our love can reach. His love certainly shatters limitations and shows us the value and importance of doing the same. Is it easy? Certainly not! It wasn't easy for God, either – to give up the best that He had, His heartbeat, in exchange for us.

Sacrifice isn't a pretty word, but I believe it embodies the nature of unconditional love, the decision to go without so that those we love can *have* and *live*. I look at the loved ones around me, and I realise that it's possible. I have done it so many times without hesitation for my husband and my children. I have *gone without* so that they can *have*, and I have done it without thinking about it. So, I know that somewhere inside of me is a dormant potential to love sacrificially.

The key question, before working our way to embracing the nature of sacrificial love, is how can we simply love better? Can we love in a way that allows others to trust us with their secrets? Can we be more understanding and see things from other people's perspectives? Can we be more patient, supportive, loving and kind? I believe that we can! We press towards the goal. We are deliberate about it and proactive in choosing to be that change. It is only through total dependence on the Holy Spirit that we can see progression, improvement and trans-formation in our marriages. I really don't have the view that love should make you timid, withdrawn and unable to assert your values, character and truth. Love is bold and fierce. When it is given relent-lessly, it is transformational and healing. If we could all learn to love this way, by depending on the One who already does (that's God, by the way), then we will truly be making a difference in this world.

So, as you continue to read the secrets of this book, ask yourself if you also have too many limitations on the way that you love. If so, how can you love better?

Prayer and Meditation

Let's pray and reflect using the mirror.

Dear Heavenly Father,

I open myself to receive the truth that I need to be freed from the weight of my secrets. Please stand by me through the difficult parts of my growth, regardless of how painful it may become. Give me the wisdom to navigate the pain of my secrets with foresight. To learn from every lesson my mistakes have taught me. To pay my dues and completely surrender to healing. May your strength truly be perfect in the places of my weakness.

In Jesus' name, Amen.

TWO

REACHING BREAKING POINT

§

> In the same home but worlds apart.
> Words are no longer spoken, yet so much seems to be said.
> Unified on the surface but crumbling behind closed doors.
> Waiting.
> Who will strike the final blow and call an end to this relation-ship?
> After all, it's something that they both so desperately crave.
> Beyond tipping point? They're not sure, but definitely beyond breaking point.

Does the strain of your marriage make you feel somewhat like a pressure cooker? Seemingly resilient, but as the temperature rises, a shrill cry seeps from every crevice of your soul. Broken by the pressure that you have no control over. Scorched by the pain that your relationship has induced. Love gone sour and all interaction becoming stale. At the cusp of complete breakdown and *almost* at the point of no return. What happens when your marriage feels like a never-ending marathon? When every day feels like you're barely holding on? You know deep down that one day, it will all come to an end, but right now, you're holding on to a glimmer of hope that maybe things may take a turn for the better?

Reasons to Hold On

Maybe there are reasons why you may be holding on by a thread. Let's look at some of these in turn:

I'm doing it for the kids: You know deep down that one day your children are going to grow up and leave home. What happens then? Even though they may no longer be directly affected, they may be more affected by the decision to divorce than you would actually think. Should your children be the basis for staying unhappily married?

My finances are going to suffer if I walk away: This is a very real concern. The question is, what if he one day decides to walk away? Where does that leave your finances? What is the real price of living a lie? Can you handle the repercussions?

We're more like siblings than a married couple: Hardly ever intimate. Separate parts of the bed, separate lives, separate worlds. Can you remember the last time that you even laughed at the same joke? Nowadays, you both seem preoccupied with the responsibilities and the humdrum of daily routine. Never truly connected. Lacking romance or the faintest form of flattery. Disconnected. At this point, it would be surprising if you had anything in common. The sad thing is that it almost feels like you're both waiting to be released from a prison that you have been held in for so long. The idea that your marriage could have a drop of chemistry left is laughable. You seem to have gone far beyond that, and this is your reality.

***

First love – deep, enriching and irrevocably entangled love. It felt like it would never end. It felt real, strong and unconditional. It felt like nothing would tear you apart. Seamless and without cracks. Now you're discontent and restless, frustrated with the state of your life. It's almost like looking at the world through shades of grey when you know that it should be vibrant colour. You sometimes imagine your life drastically improving without your husband. If you could just *find yourself* without the pressure of being attached to him, then maybe, just maybe, you'll smile harder. You may even sleep deeper, dress better or whatever it is! All you know is that life would be so much easier, so much better, without him. You just know that he somehow is connected to how you feel about the state of your marriage and lack of passion for life in general.

Abandoning Your First Love

Could *you* be the cause of your unhappiness? Could your pain or discontentment be harming your marriage? If you have no valid reason for wanting out of your marriage, if he is loving, supportive, honourable and doing his best, then my question to you is, what more do you want? Sparks to fly? A beefcake of a husband? What's making you so restless? If you've decided that you were no longer going to put effort into your marriage and no longer wish to build upon it, then why do you want to change it as if you're buying a new pair of shoes?

Every marriage loses its fireworks, no matter how many times a day that you decide to have sex. There's a familiarity that comes with years of marriage. You *know* the person so well that you can take it for granted. He stops chasing you and wooing you. You stop dressing up. The date nights are no longer tinged with an unspoken anticipation of what happens behind closed doors. The chemistry fades. Over time you no longer look at each other – I mean, *really* look into each other's eyes the way that you used to. If you ever have a chance to look into each other's eyes, what lies behind them is more like frustration than attraction. Do you even remember the very first time that you fell in love? The dedication that you put into your marriage? How the hairs on your skin used to rise as he touched the small of your back? The very first time that you made love? Your heart racing when he walked into the room? Or maybe you prefer not to remember, because all you feel is annoyed when you are with him. You crave a love that is deep, rare, rich and unconditional. However, the reality is that this kind of love is built from a sea of mistakes and forgiving each other over and over. It is built from failures, from pain and by two people that refuse to give up on one another regardless of how rough it gets or how difficult both people can become.

As the years of my marriage have gone by, I have realised that the more focused I am on my own little family bubble, the more likely it is that my *bubble of perfection* will pop. I have been a wife who has put pressure on her husband to make her happy. It was his job to woo me, his job to keep that spark going, his job to be the ideal so that we could keep this *perfect* little family together. After all, I prayed for this family. God blessed *me* with this family. Me, me, me, me, me. Everything was all about *me*. Nothing that focuses only on me blesses me. We are blessed when we serve a higher, greater purpose and meaning. It has always been God's heart that our lives, blessings, ministries and marriage impact others. What makes me happy in this very moment of my life is to see lives blessed due to my desire to give.

As I trust God with my life journey, I find true enrichment by shifting the focus from trying to make my bubble perfect. No longer do I spend my time trying to self-serve my blessings and happiness. Self-serving only leads to stale blessings that look and feel more like curses if I try to keep them to myself.

It is far better to focus on being a blessing and a light to others. Extend kindness to your husband even if you have to start with something gradual like leaving a note or a piece of cake for him before you head off to work. I am not suggesting that you sweep issues under the carpet or pretend that life is perfect, but never let difficult seasons kill the *good* in you. Trust God to work on the issues where your husband is concerned but, in the meantime, do your part. When you can accept that you are as flawed as your husband; when you can get to a place where your love will not be withdrawn at the faintest sign of his resistance; when you accept that he doesn't fit the criteria that you have in your head, then you know that you are on your way to nurturing a love that speaks volumes to the world. Yes, it is possible to exist on this planet and have true love.

It is possible to be loved beyond your flaws, mistakes and shortcomings because I have that kind of love. I give that kind of love. I am determined to give that kind of love for the rest of my life. It's the kind of love that I experienced from the moment I became aware of who my Heavenly Father is. I knew that He loved me so much that He sacrificed His best for me. He lost out so that I could gain. He taught me that this kind of love is possible. He teaches me every day how to reflect this kind of love to my husband. To give my best, even if there are times that it doesn't feel like it is good enough, even if there are tears in my eyes. As He pours into me, I pour into my marriage.

Is it easy? No. Do we ever feel like giving up? Yes. Life isn't always hunky-dory. Sometimes it's grit and pain. Sometimes the beauty of our marriage is shown through the push and struggle. We choose each other every day. We find something to laugh about. We flirt. We prefer each other over everyone else. We communicate with just a flicker of the eye. We make time to be together, even if it's just to have ice cream, watch a movie or get a quick takeaway. And yes, we do all the spiritual things together like worshipping, reading the bible and praying for all those who are wondering. We couldn't do all the other things without including God in the relationship that we have together. He is the foundation of love and marriage.

JOURNAL

- ◆ What is the cause of my unhappiness?
- ◆ Can my marriage be improved?
- ◆ What do I need to be happier within my marriage?
- ◆ What positive changes need to happen to improve my marriage?

Loving Unconditionally AND Setting Boundaries

When you know what love should look like, then this question is easy to answer. I believe that you should put this sentence the other way around. We set boundaries when we love unconditionally. Boundaries mean structure, and structure means growth. We establish boundaries to ensure that our love is strong and firm.

Having children has made me realise that even if they don't like the boundaries that I set, they are necessary to benefit their growth and wellbeing, to become stable and strong adults. It would be selfish to remove the structure because I feel bad when they look up at me with their big, gooey, brown, teary eyes and beseech me to be lax. I am looking ahead to the damage it will cause in the end.

I believe that every relationship needs boundaries to thrive. Boundaries are sustenance for the kind of love that flourishes. Boundaries say, *how can I love you better?* And *how can I understand and work with your needs?* We learn more about our marriage and ourselves as individuals when we have boundaries.

This process starts with asking yourself, *what do I need to ensure that I can give the best of myself to this marriage? What does my husband need to make sure that he can give his best to this marriage?* and then, working out how those boundaries can coalesce harmoniously. Sometimes this may mean compromise, but it always means understanding the needs of your spouse. Paying attention to the things that hurt them. When they are hurt, you are hurt. When they lack, you lack. You are one. I will make this clear. Establishing boundaries to preserve a healthy marriage only produces fruit when both parties are contributing willingly. You can't make him respect your boundaries and contribute to his. However, if you can share the value of these principles, then you just might be able to reach a turning point in your relationship. Be patient always. Focus on the good and always expect to yield the best fruit from your marriage.

> *Fix your thoughts on what is true, and honourable, and right, and pure, and lovely, and admirable. Think about things that are excellent and worthy of praise.*
> **—Philippians 4:8 (NLT)**

What does loving without conditions actually look like, and is it even possible? Loving without conditions looks like giving your best regardless of the outcome. Having the heart to serve and bless others even if they don't do the same.

Does it mean staying with someone who is a serial cheater? Not necessarily. Does it mean lying down and letting someone trample you into the ground? I don't believe that it is necessary to put yourself in harm's way to love unconditionally. I do believe that you have to condition yourself to love unconditionally. That means that you are always cautioning your heart from wanting to retaliate when wronged. It means not allowing yourself to be encumbered by the weightiness of bitterness, envy, strife and all those characteristics that can block the access of everything good in your life. Protect your heart. Nurture your heart. Watch it heal, regenerate and impact other hearts to do the same. Always remember that your first love is the best kind of love, and you can have that kind of love every day. Your first love affair with God is the kind of love that influences the love that you have with your husband. Your change of heart is going to breathe new life into your marriage. It's going to make you so grateful that you didn't quit at breaking point. It's going to make you look forward to the best days of your marriage and life.

*And do everything with **love**.*
—1 Corinthians 16:14 (NLT)

When Your Broken Marriage Is Breaking You

It's hard when you give 100 per cent, and the other person doesn't even give 20 per cent. You may think that you have the strength to carry both of you at first, but what happens when wear and tear occurs? What happens to your faith, patience and perseverance then? No matter how much you try to fix it, it just seems to get worse and worse.

The greatest advice that I can ever give to you is… let go. Stop trying to fix your marriage. Stop trying to keep together whatever is falling apart. Let it fall apart so that it can come together. Focus on your own healing. Let me make this clear. I am not telling you to divorce your husband. I will not and cannot make that choice for you. I am saying, relinquish control. Shift your efforts and energy into your own growth and healing. How can you bring your marriage together if you are falling apart? That's absolutely absurd! Stop trying to make everything perfect and look for the beauty in your own transition. Instead of asking yourself, *how can I fix my marriage?* ask, *what can I do to heal?* Change the narrative. You're not a victim, and this is not *happening to you.* There are invaluable lessons in your experiences that will draw out a stronger version of yourself. You cannot now, nor will you ever be able to control him. Start with and end with controlling yourself. You will be surprised at how much a change in your own mentality and approach to your relationship will make a difference to your situation. But what if you don't know why your marriage is broken?

It would be extremely disorientating and bewildering to know that your marriage is on a downward spiral, but you have no idea why. There is a sense deep within you that will send alarm bells ringing through every fibre of your being when you know that *something just isn't right.* The reasons aren't clear, but *the change* in the air is palpable. Like a wall beginning to crumble, you can't seem to put it together because you don't know why it's falling apart. You feel like you have every ability to navigate your marriage to safety, but no matter what you do, it still heads in the same direction. Your intentions are well-meaning, and even your actions are deliberate. You are trying your best to be what he needs, but nothing seems to be making it right. You need clarity, and you can get the clarity you need when you have the necessary conversations. Communicating about why you are drifting apart will almost always bring the clarity you need for the road ahead, regardless of how painful the conversation is. You've both got to be willing to take part in that discussion. I believe that if a man refuses to engage in communication, then:

- He doesn't know how to have a conversation.
- He places no value on open dialogue or understands little about its value.
- He's afraid of the ramifications.
- He is more than willing to let the marriage die.

None of the above is good. Whatever your husband's reason for not engaging or working through your marital issues, it cannot outweigh the gravity of the outcome of your collective silence. Lack of communication will ultimately be the reason that your marriage doesn't survive. Do what you can to highlight the need for conversation, but if you have to draw blood to make that conversation take place, then let it go. Even God has given us free will and allows us to make choices. If your husband uses his will to resist your efforts to strengthen the marriage, then you have to make peace with the fact that you have tried. At this point, you can say that you have truly made a conscious effort to build your marriage. Whatever action he chooses to take after that is in his hands.

Finding or Keeping Your Spark

It's impossible to read anyone's mind, much less your husband's mind. So, the next best thing is to talk about what helps to build intimacy for him. I talk more about chemistry in Chapter 7, *What's Your Fantasy*, so I won't overshare this topic at this stage (for fear of being repetitious). I will say this: pray for your sex life. Believe it or not, God made sex, and He cares about your marital and sexual happiness. I have found that a lot of inspiration and creativity flows from asking God for help in these areas. I know it feels weird knowing that God is the inventor of this aspect of your marital affairs, but I actually feel that it's an awesome thing. It really takes the pressure to *perform* out of intimacy. To know that you don't have to work or prove yourself is liberating.

The next invaluable lesson that I have learnt, not only in areas of intimacy but in so many areas of my life, is this: operate from a place of being extremely confident and comfortable in who you are, even if your body doesn't look how it used to, or there may be elements of uncertainty (surrounding the issue of sexual intimacy). Operate from a sense of being aware of your unmatched value. Never let sexual complications within your marriage dictate your worth. Act like you're gold, dress like you're gold and emit confidence that tells your partner: *I am irreplaceable, and you will never find another like me.*

So what if the sex is flat as pancakes?! That doesn't diminish your value in *any* aspect of your life, marriage and ministry. Be bold, don't shrink back, show up for yourself and allow your confidence to permeate and influence your life, sexual intimacy and, yes, your marriage!

Being Taken for Granted

I have seen it happen so many times, and it is incredibly painful to watch. The husband doesn't even open the door for his wife but shows up and serves every other woman that walks in the room. When she speaks, his eyes don't even meet hers with attention or care. In fact, he's more likely to roll his eyes than show any kind of positive interest. Hardly ever a kind word, flowers, or so much as a thank you. The weariness and feigned smile in the eyes of the wife that says, *he's lost me already, and he doesn't even know it.* He treats her like that worn pair of shoes that he's been wearing on his feet. When he first bought those shoes, he would polish them. He was careful where he walked in them or where he put them. But as time goes on, he doesn't even notice his shoes. He walks in the mud and allows creases and scuffs to mar their shine. He even launches them across the room when he enters the house. They've been around so long that he doesn't stop to think about what he would do without them.

It can be the same with marriage. No *please* or *thank you*. No gifts or acts of kindness. Your value has been taken for granted. That would make anyone want to leave. It's painful to be overlooked and under-valued. It's an absolute violation of the soul. But that's okay, because now is your chance to be the hero in your own life story, just the way God has always intended you to be. No more crutches or hiding. Now is the time that you *show up for yourself*. By show up I'm referring to your ability to give the very best of who you are to all that you do. I say this in the most loving way possible. Take care of yourself. Wash off the mud from your soul. Iron out the creases of neglect and misuse that you have endured for so long. Polish yourself off and be prepared for better use, because now is the time for you to be awakened to your own value. Be dedicated to your *own glow up*. Pamper yourself by get-ting your hair, nails and makeup done. Find environments where peo-ple will welcome and treat you like you are *priceless*. Take the advice of that famous shampoo advert and love yourself *because you're worth it*. Don't look to him for validation but find it in the many things that surround you. Even this book is here to remind you of the greatness of your value. Don't wait for someone to do what they may never do. Go to confidence retreats. Talk to a coach that has the gift of igniting the shero in you. Socialise. Grow. Focus on building you. If he doesn't catch on now, then, trust me, he will catch on later when the new, invigorated version of you has awakened from her slumber. I have no doubt that an extraordinary and unbreakable lioness is deep within you and ready to roar! Let her out!

When you step into being your own nurturer; when you truly walk in the authority that God has invested in you; when you start tending to the wounds in your soul – that's when you will finally be able to embrace life, like a caged bird that has been freed. Your new lens will show you that you no longer need to carry the weight of your marriage. You can give the weight of it all to God. That pressure to keep up with, maintain and make your marriage work only induces stress. Travel light and embrace the peace of God. Take confidence in knowing that the burgeoning strength within you will positively impact your surroundings. You are the catalyst for the change that you are so desperate to see. You can make that happen. It all starts with you. A change in your mentality, your faith and your growth will cause a shift in the circumstances around you. When you are ready, new doors will open because you are no longer focused on the wrong things. You will be more at peace. You will radiate the joy that you have been craving for so long. You will see the beauty and joy in the blessings that are surrounding you. No longer will your soul be tainted by the pain and weight that your marriage has caused, because what he does or doesn't do has no bearing on the brilliance that shines from within you. You're still going to live and be happy regardless. Once you embrace your inner warrior, you will have the confidence to establish boundaries and welcome new opportunities. Life will finally start to make sense to you because you are welcoming the beauty of it all instead of being focused on the challenges that once held you captive.

Prayer and Meditation

Let's pray and reflect using the mirror.

Dear Heavenly Father,

I admit that my marriage is at breaking point and that I cannot fix it with my own strength. Please mend the broken places of my soul and marriage. Heal the pieces and the broken places that I am not able to reach. Teach me how to contribute to the healing of my marriage. Show me how to improve my own life and circumstance.

In Jesus' name, Amen.

THREE

Who Am I… Again?

§

> The truth hit her like a bucket of ice-cold water.
> Every decision that she had made throughout her life was for the benefit of someone else.
> Everyone else's voices had somehow managed to drown out her own.
> She was beginning to feel like she was losing grip of who she is and what she wants.
> Not only was she afraid of what she was losing, but of who she was becoming as a result.

Maybe you are like the woman I describe above, drowning in the weight of everyone else's expectations. Maybe you haven't found the strength to challenge their expectations and feel like you are somehow being punished for it. Not knowing who you are, your value, ideals and boundaries can leave you at risk of being swept through the current of outside forces that seem to be beyond your control. Having a strong sense of identity comes with the skill of shutting out the noise around you and amplifying *the voice within you*. That voice that is a fine-tuned compass leading you to the truth of who you are – that warrior within, desperate to be freed and to be everything that God has called you to be. Please don't settle or just let life *happen* to you. Take control of it. That includes your own vision for your life, your unique voice, values, ideals, hopes and dreams. Marriage can make it so easy for you to put yourself at the back of the queue. If you have children, then that makes it even harder to prioritise your needs, but when your identity is out of focus, then it will negatively impact your life and everything around you.

Self-Discovery: The Journey

I want to speak to the dark crevices of your mind – the places where pain has been living and growing. Trapped in a place that has made you feel like you don't have a voice, you might have used spiritual crutches to limp through life and settle for not truly being aware of who you are. As a result, the symptoms and struggles of your crisis have intensified. You know what they are: any habits that you have used to escape the pain of feeling lost and uncertain. You thought that having them as your crutch would fill the abyss in your soul. The truth is that you can't cajole, spring clean, date night or manipulate the pain or loss away. You can't hide from the pain. Even worse, when you feed it all the wrong things, then it continues to grow. You have to fight it the right way. Be deliberate in finding out who you are. I am sure that there have been so many obstacles that have systematically stripped you of your identity as you have gone through life. You thought that marriage would fix it, but it has just contributed to the pain and has brought you to a place where you feel that there is no point continuing to fight.

I am not writing this to entertain you. I want to speak to that raging lioness within you that is fighting to break free. That lioness that wants you to conquer every single challenge that is thrown your way. That lioness that looks into the eye of the storm and says, *bring it on!* You've been dependent on others for validation and permission for so long. What you don't realise is that you are fierce, and when you break free from the desire to have the approval of others, you will be unstoppable. Their influence is hindering your self-sufficiency and growth. The only person that you can trust enough to be completely dependent on – is God!

God won't break your heart, send your call to voicemail, die or leave you. There's so much beauty waiting for you on the other side of completely stepping into who you were born to be. Staying in life's *safe zone* to keep others happy is robbing you. How can you possibly have a fulfilled marriage if you are existing or hiding from yourself? How can you have a thriving marital life if you're not truly living? Now is the time to shift the power in your favour. Change the direction of your life. After all, your identity, your life and your values – belong to you. Don't wait for permission to take what has always been yours. Just take it.

Hearing Your Voice

Every one of us has an innate voice filled with all our desires, beliefs, hopes, dreams and decisions. It's a unique sound only to you, and it will always prioritise your own interests. Sometimes, we go through life and allow everything else to drown out that voice, until our true essence becomes a whisper. It's from that space of losing connection with ourselves that the conflict intensifies. Your voice is priceless. It's as unique as your fingerprint – that ability to stand by your identity and fiercely protect it. Who you are is heard loud and clear when you have the courage to stand by your own unique sound: those qualities that make you rare, those important principles that you uphold. We have to protect it to ensure that we don't lose who we are in the crowd and noise of life. Sometimes we let life and others take away invaluable components to our identity. We have to weigh up what is important, what we are not willing to give up and what we want to protect.

A major disadvantage of not having a voice is feeling like a ship without sails. Effortlessly going in whatever direction that the wind blows. Never arriving at your destined shore. Never becoming the extraordinary woman that you were born to be. It is so easy to get into a marriage and let that marriage define you. There are so many other things that can deceive you into believing they are the sum total of your identity. Drifting. Following everyone else's desires and ignoring your own inner voice will cause you to drown in the sense of unfulfillment that will inevitably have a devastating impact on your connection to the world around you. When you are not self-aware, you inevitably drift into living life on everyone else's terms rather than walking a path that you are in control of, resulting in frustration and resentment. As time goes by, it becomes more apparent that you traded an unfair deal, and regret starts to weigh in.

When the symptoms manifest, no one else but you will feel the weight of your internal crisis. It manifests in the fear that you have when other people are upset by the values that you wish to stand by. It shows up in the feeling of incompleteness and the strong sense of unfulfillment – like something is missing.

Have you ever screamed out into a crowd at the top of your voice but received no response, not even the bat of an eyelid? Or have you ever had a dream in which you were invisible and everyone that you loved dearly completely ignored you? Then, like a wave, the feeling of insignificance washes over you, and you feel like you're drowning in isolation and obscurity. That experience can be summed up in a few words: You. Don't. Matter.

Maybe you haven't experienced any of the above, but the feeling remains. What's worse is that while to many, you don't seem alone, in reality, you feel completely and utterly alone. Floating through life without being able to make sense of it all. Unable to speak about the things that really matter, because the truth is you can't actually define those things. How can you know what actually matters if you are unsure who you are or what you want your life to look like? Living life on everyone else's terms has been your priority for so long that you have almost forgotten what it is that *you* want.

Every wife risks the possibility of losing her identity throughout her marriage. It seems like a moot point at the beginning of marriage, but as time goes by, it becomes harder to keep a grip on identity, purpose and values. It takes a strong sense of courage and self-awareness to protect and nurture your identity as the marriage progresses. How you view your identity (and its significance) will also determine whether your identity thrives or not. If your own sense of identity isn't of great value to you, then there is no chance that it will be of value to anyone else. That's simply because their voices will be their priority. Your voice is *your priority*.

I have spoken to many mothers and wives who have dedicated their whole lives to their families, and once they're all grown up, then all they're left with is regret – "Don't do what I did." I recall one wise woman instructing me, "Have something for *you*." I sensed the weight of regret in her tone as she spoke, and her words left an incredible impression on my soul. This is why I take the hard road and fight for those things that God has imparted in my life. To speak up when something just doesn't fit my values or ideals. To give the best of myself to ministry, my visions and my family.

One valuable lesson that can help you maintain your identity is to be clear about who you are and be unapologetic about it. I stand by this principle, and it has guided and saved me from one disastrous circumstance after another.

In the context of my marriage, I know that it could not thrive without my husband and me knowing who we are and what we both bring to the table. So much will simmer under the surface if your voice is crushed; if you are unable to set boundaries; if you cannot say for sure that the decisions, ideals, visions, dreams and expectations are being heard. You matter. You matter in the context of being a wife, and you matter in being *you* – unique, complex, brilliant *you*. How tragic is it that everyone else around you has their needs and values met, but all you have is longing? Choose to be known by the values, purpose and ideals that you navigate in your life.

Live on the terms that you set. Make decisions that are solely yours and no one else's. Speak and be heard. Ensure that your opinions carry value. A discreet but common secret for wives that have shared their heart with me is that they are aware that they could lose their identity within the roles and responsibilities of marriage. In fact, some wives have lost their voice and have no idea how to regain it. Other wives are content to pursue other endeavours.

On the other hand, some wives fight to protect and strengthen their identity while embracing their wifely and mothering responsibilities. Sometimes we do it with tears in our eyes, knowing that there will be many, many times when we fail to get the balance right in holding it all together.

You may not realise it now, but this balance is part of the beauty of it all. It can be incredibly difficult to get it right all the time and to balance the everyday. Just enjoy the ride and bask in knowing that you are valued; knowing that this is the harder road to take. Silence and compliance are easy. Following the herd without question is safe. Going for the greater thing, that greater purpose for your life, is liberating. Fighting for purpose and identity will take a supernatural level of resilience that only God can grant you.

There is such a discontentment that stirs in the heart of a woman whose purpose is multidimensional. They will never be satisfied until they have walked in every aspect of their life's purpose – until they can say that they 1000 per cent know who they are and can live in the complete truth of who God made them be. You know I'm talking to you. When did you lose your voice? Was it something that someone said to you that has broken your spirit? Did it happen over time? Or have you felt lost for as long as you can remember? It's easy to see that you've been crushed under the weight of the expectations of others. You could have had a misplaced sense of identity long before you said *I do*. Or you could be changing over time and are now starting to feel frustrated at not being given permission to express yourself as you truly are. Could it be that you didn't know the weight of sharing your life with someone else, and the reality of it all is crushing your identity? Maybe as a result of the burden of marital responsibility, you just don't want to be married anymore. There can be so many challenges to establishing your identity within your marriage, especially if you have never been assertive about your identity in the past.

Finding your identity may not be a pretty process for you. You may experience turbulence in your marriage as you find your feet. You may lose friends, family and find yourself in a place of isolation. I call this the "reset" because it seems like a disaster, but you're just being reset for the opportunities, friends and people that should be in your life and space. I am not suggesting you go around upsetting others deliberately, but when you start to know who you are and what you value, you may become intimidating to those who don't understand. It's completely okay for them to be intimidated, but your focus must be on becoming confident in who you are. Finding yourself can feel like a maze and can have you feeling like you're lost in the spiritual wilderness of uncertainty and alienation. You need to understand the value of knowing who you are and how it can enrich your life. Knowing who you are will give you your power back. It will strengthen your voice and make your life meaningful. Shift your mentality: prioritise and value your identity. Build and nurture your inner voice and make it of utmost importance. Make a commitment to yourself – that this time you will speak up and show up for yourself. You have an opportunity to shift the trajectory of your inner state. It will astonish you how much you will be positively impacted by the subtle changes you make to prioritise and build on your inner voice. As a result, your purpose be greater than you ever imagined. Before you can be awakened to the full reality of your life's purpose, you first have to know who you are.

The Cause of an Identity Crisis

What was it that has caused you to lose yourself? Do you just feel like you've been uncomfortable and uncertain with who you are for as long as you can remember? Was it something that someone said that made you question your identity, that made you feel unfulfilled and lacking purpose – never *really* happy? Discontentment is the cry of a soul that knows that it exists for more. More than the lifestyle that you are living in now. More than everyone else's hopes and plans for your life. Let discontentment drive you in the direction of your life's purpose. The discontentment that you feel is trying to speak to you. It's a feeling that is telling you that there is more and that you are settling.

It's time to become more aware of how your surroundings and others affect your ability to build on your identity. Look around you. Don't be afraid to look *within* you. Start to speak to the painful places inside that pressurise you to oppress your identity. Unearth and release it.

- Why am I hiding?
- What symptoms are indicating that my identity is suffocating?
- How is my internal and external environment affecting my identity?

Have you ever observed children and noticed that their confidence seems to dissipate with time? It seems like the world just comes in and tries to tarnish their shine. There are very few of us that will fight against being dulled down to fit in. There are very few who can resist conforming to systems *just because*. The secret to why some shine while other lights get dimmer with time is the ability to build a foundation on something stronger than themselves. The ability to keep that confidence and shine comes with knowing you have every right to be who you are fighting so hard to be.

Make your unique voice count. You are not insignificant within wifehood, motherhood or as an individual. Don't fuel the agendas of others to choke out your identity by playing small. There is something brilliant about you that you have been hiding from the world. If you could just be a little bit braver, shine a little bit brighter and be unapologetic about it, then you will reap boundless rewards as a result.

You'll be happier and have a stronger sense of assurance that your life is making a difference to your husband, family and everyone around you. You will have an impact. You will be unforgettable. First, though, you've really got to ask yourself the right questions to navigate out of the maze of uncertainty that you currently find yourself in.

JOURNAL

- How do I value and prioritise my inner voice?
- Is my voice being heard?
- Do I feel like my identity matters?

Getting to the Foundations of You

Let's start with the most obvious question: who are you?

We are born into a world that requires everything to make sense. We are given names. We are given tests when we are at school so that the world can *make sense* of who we are. We are encouraged to *fit in* instead of *standing out* for the benefit of the world's system. When we enter this world, we are born so unique that standing out is as easy as breathing, but everything around us tells us that we should fit in. Society has its part to play in this moulding process. We are expected to learn by this age. Get a job by that age. Get married by this age. Have children by that age. Adapt to herd mentality.

One way or another, we have subconsciously obliged. We have all at some point submitted to the world's herd criteria to conform, mainly out of fear of being typecast as *not making sense*; in exchange, we have stopped making sense to ourselves. We have betrayed our own values and ideals in exchange for theirs. What do you do when your life doesn't make any sense? You seem to be ticking all the boxes, but you still have no clarity about the direction that your life is taking. This can easily happen if you're not paying attention. When life gets hectic with marriage, parenting, careers and all the other engagements that ensue, it can become increasingly difficult to stop and ask yourself, *is my life making sense to me?*

It's easy to be categorised and placed within boxes that everyone else feels that you should fit into, but if your life doesn't make sense to you, how can you live it to the fullest? To be an unfulfilled wife is one of the most common secrets that women carry because it is so easy to put yourself at the back of the queue. It's also one of the most painful secrets that you could carry. It's easy to live up to your husband's dreams, your family's expectations and hopes for your life and feel like you're choking. Feeling enslaved and trapped while trying to keep it all together on the outside. Gaining clarity on what you stand for and understanding your values and beliefs are the first steps to truly owning your identity.

There are various dictionary definitions of "identity", but the ones that stand out to me (and the most applicable to this chapter) are:

> *1. The prestige, features, etc. of a person or organisation that makes the public think of them in a specific way.*
> *2. Who a person is or the characteristics of a person or community that differentiate them from others.*

All definitions allude to the objective of trying to make sense of you and me. Every day you choose to embrace values and beliefs that contribute to your condition and character. They are the sum total of your identity. These sets of ideals, values and beliefs are chosen consciously or subconsciously. These ideals help you navigate the direction of your life. It is a devastating thing to go into a marriage without really knowing what your values, ideals and identity are. Having a strong sense of identity will give your life direction. Knowing who you are will help you to make your choices clearer and add value to your life. It means that you get to take the steering wheel and control where your life is heading. No one else has the right to take control of your voice. There's nothing worse than sitting on the sidelines of life and watching it all pass you by. Existing without living. Aimless. Directionless.

Marriage can contribute to this loss of identity. Trust me, I've been there. Having moments of *is this it?* Feeling like you're spiritually standing at a brick wall that you just can't seem to get over. Stuck. So lost in the identity of wife and mother that you simply can't find *yourself*. What makes you – *you?* What is it about you that is so unique that nothing and no one can imitate – that thing about you that makes you as unique as your fingerprints? You are the reason that God doesn't do carbon copies. God decided that throughout the existence of this planet, there would only be one version of you.

Never mind that there are nearly eight billion people on the planet. No one can ever do it your way or be *you*. It's all those little things that you do without thinking and it comes to you as easy as breathing. That thing will tell you who you are.

JOURNAL

- ◆ What is unique about you?
- ◆ How does your identity positively impact your marriage?

Don't suppress *you* anymore. Breathe. Release yourself as a gift to the world. In doing so, you cause a chain reaction in those around you – including your husband. To make the journey to complete self-discovery, you have to quiet the noise around you. Make time to listen to your own thoughts. Let your heart speak to you about what you love and what you've always wanted to pursue. It is not selfish to take time for you. In fact, it is selfless. You're taking the time to gain clarity so that you can impart and give the best of yourself to others. It takes time to learn who you are. It takes time to build on your values and principles. It takes time to connect with God to gain clarity on your true identity. You have to be relentless in your pursuit. Give it your everything.

There is a person whose identity is so potent that it has profoundly impacted my life over the years. This person is the reason that I am deliberate about having a powerful impact on everyone that I come into contact with. When I studied the life and ministry of Jesus, I noticed that He has something that I call "a super identity". It is an identity that is so supercharged that you can't hang around Him and stay the same.

When He was with His disciples, He wanted to show them that He was a whole class syllabus, course and certificate all in one. You were always going to learn something, push yourself, develop and grow. He was always going to call out the best in you. He asked them, "Who do men say that I am?" The disciples didn't know who they were, and if they could understand who He was, then the realisation would activate their own value. He asked them, "Who do men say that I am?"[6] And they gave a variety of answers. Then Jesus said, "Who do you say that I am? That is, what do you see? What have you observed? What

---

[6] Matthew 16:13-20 (KJV)

has been revealed to you about my identity?" Jesus wanted them to be impacted by the power of His Divine identity. He was 1000 per cent sure of who He was.

When you are that sure, you will not only repel anything that goes against your identity, but you will have a profound impact on anyone who comes into contact with you, with your values, with your standard and with your nature. Jesus set the standard so that we could imitate and learn to strengthen our identity in Him. I am a carbon copy of Him because I am impacted by this truth. You can't hang around me and stay the same. You will always be provoked, inspired, energised, encouraged, uplifted around me because I have learnt (and am always learning) to be more like Jesus every day.

I urge you not to allow your identity to be built upon fickle things that can be taken away from you. Your house can be taken away, your car, your career, even your family can be taken away from you. You can raise your children, and they will leave. If your identity is tied up in your children, then they will take every piece of you with them when they leave to lead their own lives. Your identity needs to be invested in the things that *cannot* be taken away from you. Know your identity so well that when you are asked who you are, you will not hesitate to declare the *real* truth of who you are. If you asked me this very question, I would say:

> *I am a daughter of the Most-high God, a joint heir with Christ.*
> *A changer of worlds. I don't play small to make others feel better.*
> *I set a standard of Holiness in my life that challenges others to come up higher.*
> *I am driven by the light of God that burns within my soul.*
> *I don't waste my time, gifts or God-given resources.*
> *I fight for truth and protect the Divine mandate upon my life.*

I do everything that I do because of what God has designed and made me to be.

I am a warrior, a lioness, royalty.

I am fierce. I am the fire of passion for Divine cause, a true ambassador of heaven.

Low self-esteem, suicidal thoughts, confusion, lack of direction, lack of faith, anxiety, depression are all symptoms of a deeper root issue. You don't operate from a place of truly knowing who you are. You don't know your power and your value. It comes out in the way that you stand. It comes out in the things that you say. Your boss knows. Your colleagues can sense it. Your husband is most certainly aware (whether consciously or subconsciously); your journey to self-discovery is nowhere near complete. Now I am not saying that you may not feel these emotions from time to time, but when they are consistent, intensified and left unchallenged, it speaks volumes of your awareness of the power that lies within you. There is a different kind of fight that is born out of the place of self-awareness and a strong identity. It comes with unshakable grit and relentlessness. That ability to bounce back comes from the place of knowing who you are. Lionesses don't cower at the sight of their prey. They know that *they* have power. They even pick up speed at the sight of their target. They are fierce. They pursue, overtake and recover their prey without apology. You, too, can have this level of self-awareness, but no one is going to give it to you; you have to take it.

Pressure from the Outside…

Are you paying attention to the outside influences that may be having an impact on your identity? Your husband, your family, the media, friends, social media… anything that you let in is having an influence on who you are. What are you making yourself susceptible to that is having a detrimental effect on how you see yourself and everything surrounding you? If you want to make real strides in building the right foundations and self-awareness, you will need to be deliberate in guarding your mind. There is so much danger in focusing too heavily on others' opinions and allowing their voices to be more amplified than the sound of your own. Focus on the voice that speaks to the truth of who you really are and how you want your own life to be played out.

I have seen it happen way too often – the opinions and subliminal control of others crippling the direction of women. Women who have so much potential, greatness ahead of them, allowing their own voices to become insignificant and drowned out. Keep in touch with your inner voice as it guides you to the truth of who you are. I'm talking about the voice that is the sum total of all your hopes, dreams and the things that you have always loved to do. That's the place where you will build a strong sense of self-awareness. You can do this by creating a sacred space in your environment.

In that space, you start to build on your voice by using vision boards. A vision board is any type of board on which images representing everything you want to be, do, or have in your life are displayed. You could also arrange to have a wall of answered prayers and meaningful furniture. In your sacred space where you can build on your inner person and observe the progress. It's a space where you can pray and listen to the unique sound of your own soul. Where you can download guidance and strength to face anything that will challenge your identity in the world outside. Don't feel guilty that you were not aware of it before you made many major decisions in your life. You can make amends with yourself as you continue to grow. Right now, just be glad that you are one of the special ones. You're about to make tremendous changes. You are about to find your own unique voice, that voice that does not belong to anyone else – treasure that voice.

Some people go throughout their whole lives without ever being heard, but you, you're about to amplify your voice. It's the voice that will speak to you and encourage you to set the boundaries you need to set to move forward. It's such a privilege to speak and be heard. You can now exercise that privilege. Nurture that voice. Spend time alone. Listen to the cries of your heart. Be in tune with the condition of your spiritual state: the pain that you have felt, the weariness of the journey. Take the time to rediscover the beauty of your own uniqueness. Then, share it all with the One who wants to be your best friend, God. He is listening. *He will lead you into all truth.* The truth of who you are and why you are here. He will give your life a strong sense of purpose. He will give you the boldness to execute your purpose's complexities in a way that only you can. Remember, clarity comes with solitude, with quieted noise. Those are the moments when everything becomes clear. Make the time to discover yourself in that space, and you'll be astonished by the strength and growth you experience.

Pressure on the Inside...

Isn't it easy to make our lives unnecessarily busy to avoid the noise that is going on within us? Especially if your marriage is under strain, you're hiding secrets or even having an identity crisis. The complexities of your secrets are only symptoms of a deeper issue. Whether it's resentment, lack of confidence, unforgiveness, hate, bitterness or any of the other secrets that quietly and viciously cripple your marriage, they're just the outcomes of the pressure that's on the inside. Like a stovetop kettle, there is heat on the outside, but it is the hot water and steam on the inside that causes the shrill whistle to be released. Just like that kettle, your symptoms are the cause of the heat that you feel inside. You can feel it as you read, continuing to rage as the pressure continues to increase. You just don't know how much more of this you can take. The solution is to continue purging your soul by evaluating the state of your identity and how you can strengthen it.

***

True self-discovery and enlightenment can only come through our discovery and enlightenment of who God is. You will never come into the true realisation of your own unique strengths, purpose and value without a direct revelation of who you are from the One who created you – God. He says:

> *I knew you before I formed you in your mother's womb.*
> *Before you were born, I set you apart.*
> **—Jeremiah 1:5 (NLT)**

When David received enlightenment about the brilliance and beauty within, he exclaimed:

> *Thank you for making me so wonderfully complex! Your workmanship is marvellous.*
> **—Psalm 139:14 (NLT)**

Every detail, every single hair on your head, has value, purpose and is incredibly precious. God is in the detail of our lives, its intricacies and complexities. You are a child of God. The lack of understanding of the greatness of your value is your way of *playing yourself down*. You are a jewel in the depths of the dirt. Waiting to be discovered by people who will never see your value. That is, of course, until you do. Be completely dissatisfied with being in the dark about who God is. Relentlessly and desperately pursue Him, and in return, He will give you – *yourself*. The truth is, by then, you will want so much more. Ultimately, God-discovery trumps self-discovery every time. How do I know this? It happened to me. God encounters are transformational. An encounter with God will make you so much better than you ever thought that you could be. He will teach you more about yourself than any self-help book or seminar can ever do. It's something that only happens when you search with all your heart.

> *If you look for me wholeheartedly, you will find me.*
> **—Jeremiah 29:13 (NLT)**

Ask God to reveal to you the truth of who you are. Your purpose, value and identity are not a mystery to Him. I have found that when you open yourself to God and ask for the revelation of self, He will share so much more than you imagined that He would. Finding your God-given identity may not be a pretty process. You may have turbulence within your marriage as you find your feet. You may lose loved ones. You may find yourself in places of shame and isolation. It may seem like a disaster, but you're just being reset for the opportunities, environment and people that should be in your space. I am not saying to start upsetting and alienating others deliberately, but when you start to know who you are and your values, you may be misunderstood or intimidated. It's okay.

Defining Your Identity

Not all identity crises happen in mid-life. Maybe it's been the theme of your life, or maybe there are elements of your life where you have felt like something has been missing: the feeling of being tossed to and fro on the whims of others' agendas or unsure of what you should feel, believe or even live for; the uncertainty that you are at the helm of the choices and direction of your own life. When the right things fuel the truth about who you are, you will set the foundations that will enable you to thrive instead of self-destructing. There is nothing more alienating than living life with no awareness of your values and operating from that lack of certainty. There is also something extremely invigorating about having a strong awareness of your identity and making confident decisions from that space.

There have been pockets in my life where I have felt like I was drifting and just going with what everyone else was doing. It's only when I took time to self-reflect that I would realise that I needed to examine my values and operate confidently in who I was. Having a strong identity always has to be of utmost importance if I want to make sure that my life doesn't spiral out of control or I feel like I am losing myself. I have always known that I was valued and precious in the eyes of God, but there have been times where I just wanted to have a strong sense of purpose and direction for my life.

Looking back, I would always have a crisis when something crucial happened. They seemed to go hand in hand; there were moments after I got married and when I had my first son, Ezra, where I craved clarity and direction. I was feeling lost and uncertain about who I was or what the future held. I knew I had to reset. I spent a lot of time talking to God, writing and visualising what I wanted from life. Then, when I took the time to get the clarity and direction that I yearned for, I began to walk confidently in my newfound self-awareness.

It's the moments that I take alone to reflect, develop, grow and assess the direction of my life that ensure that I am constantly nurturing my identity. The truth is that a strong sense of identity is deliberately built. It is built through prayer, reflection, isolation and meditation (on the right things). It is also built through allowing God's word to speak concerning my identity and to remind me of who He created me to be. I am always making sure that I am paying attention to the direction that my life is heading in. I don't have the mentality of expecting God to do all the work for me. I partner with God by trusting that He orders my path, but I also know that I have a part to play. I make the time to pick apart the pieces of my life and life choices. I evaluate relationships and how they make me feel. I ask myself if there are areas of my life that I can improve. I treat my life like it is the last bit of change in my purse. You know what I am talking about, right?! When you have lots of money in your purse, then you spend it like Christmas has come early, but when you have that last bit of change, then you carefully spend it.

In the same sense, I am carefully spending my life. Deliberately spending my life with the right people and in the right places. I am carefully making the choices that yield much fruit and are productive. I am carefully assessing what I let in and what needs to be kept out. I am deliberate with my life choices. This self-evaluation level may seem intense, but what's more intense is looking over my life and realising that I never made any productive choices and that my legacy was weak. It's knowing I finished a race, deserve self-approval, satisfaction and true happiness because I achieved my own personal best.

Living on purpose gives me a sense of confidence and boldness. It assures me that I will reap so much more fulfilment than I ever imagined. Why? Because I understand that every action has a reaction, and every decision will have a positive or negative consequence. There is nothing more empowering than knowing that you are making the right choices. We are emboldened and confident when we know that abundance flows from the work we invest into building our identity. Boldness is a skill and a gift. It's a skill because you have to be deliberate in strengthening your self-awareness. It is a gift because its unique value and impact will remain long after you're gone. The boldness to set standards and ensure that others respect them speaks volumes about who you are. Boundaries and identity are interlinked. You set boundaries because you know who you are. Firstly, you have to know who you are before you can set boundaries. How do you discover yourself? It seems like a simple question, but it's actually harder than it looks if you haven't done it before. Let's always start setting foundational values that are not necessarily about *what we like* but more about what is necessary, the right values required for us to thrive. The most powerful principles that have guided and enriched my life (in epic proportions) that are foundational for building a strong identity are expressed in the following verses:

> *You are made in the image of God.*
> **—see Genesis 1:27**

A statement that should never be taken lightly because it speaks of how powerful we are because we reflect God's image. That is an incredible compliment, encouragement and indicator of our value! The Person who spoke the world into being. A timeless, royal, omnipotent Creator who isn't controlled by time or space. We are a reflection of God! Wow! That's enough to have my shoulders squared and head held high. How valuable are we!

> *You are of Great Value.*
> **—see 2 Corinthians 4:7**

Within us are treasures that we haven't discovered or tapped into. More valuable than any jewel that can be found. The treasures within us testify immensely to our worth. How would you live if you were aware that you were priceless in every way? If you had the answer to this question, I believe that your life would never be the same.

You are Royal.
—see 1 Peter 2:9

You may be overlooked by earthly kings and queens on this planet, but the most important and eternal King knows you. He is affiliated with you and even has bestowed upon you the title of the greatest honour. Not only that, but He bestows upon you the privilege and power of being royalty by Divine association.

These are awesome principles and ideals to hold onto as you continue to build on your identity. I am not talking about repeating them in a clichéd way but really owning your identity. Hold your head high, dress like you're a Queen, assess your surroundings and be intentional about building relationships with other royalty. Have poise and dignity. Be gracious and stand by your values and principles. Be a woman of your word.

I don't just impart these precious jewels of truth to you; they are principles that I live by, and they have helped me thrive. We have to tap into that value and awaken to the truth of who we are every single day. There is really no need for you to play small. If only you could realise that you are so great a giant that, when you are ready, nothing in the world will hold you down. You will be tested. That's absolutely okay because when you are tested, you will "come forth as gold".[7]

It's okay to go against the grain and not follow what everyone else is doing. You will flourish because you are breaking away from negative patterns, traditions and expectations in your life. You are looking

---

[7] Job 23:10 (KJV)

ahead to theologies, ideologies and perspectives that are being de-
manded of you. You are asking yourself:

* Are they the truth?
* Do they bring out fruitfulness and value in my life?
* Are they helping me to grow, or are they doing the opposite?

You are fully aware that neither mummy's, daddy's, nor husband's
opinions can trump God's opinion of you. However, even He leaves
the decision to act, accommodate or accept the truth about who He
says that you are – in your hands. You have to partner with God to
allow the fruits of your identity to be activated within you. When you
understand your identity, then you will operate from that truth. It is
by understanding your identity that you will be able to strengthen the
core of who you are. You can ensure that others meet you at the values
that you set. You can remove yourself from the table when what you
have ordered is not being served.

Being a woman of high standards is a powerful position to be in as
a wife. Why? Because it steers the direction of your home. You are the
rock that your family depend on in times of crisis. I believe that a wife
has a great impact and influence on her family. Especially when she
allows God to guide her on her marital journey. She holds everything
together in the home. She is the one that everyone comes to when they
are in need. She sets the pulse and environmental thermometer within
the home. If she is angry, then she will be impossible to ignore. If she
is at peace, then it is so much easier to have a peaceful home. When a
woman knows her power within her marriage sphere, it ripples
throughout her home, life and environment. It speaks for her, and she
doesn't need to open her mouth to declare it. There is great skill required in partnering with our husbands to steer the direction of our
family's circumstances, legacies and future. It takes great discipline to

change negative patterns and establish new ones. You have to see where you want to go ahead of time.

One way that I have personally worked on my identity is by envisioning the woman that I wanted to become. I wrote all those characteristics down in a prayer diary. I did this a few years ago, and I focused on the growth of those qualities, so much so that the vision of myself has now come to fruition. I will give a light example below (but I won't share the full extent of the vision of my future self that I wrote down due to the sensitive nature of some aspects).

I am a woman of integrity, grit and heart.
I am a ray of light.
I do not gossip.
I am a lover of the underdogs, and I support the growth of those struggling to bring their visions to fruition.
I am a great example of Christ on this earth.
I am a woman of impact and great vision.
I have poise and grace.
Haters, opposition and negativity ricochet off of me.
I am bold, unapologetic and shine effortlessly.
I physically don't reflect the pain that I have overcome.

- ◆ Write down the woman that you visualise yourself becoming.
- ◆ Write three simple steps that you need to take to become her.
- ◆ Put your notes in a frame and in a place that you regularly have access to.

The list above is similar to the ideals that I wrote down, with more details about how each would affect my everyday life and the people within my reach. I was specific and deliberate. I am a firm believer that when you write on paper, it is sealed in your mind. You begin to gravitate to and see those things become a reality. I don't believe in manifesting in a hocus pocus kind of way, but you deliberately work towards those things that have been written down. When you write the vision and "make it plain... it will surely come".[8] There is something final about writing things down that can profoundly impact our minds and actions. I am certain that this scripture sheds light on this truth.

If fear is holding you back – the fear of speaking up, setting the standards, staking your claim on what belongs to you – it can hold you in bondage. Our inability to be confident in who we are is the very thing that robs us of what rightfully belongs to us. It is so important that we take responsibility for the nurturing of our identity. We need to avoid being pushed and pulled in every direction other than the

---

[8] Habakkuk 2:2-3 (KJV)

road that we are *meant* to take. It can easily happen in marriage because there are two of you, and you are unique individuals – trying to build together, but you are bound to have different building methods from time to time. It's helpful to check in on each other to ensure that you both have the time to navigate the direction of your own lives individually and jointly.

A Crisis of Faith

The level of faith that you have will determine the strength of your identity. It is God who declares who we are from the beginning of time. When we are born, we do not question our greatness. We are just born great. Over time, we lose touch with the innate gift of greatness that God has already imparted to us. What's worse is that we let it slip away. When we refuse to fight for our birthright, it becomes easy to drift throughout life with a strong sense of purposelessness.

Maybe it's not just your lack of connection to your purpose. Maybe you're trying to fly, but your husband keeps trying to clip your wings. Maybe he plays on your pain and your insecurities, or reminds you of past failures and invokes a sense of worthlessness? With every patronising act of belittlement, a piece of you has died inside. Lack of confidence and fear take hold. How do you expect him to know who you are if *you* don't? Finding yourself is the gift that you give to yourself. If you've gone into the marriage without a strong sense of self, faith in God and principles that you stand by, then it's so much easier for someone else to take you along for the ride in their dreams, visions and values. You both may have started the marriage with the same values, faith and vision, but your strong sense of identity and faith in God are what will anchor you if he changes. The reality is that people change – sometimes for the better and sometimes for the worse. It is knowing how to anchor yourself in God that will steady you through the tumultuous times when there are differences in character.

> But they delight in the law of the Lord,
> meditating on it day and night.
> They are like trees planted along the riverbank,
> bearing fruit each season.
> Their leaves never wither,
> and they prosper in all they do.
> **—Psalm 1:2-3 (NLT)**

The roots of your foundation need to reach so deep into God that nothing can shake your faith. That can be extremely difficult when your husband has different ideas. This is a test of the fortitude of your identity and your character. This is going to show the adverse situations you encounter and your adversaries just who you are. You are a champion with the army of heaven on your side. The odds are stacked in your favour. When you are ready, you will win every battle that you set out to fight, including the battle for your dreams. If you look closely, you will see that whatever you do will prosper, and you have won already. You have to let this truth cascade over every ounce of your soul. These are the ideals that will anchor you throughout the difficult aspects of your marriage.

Some limitations can suffocate your greatness. You were born to fly, but you have to trust in the One who gave you wings. Believe again. Trust that as you place your eyes on Him, God will transform everything that you are. In essence, your transformation will permeate your marriage. The journey starts with you recognising who you are. He calls you Queen; don't say you're worthless. When He says you're a ruler, embrace your authority. Walk tall and worthy of the calling that He has given you and never question your value.

The Value of Having a Strong Identity

In the early stages of our lives, there is no active teaching about self-discovery and awareness of who we are *becoming*. There are so many things that we subconsciously and intentionally *let in*. There are many factors involved in why some stumble upon their Divine identity, while others never find it. Some are living the hopes and dreams of those who influence them. It could be a parent, a boss, anybody. Knowing who you are is a gift and a compass to your Divinely ordained course to greatness. Your strong sense of identity will be why you are not dragged to and fro in life. It will be the reason that you know and protect your ideals. It will also be the reason that you have the courage to say, "That doesn't fit my values," or "I'm not available to that agenda," or "This is my calling." It will enable you to stand up for your values without shrinking back. It's actually never too late to do the inner work on yourself and be proud of yourself for pushing through. Of course, it's harder because you've already started on the path of building a life with someone, and they may have preconceived ideas about who they think you are, but you can rectify that by being clear about who you are. Communicate. No rule book says that you don't have a right to grow, be better or want better for yourself. So, whether you were uncertain of your core values before you got married or you are years deep and still uncertain about who you are, remember that every day you're breathing gives you another chance to make positive and strong changes that will truly enrich your life.

Sometimes there is a high price to pay for standing by your ideas, but there are always rewards for defending who you are in Christ. Our identity is only fortified by our relationship with Jesus. Outside of Him, there is no identity worth clinging to. Without Jesus, saying we have a strong sense of identity would be like having a tree without roots. It would look sturdy and strong on the outside, but as soon as the wind blows, that tree would not be able to withstand it. I believe that God made all of us great in a unique way, but so many get lost on the journey to their unique calling.

There's a scripture that talks about the wide path to hell and the narrow path to heaven. This is literally true, but I also believe that identity has a big part to play in many finding their way to hell or heaven – even in this life. Consequently, many live in their own personal hell of confusion and aimlessness because of a lack of identity. Others will die happy regardless of the price of finding their identity because they know the value of truly *being aware* of who they are. To know who you are, what you stand for, what you tolerate, what you're driven by, is a gift and a blessing. It is the anchor that steadies you through the course of your life and makes life worth living. Knowing who you are will give you the potential to leave a legacy as unique as your fingerprint. Start building your identity by having the courage to face yourself. Gravitate to anything that will help you to find your voice and build your identity. Start to look around and observe how your surroundings and resources affect your identity. Solitude and dialogue with God will also enlighten you on the steps that you need to take to strengthen the vulnerable facets of your identity.

Personal Boundaries and Resolute Identity

Identity gives you the strength to work out and set boundaries. Knowing who you are means knowing what you like and what you don't like. From there, you then work out what you tolerate and what you don't accept. You will learn what's for you and what will weigh you down if you give it too much access. There's a great chance that you will be liked a lot less. After all, you know when and how to say no, but you'll also be happier for it because you are protecting your standards and your identity. Having a strong sense of identity will repel what isn't true and attract gold. Golden relationships, golden friendships, golden opportunities equal a golden life. When you recognise that you are gold, then gold will overflow from every area of your life. All of your struggles will be worth it because they taught you the lessons that brought you to this part of your life. The years of turmoil, pain and confusion will become inconsequential because greatness is all you will see before you. Your newfound freedom will light up your soul because you didn't settle for less.

I know that you have felt like you have been stumbling in the desert of mediocrity, but that's only a fraction of your story. Your future years will be so bright and powerful that all the years of instability, loss and uncertainty will seem like a distant memory. The strength you need will come to you to protect and assert your identity because you've taken the time to discover who you are and *KNOW YOUR VALUE*.

There will be times when you will need to have necessary conversations with others, even if you have to initiate it through text or letter(s). Push through and speak about the ugly things, even if your voice trembles. Stand for something so that you don't fall for everything. Sometimes you will have to walk away from relationships that don't serve your peace of mind, not because you are resentful but because you have to protect the person that you are becoming. Be brave enough to say, "This isn't working for my marriage. This doesn't serve my faith or values." You have a right to say no. It's a British thing to explain why they don't want to do something because they are so polite, but it's okay to just say no without excuses just to make the other person feel better.

We can also be so concerned about the other person's feelings that we become afraid to boldly take everything that rightly belongs to us. Sometimes you just need to say how you feel and work it out with that person. If your husband is going to be angry, then that's okay too. I just believe that it's important to establish some guidelines between you as a couple to preserve respect. For example, my husband and I don't call each other names. It's okay to say, "You make me so angry when you…" But if I say, "You're such an *idiot* for doing that!" it becomes disrespectful. It shows mutual respect in a marriage when both parties can agree to express pain or dismay but not at the expense of attacking the other person. I love my husband, and I am not willing to attack him at the expense of trying to heal my wounds. That being said, I don't believe that we should ever ignore the elephant in the room. I am the type of person that will want to give the elephant a poke and a nudge. We address painful topics directly and move on.

What are you willing to compromise? Your boundaries have to work well with your husband's boundaries; otherwise, there will always be conflicts. Effective communication means that you've got to know when to speak up *and* listen. This will determine your success at establishing those boundaries. So, you have to weigh up what's most important to preserve your identity, your values and how willing you are to adapt to your husband's. Are there boundaries that are needed to achieve a new goal? Or for self-preservation? Or self-development? Knowing why you are setting boundaries will help you weigh up whether they should be prioritised jointly. I've found that as life changes, boundaries and standards have to constantly be reassessed. Life changes as your marriage develops. There will be different demands, such as children or financial changes, so you'll need to discuss what works for you both when you feel that those boundaries need to be reassessed.

- How will I have the necessary conversations with my family?
- What boundaries do I need to introduce?
- Why do I want to introduce these boundaries?
- What aspects of my boundaries am I willing to compromise on?
- How will these boundaries strengthen my identity?

Build upon the resilience of your mind. Weakened facets are a result of allowing doubts to creep into your mind about who you are. It's a dangerous thing to let every theory, notion or ideology have access to your mind, heart and even your emotions. Guard your heart. You are too precious to let everything have access.

In the same way, we have society telling us that we can change our identity, give in to urges and neglect our place of power. For so many, this has initially brought a false sense of liberty, to be left with despair, devastation and pain. What's tragic is that the suffering intensifies, and many suffer in a silent prison, knowing that the pain still remains but pretending that it isn't there.

Marriage can be a beautiful and complicated thing for so many. It can lift you up and have you walking on cloud nine in one minute; then the next, you could be wondering what has happened. Where did you go wrong? How did you both end up here? The things that you overlook initially can seem so minuscule and insignificant, but they can become gargantuan over time. They could have your marriage so close to the edge because no one had the confidence to call out the issues initially. That's why I believe that it's so important to have the necessary conversations about your values, identity and boundaries from the beginning. What will you not tolerate? How is your voice being received? Are you being patronised, belittled or ignored? Do you feel like you are *really* being listened to? It's the strangest thing to be loved and not understood. To be embraced but not heard. Your heart can be yearning, screaming out, but your husband can be speaking a different language. It happens so much within marriage. There has to be such a deliberate effort to communicate nuances and unspoken things: the looks and the actions; the misinterpreted statements. There has to be a trust that no ill will was intended. That takes deliberate effort to clarify.

For Paul and me, we have to dumb it down for each other. It doesn't matter about political correctness or how blunt it may sound. Just so that we can make sure that we are on the same page. So many marriages die because everyone is speaking from different chapters. We have learnt to take our time to find out if we actually hear what each other has to say. It takes trust and teamwork to do that. Sometimes you just have to go back to the basics. Learn to listen again. Speak plainly. Pray and laugh together. Connect. Then build from there. It's not always easy, but it's worth it.

"Two Shall Become One Flesh"[9]

Becoming unified within marriage but still having unique values, perspectives, and ideals is hard. It's so important that you find ways to agree without crushing each other's uniqueness. Make room for one another's growth, and sometimes you have to be okay with the other's resistance to do things your way. It's all about allowing and giving

---

[9] Mark 10:8 (NKJV)

space to one another to explore who you are. We naturally change over time. We may not like the same food, colours, clothes, and even how we look will change over time. In a lot of ways, change is inevitable. A great marriage allows space for growth.

What happens if you're hitting brick walls regardless of how much work you put in? The fight to get it right can be exhausting. It's time to let go. Stop fighting. This may mean that you have to bring in a mediator or counsellor. It may mean that you give each other space to work out what's most important. There is nothing wrong with being still and not trying to *make* things happen. Depend on God to take you through the process without forcing your agenda. Sometimes you win by being still. Trust me, this is a lesson that I have had to learn over and over again. I am a natural fighter and a fixer, so I will force and push until nothing is left for me to give. Pause, look closely at your situation and ask God, *what are you trying to teach me?*

As long as we are living, there will always be lessons to learn. We just need to make sure that we are learning those lessons and paying attention. You may not be aware, but there is such trauma with not being able to shine; with being suppressed and oppressed. Silenced. Overlooked and underestimated. It can burn holes in your soul, leaving you without the ability to stand in the truth of who you are. When you stop trying to make your husband see you or hear you or fall in line with your agenda, then you can start to focus on building yourself. You can control yourself, and you can fix yourself, but it is not always an easy process. It takes ownership and truth to say, "Hey! I messed up here!" or "I need to work on that." Self-reflection is not as common as you may think it is. I am not talking about the self-reflection that just requires acknowledgement; I'm talking about making deliberate steps to change, grow and develop. It's hard, especially if you have been doing whatever you've wanted to do for most of your life. There has to be a great amount of self-discipline, and you literally have to hold yourself accountable for taking steps to change. However, it is possible. You've just got to take the energy you have been using for the *push-and-pull* with your husband and use that energy to build on yourself. Watch the brick wall come down. When there is no struggle, then there is peace.

Marriage in Crisis

Sometimes we can spend so much time trying to *fix* everything and everyone that we don't focus on the things that require the most fixing, which is ourselves. The role of being a wife and nurturer can shift us into constant superhero mode such that we forget to save ourselves. Have you ever found yourself pointing the finger at your husband's flaws, dictating to the children what they need and how they should improve their lives, but who's left with the life that is in a car crash state? You got it! You are. Miserable, unfulfilled and empty. You let everyone take and take and take until there is nothing left. This is what I call a sad case of the "superhero complex".

How do I know so much about this complex? I was the embodiment of it. I would give to everything and to everyone until there was nothing left to give. "No" wasn't in my vocabulary when it came to those I loved. They are, of course, the hardest to say no to. If you're like I was, then you'll know that you're the one left holding the bill. One of the most dangerous things is to enter a marriage with an intense desire to *save or fix your* husband. You see what a mess he is and overlook those red flags at the beginning of the relationship, hoping that you can change those things as you go along – *big mistake*. Not only do those flaws remain, but they grow and become intolerable because there were no boundaries established before the marriage began. So you suffer in silence, in the hope that there will be an opportunity to escape the mess that you allowed to grow and fester. I have found that when you allow your loved ones to take an inch, then it becomes increasingly difficult to prevent them from taking a mile. I'm going to tell you the painful truth: it's not their fault   it's yours! It will always be up to you to kill the superhero complex. You just have to exercise that authority.

I remember getting to a point where I was so burnt out from being used and taken advantage of. When I was broken enough, a wise woman I confided in said to me, "Let them drop." At the time, it was so hard to hear. How could I let the people I love *drop* and resist the urge to save them? I wanted to prove that I had a good heart and that I cared. What I didn't realise was that my care was crippling our growth. By *dropping*, they would learn lessons that my *saving them* would not teach them. They would grow through the pain. I had to learn to pull back and watch them learn the lessons that I inadvertently foresaw. I had to shut up, wait and (if required) love and comfort them when they had learnt the lesson. My mother often used the saying, "Those who don't hear must feel." I will add a more appropriate saying (that applies to the topic at hand) and say sometimes you have to *feel* to be willing and ready to *hear* the lessons that life has to teach. God is speaking through the pain of those lessons. I bet you can think of a few lessons you have had in life that God has had to speak to you through. I know that I am thankful for those lessons, including this one. Save yourself, save your energy and invest it in your own growth. Trying to fix your husband, family and everything else will eventually send you into a frenzy. Support where you can, but wait, pray, be uplifting and allow God to do the talking. Cause when God talks, we all have no choice but to listen.

I know that this process is tough, and it highlights so many aspects of marriage that can be difficult to work through, but well done for sticking with it. I just know that you will come away from this process with direction if you want to. Keep pushing through, and you will reap if you don't give up.

Prayer and Meditation

Let's pray and reflect using the mirror.

Dear Heavenly Father,

*Please be my guide and usher me on my jour-
ney to self-discovery. Give me the courage to
face myself, even if I am afraid of what I
might see. Help me to embrace the truth that
you love me regardless of how much mess that
I am in. I embrace your hope, strength and
peace as I progress past this pain.*

In Jesus' name, Amen.

FOUR

DROWNING IN EMOTIONAL WAVES

§

"I must admit that there were times..." My husband's voice trailed off as he looked sheepishly in my direction to assess whether or not I was able to handle his confession.

"What?" I responded, curiously confident.

"There were times that you wouldn't speak to me, and I would think, *this is it.*"

It seemed like we were about to turn a corner and venture into dangerous, uncharted territory, the beginnings of marital breakdown. He was right. If I continued to put the walls up and not communicate, then it would put our marriage under immense strain, and it would eventually come to an end. That doesn't always mean divorce. We could easily have performed a happy, loving married couple act over choosing to be genuinely happy. There are so many skeleton marriages out there. Fundamentally, they look like they are working, but if you look closely, you will see the absence of any flesh while performing very well on the face of it. Loved up in public but in separate rooms when the doors close. United in a crowd but divided in the bedroom. Loveless, hopeless, dysfunctional and directionless.

I was taking us on a rollercoaster of emotions that risked leading us into an abyss of division. Drowning in emotions. Constantly irritated and unhappy. Disengaged and withdrawn. My husband would walk on eggshells and, in his own unique way, defend himself. He would meet my defensiveness with feigned chirpiness, hoping that the atmosphere would improve, but instead, it would intensify. We couldn't go on like this, but it was a self-perpetuating cycle. I had got stuck on this rollercoaster many years before I married my husband. I remember being a child in a broken home. My siblings and I lived with my mum. My dad would frequently come to collect us and take us to do fun things like go to the zoo, but, every now and then, he would forget or change his mind. The feeling of being disappointed was too much to bear. Growing up, I told myself, *no one will disappoint me like that again.*

I've had many relationships and friendships that I thought would last a lifetime. One after another, they expired, and I was left in that space of brokenness, like the little girl whose daddy didn't come to get her. With every disappointment, I built another wall. Fortified and impenetrable. Strong enough to hide my fragile heart. A heart that was so wounded and fearful that the next blow would be the end of it.

By the time I married Paul, the protective layers were so thick that I no longer noticed until he pressed against them. *How dare he?* I would think to myself from time to time. Paul would say or do something, and I would react by becoming withdrawn. No touch, no smiles, no eye contact and definitely no speaking. I call it the 'calm before the storm' because I would habitually withdraw before I attacked. That is of course, if the warning signs were left unheeded. Yes, my husband was the enemy – I would defend my territory. I was in fighter mode, and he was about to lose.

This perspective held me ransom for the first few years of marriage, and every time he disappointed me, I would retreat to defence mode. Even now, I can be incredibly guarded internally, while my outward demeanour remains open. It has almost been ingrained into my personality to put up walls if I feel like I am being attacked. It is something that I am aware of and something that I work on every day. I can easily attack when I feel like I am threatened emotionally. But if I go on the defensive, that usually means that I no longer want to waste my energy on a situation or person. They are absolutely and irrevocably cut off. It's something that the Lord has been working on with me recently, and I have been challenged in many ways not to burn bridges. Everyone has a defence mechanism, and naturally, this is mine. Silence. Emotional disconnect. Move on and wipe my hands clean of it. Some situations require this kind of reaction, but in other situations, it's like using a sledgehammer to crack a nut.

Surfing Emotional Waves

It is not a crime to have emotions. I admit that I've experienced my share of emotional turbulence, so I recognise how much managing them benefits my marriage, career, lifestyle and faith. Sometimes turbulence happens due to hormonal changes, menstrual cycles, lifestyle changes, responsibilities, having a new baby, or it might be due to being hazy, imbalanced and allowing the environment around us to dictate how we feel. Fundamentally, there is something quite beautiful about being emotionally healthy, but if we constantly have excessively tumultuous emotions, these can weigh us, and those around us, down. We can also stifle the blessings that we have, or eventually, will receive. That's why in this chapter, I want to talk about emotional turbulence and surfing the emotional rollercoaster. I call it "surfing" because the waves (of our emotions) will always be there, but it's how we handle them that determines how we move forward. It's okay to feel what you feel, but it takes incredible skill to surf our emotions' waves.

JOURNAL

- Do you find it difficult to control your emotions?
- Are you happy one day and sad the next?
- Do you allow your emotional state to take you on a rollercoaster that leads to no end?

Emotions will come and go, but if life is to resemble the Christlike nature that we are called to or even the abundance of peace and success that God has always planned for our lives, then we must learn to master our emotions. The key is being aware of these feelings; we are entitled to them, but they have the potential to derail our ability to thrive.

> *He who is slow to anger is better and more honourable than the mighty [soldier], And he who rules and controls his own spirit, than he who captures a city.*
> **—Proverbs 16:32 (AMP)**

This scripture aptly emphasises the importance of controlling our emotions. But how do we control our feelings and not allow our emotions to control us? How do we remove the toxicity of emotional overload from our environment? How do we build the harmonious lifestyle that we all crave in marriage, family, career and environment? Self-control. This is important because allowing our emotions to navigate can suffocate our blessings. One of the most underrated fruits of the Holy Spirit is temperance; that is, self-control: "the fruit of the Spirit is love, joy, peace, longsuffering, kindness, goodness, faithfulness, gentleness, **self-control**. Against such, there is no law."[10]

Self-control allows us to feel an emotion without drowning in it. It is the reason you didn't attack your dictatorial boss and lose your job. Sure, you felt the emotion, and there is nothing wrong with that. However, it stopped there. So, if you can manage to have that self-control at work, then you can go home and exercise that level of temperance with your husband. Of course, it takes practice, and that relationship is different, but it speaks volumes of your Divinely imparted power when you can exercise restraint with your husband.

I can hear you saying, "Sal, you don't understand… he works on my last nerves!"

Trust me, I understand, but husbands may need equally as much temperance to handle their emotions when interacting with us. Nothing tests your patience like someone who can access almost every aspect of your personal space. The only other person that should surpass the closeness of this relationship is God. I'm sure you can agree that God doesn't burst into the toilet uninvited when you need space to finish your "business". Yes, marriage is VERY personal. It's easy for your relationship to become overwhelming and for the walls to feel like they are closing in. The waves of emotion can easily rise under such extreme pressure.

---

[10] Galatians 5:22-23 (NKJV)

When you first fell in love, you could have easily been classified as joined at the hip. Where one was, then the other one would almost certainly be. It's such bliss in those early days, but when life and responsibilities set in, our needs inevitably change. I want to make it clear: it is completely natural for our emotional and spiritual needs to change as we journey along in marriage. Life pressures can require different aspects of us, and that's absolutely nothing to be ashamed of. I know for sure that I have changed so much since the early days of my relationship with Paul. However, I am vocal about the change in my preferences and taste. I don't shy away from speaking up about the things that I have outgrown, especially where my husband is concerned. Even little things about me have changed, down to my favourite colour. Many other things have changed in the last seven years, such as our ambitions, careers, routines etc. With this knowledge, he can now agree on how to accommodate those changes and vice versa. We both understand that we will grow over time, and we give each other the space to do so. If we resist growth, then we can cause stagnancy and frustration in our marriage; this is where the emotional waves start to rise.

Roots That Run Deep...

Something much deeper has taken root within the soil of your spirit. Something that seeps out of every crevice of your being. Something that you find incredibly difficult to admit and acknowledge. It's the elephant in the room, whether you realise it or not. Those roots have taken hold and are painfully, relentlessly, gripping you in this perilous position. Your experience has sown the painful seeds of animosity and discontentment; it has led you down this road, and you feel like there is no turning back. I should know; I have had to identify these roots in my life and why I responded to anything that I considered an attack, with a defensive wall. I have fought many battles and won so many, which was my justification for fortifying my walls. This time, I was fighting when there was no war and under immense spiritual torment and strain. I found it difficult to trust anyone, including my husband. My most honest answer is that it came from a deep-rooted sense of rejection. *Are you going to leave too?* It was always my mind's default question when challenges arose with my husband or those closest to me.

Even today, I instinctively hide behind the walls whenever I feel rejected and still struggle to conquer them. *She's so moody. She's sensitive! Oh, that woman is so unapproachable.* I understand that sometimes the lioness's roar is due to her pain. I know that you need to heal, and you are trying to find a way to move past the pain. All they see is the tree of symptoms, but they don't look at the roots. We all have this battle to fight. When times get tough, our emotions can run high. When someone loses a job or a loved one, emotions are likely to fluctuate. The challenges of managing a career, business or raising a family can cause emotional turbulence. The battle for our wellbeing happens every single day. Sometimes we will feel overwhelmed, but we must be vigilant in the battle for our minds, emotions and marriages. It's got to be deliberate and conscious.

You may find that the toughest challenge is working through some of the aspects of building your character. But persevere. To uproot, you must discover and cling to the truth about yourself, regardless of how painful it may be. Why do you feel the way that you are feeling? Is it something that your husband did? Or is it something that you have been trying to avoid within yourself? Have you been trying to convince yourself that it doesn't bother you, only to face struggles wherever you turn? It's not going to go away until you face yourself.

I consciously observe my emotions and focus on finding a safe space inside my spirit. Self-control is a daily choice and habit that I must practise whenever I am tested. We will inevitably be tested more often than not. The realisation that fear is not my truth has brought about a peace that lightens my journey. I am no longer governed by the fear of rejection that once caused me to hide the bubbly, sharp-witted and brilliant personality that makes me… me! I protected myself against anything that I felt might attack that beautiful individual I had worked so hard to become by pushing the opposition away. I believed the *wrong* perspective of others damaged my ability to have beautiful and thriving relationships. People caused me too much pain and rejection, and I was absolutely safe behind my walls. That perspective is so untrue. I was absolutely trapped behind the walls, and God clearly saw that. How can you be yourself if you're always hiding and unable to shine, to trust, completely?

I'm so thankful that God sent me Paul, and every single day, we work on breaking down the layers of pain and defences that we have both worked so hard to build. We discuss how to communicate better, how to be more open, and we challenge *the way it's always been done*. We do it with big lumps in our throats (that's our way of swallowing our pride). It's the way that Christ has called us to be. Marriage epitomises the denial of self and the nature of selfless love. That means we constantly show each other those parts of ourselves that we don't show to anyone else. A no-condemnation zone makes it even easier to show each other why we respond to things the way we do. It means that we are paying attention and giving each other the floor to share whatever is in our hearts. His whispers are heard, and my roars are understood.

You are welcome to try it – open up to God and allow Him to heal your pain. God is close to those who are crushed at heart, and He knows how to mend it. If this rings true, ask, *what hurts so much that I am determined to keep my guard up?* You know you are losing in this state. There are so many blessings in the people that God wants to bring into your life, and one of those blessings is your husband. God wants you to bloom so much that you become unrecognisable. He wants you to radiate from your soul so much so that your own husband will marvel at the brilliance that you exude. You need to go to the source of your joy. Only Jesus can be that level of joy and freedom for you. Let's admit it: without Him, we haven't got a clue what we are doing.

I fiercely contend for and protect my marriage. I look ahead to assess any potential threats coming against us. I handle every battle with wisdom and look to God for opportunities to masterfully defend our marriage. It's easy to consider my husband as a threat, but could it be that the enemy lies within the extremities of our waves of emotion? One day we are easy to approach, and the next day it's like walking on cracked glass. Does your husband retaliate with vehement arguments, or does he retreat? He's trying to understand but just cannot get through that wall. Should he hug you? Or should he give you space? It's difficult for him to love you when you experience emotional turbulence because it's difficult for him to understand you.

Getting Off the Emotional Rollercoaster

There is nothing worse than feeling stuck. Stuck in an unfulfilled life, career, stagnant friendships; stuck with unused talents and abilities or stuck in spiritual blockage. There are so many ways that we can get stuck in life. It can be so restrictive and suffocating. Sometimes, I see it in the eyes of the people that I meet. Their mouths say that they are fine, but something else is in their eyes. Paralysis oozes from their pores. If you are stuck, then it's going to have an effect on your marriage: your attitude, talk and perspective of your husband. It will be easy to attack your husband for what he didn't do or the things he did wrong. Think of the times that you argue about things that don't matter because you're avoiding the things that DO matter. It's your emotions that are erratically swinging back and forth like a pendulum. You are not addressing the real issue – the feeling of being stuck. Many root causes can lead you to this place, but the result is always the same. Pain. Discontentment. Frustration. You're in pain because you are paralysed in life. Maybe you aren't acknowledging that you gave YOUR life away, and it's YOUR choice to remain in that space of being unfulfilled.

I completely understand because I have been there. God has given you unimaginable power, but He is not going to force you to use it. The power lies in your own will and ability to run with what God has given you. It's not in your husband's hands; he can only be your cheer-leader. You have to be your own champion. When this truth became my reality, I was able to soar to new heights. As a result, I feel better connected to my husband and more understood; what's most im-portant is that I understand myself. Being aware of my emotions has given me the ability to know when I need to tend to my emotional state. I can ask for support when I'm in a state of emotional turbulence. I even feel more confident about my emotional state and space. Has it been a challenge? Yes, with my newfound power are newfound chal-lenges, but each one contains a lesson that brings forth new growth. I feel so released into my Divinely orchestrated purpose that I can in-spire my husband to be the king that he was always meant to be. It takes strength to birth the king in your husband, but first, there has to be a birth of the Queen in you. It starts with realising that you are a Queen, and you have the power to change the narrative in your life regardless of how difficult the circumstances may seem. As a mother of two, I know that giving birth is one of the hardest things that a woman will ever do in her life, but there is also a tide of joy, satisfaction and happiness that washes over you. You feel complete, and a wave of love overtakes you when you look into the eyes of your baby. As it is in the natural world, so it is also in the spiritual. You will see your life and value in the same way that God does when you live out your purpose. There is so much locked up in the depths of your heart and spirit that is waiting to be released, and when it is, you'll recognise that your husband wasn't the problem.

Don't get me wrong, you may have an unsupportive husband who doesn't understand your heart or why you are so unfulfilled, but you have to respectfully continue to be an example and a light to him until he captures the vision. Am I asking you to be deceitful, scheme or lie? Absolutely not. I'm asking you to own your truth boldly and push your way through the dirt until the rays of truth and purpose cascade over you like a waterfall. Make it a challenge for you and your husband to work towards. Encourage him to be a part of the process to the benefit of your marriage. It's necessary and important.

In 1 Samuel 25, notice how Abigail took drastic action to save her husband from King David's anger. She tried to use her vision to save her husband's life and was ultimately honoured for it (even though her husband died, but that aspect is for another day). I would never encourage you to withhold information from your husband that benefits your marriage and trust. However, I would encourage you to have the foresight to see that marriage needs two FULFILLED people to be enriched throughout a lifetime. So, start by working on yourself.

Fight Mode: Attack and Defence

I describe the disagreement between husband and wife as "the war" because there is a point where our primitive human attack or defence mechanisms are triggered, and we engage in battle with our spouse. He becomes the opposer, and we are determined to be the victor. There is a point during the war when we decide to attack or defend, and it's usually when we feel like we are being attacked. In response, we argue, snap, goad. Or we defend: we employ the silent treatment, emotionally disengage and withdraw. It is our way of protecting ourselves when we feel like we are in danger – whether consciously or subconsciously. When there is no communication, we go into fight or flight mode. Do we run or fight for our territory?

Asserting our dominance is a futile move for marriage. It's not about *you* or *me*; it's about *us*. How can WE move forwards? How can WE change the narrative? How can WE flip the script? We can either deliberately or subconsciously put up defences regarding emotions and matters of the heart. The story that we tell ourselves might sound very powerful. Either our husband is our enemy or our friend. When we choose to make him our enemy, we can become guarded, defensive and protective. These traits are needed when it comes to dangerous adversaries, but with the love of your life? I don't think so. The defences are also necessary for when you are in harm's way, for example, in an abusive marriage. However, in a healthy marriage, these walls are counterproductive. We don't consciously set out to suck the life out of our marriages because it is like draining our own life force. We unify with our husbands, and we suffer when they suffer.

Men usually respond to any attack from a logical perspective. In their minds, it seems that if there is a problem, then it can be fixed immediately. Whereas a woman usually has to ride out how she feels. If I'm angry about something, then the last thing I want to hear is, "It's over now. Just forget about it." I need an opportunity to ride out the feelings of anger, frustration, etc., although I may use distance or distraction as tools to help me calm down. Women are all about the journey rather than the destination. Men are usually the opposite. Women are about the details and men prefer the overall picture. Don't believe me? Ask your husband what one of your friends was wearing at an event that you recently attended. Most of the time, the response will be vague and non-committal. However, if it is a friend we admire, then we're more likely to describe the details of the hair, shoes, dress or suit. Women tend to care about the details. We even notice if someone has worn the same outfit twice! Men and women can be so opposite, but the beauty of it is that no ground is left uncovered. When women and men come together, then logic and emotion will either collide or unite. There is absolutely nothing wrong with logic or emotion because they are God-given gifts to help us connect with one another. How can we use both our logic and our emotion to enhance our ability to agree instead of fuelling discord?

Communication and patience are the keys. Appreciating the value of logic and emotion within our family is vital to our ability to thrive. We take time to learn how each other works, and it's okay not to get it right the first time. We need to be as patient with one another as Christ has been with us. How many times have we made mistakes, and how many times has God forgiven us? He sees an end goal, and He is patient with us until we get there. This is the same approach that we should have with our marriages. What is your end goal? Mine is that my husband is excited to come home to a wife who is equally as thrilled to have her husband home. There is nothing worse than being with someone who doesn't want you there. I am not painting a picture of perfection. This isn't *Stepford Wives,* and we aren't trying to become women that mask our feelings. I believe in emotional health, and I am certain that God wants us to function at our best emotionally. It's okay to journey through emotional valleys because we won't be happy all the time. Sometimes events will cause us to struggle emotionally; for example, bereavement, job loss, financial straits, problems with parenting, anxiety, and the list goes on. My emphasis is on being vocal and sharing how you are feeling. Let your husband into that sacred space of your heart and soul and allow him to journey, pray and support you through it.

Identifying Triggers

What's bugging you? Maybe you have a hectic schedule, and it is affecting your mood. Or you have a house full of children, and the responsibilities are overwhelming. Or maybe it's something deeper. Maybe your husband has let you down in some way. Some triggers are valid, and some are not. Some triggers can be avoided. Others aren't that easy to deal with. As I write this book, I am currently teaching my four-year-old son about emotions and to name how he is feeling. Sometimes he is so overwhelmed by his emotions that he can't explain how he feels. Some emotions are too complex for him to identify (like jealousy, for example).

It is the start of the Covid-19 pandemic. We have been at home for three weeks without school and unable to go for regular walks due to the rise in infection rates. Needless to say, there have been waves upon waves of emotional turbulence. Ironically, I am writing this chapter now because it has really helped me to become more aware of how I feel about the current situation and the emotional impact that the world events are having on my family. My eldest son has been crying more often than usual, and when I ask him, "How do you feel?" he anxiously replies, "I don't know!" I was at a loss as to how to help him cope with his despair until I found a book that has been a game-changer in managing his feelings.

"There is nothing wrong with feeling emotions, but it is important to work through your feelings," I have told him over and over again. In one of my repetitive lectures, the penny dropped. This is it! Something so basic and powerful. We can become victims of how we feel and think that we deserve punishment for how we feel. There is nothing in the Bible or in society that punishes us for feeling emotions.

On the contrary, emotions are a sign that we are alive. They are the reason that we don't harm our babies out of frustration. They are the sign of an effective nurturer. Emotions help us sense danger or truly enjoy life's experiences. They are vital to our spiritual, mental and physical health. They are a God-given gift. I believe in the power of emotional health.

I teach my family to be aware of their emotional health, because I truly believe that it sets a strong foundation for wholeness and will help our children grow up balanced and with the best potential to thrive in life. My belief has been cemented by a variety of life experiences that various people have shared with me. They have shared how their lives have spiralled out of control due to addictions and self-harm. A young woman addicted to pornography, another woman addicted to cutting herself, bulimia and suicide attempts. What set them on this path to destruction? Depression. Anxiety. Being unable to cope with the emotions that they were feeling?

We are not taught at school about the importance of emotional balance and how to nurture our emotions. They are seen as insignificant. No big deal, right? Our emotions can derail our logic and lead us to find self-destructive coping mechanisms. Feeling stressed after a hard day at work? Had an argument with a member of your family? Failed at an exam? That can drastically impact how you feel. You may not have the most extreme crutches to deal with, but when it comes to the long-term sustainability of your marriage, emotional management is crucial. It's something that I wish someone had taught me. Even though I am married to my best friend, there are times that I have to be silent when I want to scream at him from the top of my lungs. There have been times where I may want to share information with others that I think, *hmmm... my husband wouldn't want me to share this.* Then, regardless of how extrovert I am, I choose to exercise restraint.

Direct, Flow, Release

Emotions are like a river. They surge from within, but they need direction, flow and release. Proverbs 4:23 says, "Keep your heart with all diligence, for out of it spring the issues of life."[11]

Whatever you feel inside is going to overflow and come out in one way or another. The only thing that you have control over is releasing your emotions the right way. This is where you will really need to know how you're wired. What are you passionate about? How easy is it for you to shout, cry or let off steam? Emotions need a place to go. If they aren't dealt with, then they will come out the wrong way. If you can manage your emotions well, then you will know when you need a safe place to let them out. Where is the safest place for you to let out your emotions? How do you let out your emotions? Do you find it easier to let out your emotions during your prayer time? Or while you are painting a picture? Or making music? It must be obvious to you that writing is a great way for me to navigate my emotions. I write more passionately when I'm emotional. Some of my best work comes from expressing my emotions through writing. When I find it hard to pray, lose the words and feel like there is an emotional blockage, I just write letters to God.

Some people bring out the worst emotions in us, and in those situations, it can be so difficult to exercise self-control. Switch your focus from that emotion to something that is going to ease the emotional pressure that you are feeling. Why does that person make you feel how you are feeling? Is it how they talk to you or the things that they do to

---

[11] Proverbs 4:23 (NKJV)

or around you that make you feel like you're going through emotional loopy loops? Fight for your peace. That may mean that you need to be silent when you are around them or avoid them when you can. It may mean that you may have to have a frank discussion with them. Your peace will be a great indicator that you have made the right moves.

Sometimes there are no solutions to your emotions at a particular time in your life. Just know that you are not alone on that journey and that God is with you. Even if you cannot find concrete solutions to how you are feeling, find a safe space to express your pain. Talk to God. Seek Godly counsel and someone that will pray with and support you as you go through your journey. Some situations simply don't have quick fixes. If there is a bereavement in the family, and your grief is raw and long-lasting, God understands. You may have to journey through those emotions slowly and delicately while you grow from the pain of your experience. Being in touch with your emotions is a skill, and it takes time and great self-awareness to learn how you feel and what you need to fuel your emotional health. Are you burning out? Do you need time away with your girlfriends? Have you been struggling mentally? All these things affect how you feel, and your emotions affect your home.

A phone call, or coffee with a friend and a shoulder to cry on, can have a massive impact on balancing our emotional state. Sometimes we don't need solutions. We need to release our emotions in a safe space and move past them. We learn as we go along. We make mistakes. We read books and evaluate. We cry. We process, work through and recognise that we are going to be OKAY. Your journey is yours. You are growing all the time, even when you don't recognise it. This is a lifelong battle, because it is easy to become emotionally imbalanced but can also be easy to rectify. I have learnt the value of listening to the observations of the person closest to me – my husband. Pay attention to your husband's observations. Especially if he has a proven track record of being right. If he says that you are going on a downwards spiral, then this is a clear indicator. Time alone with God is so important. Pray, reflect and meditate on God's word. It can be cliché, but I want you to hear me out. When you really make time to connect with God, then that connection has a massive impact on your emotional state: "In Your presence is fullness of joy; At Your right hand are pleasures forevermore."[12]

Having a Bible app is great. I love to use it to help me to relax, meditate and focus on God's presence. Exercise, rest, a healthy diet and plenty of water can also work wonders on our emotional wellbeing. If you take care to nurture your body, it can have a positive effect on your emotions. If you aren't able to avoid the things that bug you, then articulate how you feel. Identifying and communicating how I have felt has massively contributed to the progression and success of my marriage. I would like to challenge you to change one of these things every two weeks and keep a diary about how it makes you feel at the end. I am more than certain that you will see such a transformation and, even better, your family will too.

JOURNAL

- Discuss your emotional health with three of your closest friends and family.
- Pray about your emotional state.
- Write down three activities that you will use to nurture your emotional state.

---

[12] Psalm 16:11 (NKJV)

Developing Perspective

Marriage is a journey and is not always easy. I am incredibly blessed to have Paul in my life. His attentive nature, openness and sincerity have brought down the walls, layer by layer. I prayed for someone that would exemplify the love that Christ had for His Church and for me, and God sent me Paul. However, over time I began to realise that I could potentially be a threat to my own blessing. To fuel and nurture my blessing, I would have to let go of some deep-rooted habits and allow new practices to thrive.

One of the first practices I had to change was my perspective. To strengthen and improve my marriage, I had to recognise that we had to unite against any enemy attacking our marriage, and I had to stop making Paul my enemy. It was incredibly difficult, and it took a long time. He had, and still has, good intentions towards me (even though he may not always understand quickly) and does everything in his power to ensure my *wellbeing*. When I stopped morphing him into a bad person every time he did something that I didn't understand, or I disagreed with, then I was able to communicate with him better. Now, when I feel frustration, pain, sadness or anger, I let my emotions placate before going to him and saying, "I *feel* so angry *when you speak* to me like that."

His response has sometimes been that he didn't realise I was feeling that way. He wasn't observing or didn't agree with me. However, once the lines of communication are open, then hope reigns! When you know your husband's heart, then it is easier to trust him with yours. How open are you with your husband, and how well do you understand him? Having the right perspective will save you from the wave of emotions, and, even better, it will save your husband too! These habits can take a lifetime to build, and it takes the Holy Spirit to remind me to use these new practices whenever I go on this roller-coaster of emotions.

To nurture your spirit, get better at identifying what you need and conveying those needs to your husband. You can have this dialogue in a variety of ways. If you find it hard to be verbal, then you could write a letter or make a video and leave it for him. Speak the truth even if your voice shakes and even if you have to use other means to make sure that your needs are heard. It may mean that your relationship becomes difficult for a time. Make it clear that it's your heart's desire to ensure that your relationship goes from strength to strength. Pray, hold onto your truth and integrity and be patient. The end outcome will work out "for your good".[13]

It's that time again! You've come to the end of another difficult chapter and are making waves that will change the course of your life! Stay focused and prayed up as you continue to move through the other chapters of this book. It's about to get steep but stick with me as we show the world what a real glow up looks like. Now let's go back to that mirror and pray.

---

[13] Romans 8:28 (KJV)

Prayer and Meditation

Let's pray and reflect using the mirror.

Dear Heavenly Father,

You see my emotional wounds, and you are my remedy. Please continue to guide me to the right people, places and resources that will support me as I heal. Give me more of an awareness of myself. Show me the triggers and healers of my turbulent emotions. Heal my family and relationships from all of the damage that the fluctuations of my emotions have caused. Thank you for hearing my prayer.

In Jesus' name, Amen.

FIVE

IT'S THE THOUGHT THAT COUNTS

§

She seems like the perfect wife, with what appears to be the most amazing family. She seemingly has a perfect life.

On the outside, she is a flawless example of a wife. She appears to have it all. If only you knew that she is consumed by the lies that she tells herself every day. There's an emptiness in her soul that seems to get bigger as the days go by. She is acutely aware of the pressure that weighs upon her mind and the decline in her mental health.

Still, she stays silent. Afraid that asking for help would make her look weak. No matter how hard she tries to shake it off, a dark cloud hovers wherever she goes. Engulfed by the maze of confusion inside her mind, she stumbles on, hoping that help will come.

Yet it never does. Of course, not until now.

Maybe you're having similar struggles to the one described above. Perhaps you are finding it difficult to give the best of yourself because your mental fight is so intense. Your mind is the steering wheel of your vessel. Your whole being and way of life depend on your mental health; it affects your emotions, your spiritual wellbeing, your dreams, your visions, your relationships and, of course, your marriage. It's not easy to maintain a healthy marriage if the facets of your mind are crumbling. When your mind goes unnurtured, it becomes hard to move past the hazy confusion and help anyone else. It may even feel as though you're in deep waters and have lost control. You are kicking your arms and legs so hard, yet the waves keep crashing overhead. Imagine the feeling of briefly coming up for air and, just when you feel like you've got control of the waves, you are pulled back under. Your heart seems to expand as the fear washes over you. You completely lose control. Somewhere in your mind, there's an awareness that you should be on the shore where it's stable and balanced, but you've forgotten how to get there.

When the mind loses its stability, it can feel exactly like this. You yearn to be in a stable and balanced position, but there is just nothing certain to hold onto – nothing to give you weight. How do you keep it all together when you are falling apart? You can feel yourself losing control, but how do you ask for help? How do you stop yourself from drowning, especially when no one knows how much you need saving?

Dealing with Pressure

The mind is complex and beautiful. Brilliant like a diamond yet as fragile as glass. When put under enough pressure, stress, worry and without the right support, it can splinter, and eventually, the cracks will start to appear. Mental strength varies from person to person; what one person's mind can handle could potentially break another's.

The pressure could mount due to a minuscule issue, like worry over a child; the pressure could grow exponentially due to life-altering events, such as bereavement, illness and so on. Maybe that's your mind. Maybe you're reading this and wondering, *will my mind ever be okay? Will I ever wake up in the morning and be happy with the world of wonders that is buried within the depths of my mind?* No longer lost in the maze of it all but finally emboldened by a newfound clarity. Free. More than able to move forward with plans for the future without fear of jeopardising it all. No longer bound by the secret of being the victim of a fragile mind. Able to be the best wife, mother, family member, friend that you can be because your mind is liberated from the baggage that has weighed you down for so long.

Thinking, *I can handle it*, is one of the most deadly and deceptive thoughts. It's easy to feel like you are stronger than you actually are for fear of being exposed, seeming out of control or weak. Or maybe you tell yourself that good ol' Christian jargon that you're trusting God that your state of mind and situation will improve. But are you actually trusting God, having faith and looking to see your situation improve? I believe that it is crucial to take steps and do the work to see true progress. "Even so faith, if it hath not works, is dead, being alone."[14]

You can start reassembling the fragments of your mind by admitting the truth: you need support to thrive. Show good faith that your situation will improve by taking action. We all need a lifeguard to guide us to shore when the waters of confusion, instability and mental challenges feel like they're closing in. It can happen to anyone at any given point in their lives for any given reason. The lifeguard can take many forms, whether it is a counsellor, a psychologist, a doctor, worship, prayer, expression through hobbies, meditation or a combination

[14] James 2:17 (KJV)

of the above. We have to become more aware of drowning and be brave enough to ask for help.

Knowing When You Need Help

I have found that those who are closest to us are the most honest observers. When I have struggled with depression, my mum and husband have brought it to my attention and helped me own up to it. I have learnt that you have to trust someone to be completely honest with you, even if you don't like it. Not only do we need honesty from our loved ones, but we also need them to stand with us and help us to start taking the steps towards healing – even in the toughest and darkest times. To show you that you don't have to be afraid of your struggles. To pray for you when you find it hard to pray for yourself. It's even more uplifting when others don't make assumptions about why you have come to this place and believe in you when you doubt your own ability to triumph. There are power and strength in the community, and it is absolutely necessary for mental health. When you are supported by people who know God, you are in an unbreakable position, regardless of what it feels like. You dramatically increase your chances of pulling through because your back is no longer exposed. In other words, they've got you covered.

If left unattended, depression, anxiety, panic attacks, insomnia and stress can consume you and often result in disassociation, heaviness and exhaustion. Its weight can leave you wondering if you will ever overcome it. Then there are the days where you just want to hide and hope that it all goes away, making you feel like you're losing fight, faith and the strength to move forward. It's almost like the worst kind of insanity: a festering wound. You may keep looking ahead but see nothing but confusion and uncertainty. Your road has not been a smooth one. It's easy to wonder how you've made it this far. How have you managed to take on the responsibilities that come with marriage while grappling with your mental health? How have you managed to keep it all together when you are broken inside? The mind is supposed to be a safe haven, but it can easily feel like a war zone. It's difficult to keep your battle a secret forever because, eventually, the weight becomes unbearable.

In the previous chapter, we explored how emotional imbalance can strain your marriage. In this chapter, I would like to talk about how mental challenges can also be detrimental. Many marriages fall apart due to mental health issues not being brought to the light. I meet so many women who have mental challenges but refuse to nurture their minds. Sometimes they are unaware that many of their struggles come from refusing to tend to their mind's deteriorating state. Your mental agility and resilience are your most necessary and powerful resources. You are the guardian of your own mind by Divine designation; it is invaluable and precious and should not be trivialised or ignored.

JOURNAL

- How are you taking care of your mind?
- How do you guard it against the pressures of everyday life?
- Do you know how to take care of your mental health?

Did you know that you're more susceptible to drowning in emotional waves if you neglect your mind? Our mental and emotional states are intrinsically linked. It's crucial to check in with yourself to make sure that your mind and emotions are nurtured.

Self-awareness is such an important aspect of maintaining and restoring mental health. Knowing when your emotional and mental resources are becoming depleted and finding the support you need will tremendously aid your mental development. It's also important to note that so much of what we feel comes from what we feed our mind; it's crucial that we are aware of what we are exposing our mind to. There is so much out there that can affect how we think and how we feel that I have become wary of what I allow in. Also, who I allow into my space can have an effect on my mental state. I am at my optimum, mentally, during the first part of the day, but I am more exhausted in the evenings. Everyone's mental patterns vary. Self-awareness will allow you to assess your mental patterns and be in sync with your mental rhythm. There are so many factors that can contribute to the improvement of the mind; how much rest and relaxation we have, having a balanced diet, exercise, and human connection can all play a part in our mental state's progression. That's why meditation (taking time for mental stillness) is so important, because it brings awareness of what needs tending. Running around with your family, frantically fulfilling duties without taking time to tend to your spirit will damage your mind. You will find that while tending to your spirit (during your time of meditation), your heart instinctively starts searching and talking to God. It's in that safe and sacred space that we build on our inner state. In the scriptures, David wisely and aptly declares, "He that dwelleth in the secret place of the Most High Shall abide under the shadow of the Almighty."[15] It's in this secret place with Him that you can receive rest, healing and strength for the road ahead.

---

[15] Psalm 91:1 (KJV)

Fighting for Your Marriage and Mind

It can be so easy to hide personal struggles out of a misguided sense of protecting others. The fear of letting them down or being seen differently can be a heavy burden, and how can you support anyone else if you can't support yourself?

A simple change in perspective can help you show up for yourself and, eventually, others. The mentality of feeling like you're letting someone else down by sharing your fragile mental state will limit your growth. Stop hiding behind the mask of having it all together, because it is causing you to suffer. What others think about you is none of your business. Even if it is your husband's disapproval. He should applaud you for taking the necessary steps to recover and heal. Your journey to mental wholeness is pivotal in how you view yourself and your ability to fly light. You don't need the added pressure of anything or anyone that wants you to stay trapped in the cage of mental torture. Shift your focus to those things that you need to thrive. Focus only on finding the support you need to nurse the delicate areas of your mind back to health.

How Does Marriage Affect Mental Health?

Abuse, dysfunction and discord can be triggers of mental turbulence and distress within marriage. Maybe you feel a gradual decline in your mental state, or you have felt like a weight has abruptly descended upon your mind. Lack of sleep, a decline in social interaction, overwhelming anxiety and fear can be the signs of a weary mind. If all your symptoms intensify when he walks into the room and the temperature changes; it's time to face the truth. The cause of your turmoil is him. We all crave peace, especially within our marriages, but sometimes marriage can be the hardest place to find it. When you get to the point of despair because you have tried everything to make your relationship harmonise with your mental state, then it's clear that you're hitting a crisis. Every marriage is different, and there may be a variety of reasons for mental health decline. Sometimes the marriage might not be the fundamental reason for mental health challenges, and they can also exist within a perfectly healthy marriage. However, I want to specifically discuss the impact that a dysfunctional marriage can have on the mind. The turbulence in your relationship can be the root cause of depression, including personality incompatibility, lifestyle changes and relationship disconnect with people surrounding the marriage. Many suffer in silence, until one day they take drastic action to the detriment of themselves and others around them. No one saw it coming. Unable to bear the façade any longer, they make decisions that could end in the destruction of themselves or their family. Why? They don't have the tools needed to be liberated.

So, what happens when the pressures of marital life affect your relationship? Challenges of living with a difficult partner or a change in health, connection (including challenges with sexual intimacy), loneliness in marriage, lifestyle changes, having children, and spiritual disconnect can all harm your mind. Behind closed doors, it can feel like the walls are closing in. It's so easy to become weary as a result of trying to hold it all together. Firstly, I want you to know that you are amazing for keeping it all together for so long. That is a sign that you are stronger than you think you are. My Queen, it is time for you to use the strength that you have left to find the nourishment that your mind craves. Take a few minutes in your day to reflect and even make a few notes to get the clarity that you need.

- What are the *external* challenges that have been affecting my mental health?
- What are the *internal* struggles that have been affecting my mental wellbeing?
- What three steps will I take to build my mental health?

Journaling is a great tool to get the clarity that you need. It allows you to see and assess the state of your mind. You can learn a lot about yourself by looking at what you write. Please don't take this process for granted. It's important to be honest and clear about what you think, how you feel and what you need when you are journaling. You'll be surprised at how much enlightenment and direction you receive from those moments of reflection.

If you feel like your marriage has affected your mental health, then I believe that speaking to a counsellor is important. Having your partner present may be helpful, but I urge you to talk to someone even if you have to do it alone. Do it for *you*: your growth, your mental healing, your life's direction and the development of your whole person. It's okay to get outside support to help you to feel like yourself again.

Your marital situation may be in too dire a state to be resolved by just seeing a counsellor. Maybe you are being oppressed and abused by your husband, and you are certain that you will have to leave your marital home to save your mental health. There is a journey of realisation and pain that can have even more of a detrimental effect on your mind as you come to terms with your situation's weight. We will delve deeper into the challenges that come with leaving your marriage in Chapter 12, *When Marriage Is Killing You*, and Chapter 13, *Life After Marriage*. It is for that reason that I won't explore the complexities of divorce in this section, but I encourage you to glean strength as you journey through those chapters. And remember, it's okay to share these difficult challenges with our Heavenly Father. Pour out your heart to Him and ask Him for the strength that you need to journey ahead. He genuinely cares, and you will be amazed to see how He works it all out for you and your family.

Mental challenges equate to behavioural changes, which eventually impact everyday life routines and relationships, putting pressure on your marriage. If you suffer from anxiety, stress or panic attacks, you may find it difficult to deal with everyday routines. You may even try to avoid people, events, situations and activities for fear of onset. But what happens in unavoidable situations? How do you cope? It won't always be as simple or as easy as walking away. That's why you must nurture your mind so that you can confront the challenges.

My Journey to Mental Recovery

One of the most notable and memorable mental challenges that I have faced is depression. I remember having this immense feeling of loss, incredible sadness and numbness. At times I have even felt that no one would notice if I took my own life. I felt miserable, worthless and stuck. Two definitive moments were just after having my first son and losing my job – painful triggers that were ignited due to drastic life changes.

I understand how it feels when everything around you keeps changing, and you feel like you have no control. Marriage couldn't save me. My husband would come home from work and just hold me, encourage me and pray for me. I could feel myself stare blankly into the distance as his encouragements would fade into a dull hum, and the intensity of my pain would increase. Over time, I discovered that purpose would be the key to my mental development and recovery from depression. I looked ahead, and my future began to take shape as a result of prayerful planning. I became hopeful that everything could get better. I realised that the power to make positive strides was in my hands alone.

No one was going to steer the direction of my life. I had to take control of it. Another incredible truth that transformed my life was the healing power of impact. When I started to look around me and ask, *whose life can I be of service to?* When I took the focus off of myself and began to be a blessing to others – healing came. I remember starting a children's group and looking into the little hopeful eyes of those babies. They were my inspiration, and they kept me going. What's fascinating is that they had no idea! I no longer run a baby group, but I still have two pairs of little hopeful eyes that look up at me, cheering me on. They're my sons. They are two of the most invaluable reasons that I continue to make my mental health a priority. If you are feeling weighed down by your mental state, try being a blessing to others; you may be surprised by how much their lives impact your own.

The Coward and the Warrior

When you have mental health struggles, it inevitably negatively impacts your loved ones, especially your husband – whether consciously or subconsciously. Even if you try to hide the struggle within, it will eventually show up one way or another. Ultimately, as time goes on, the burden becomes too much to bear, and the weight of your struggle comes spewing forth. A man that loves and cares for you will agonise over your distress. How you feel and your wellbeing are important, not just to your husband but to all your loved ones. It's so easy to feel insignificant or that your feelings don't matter, but they do. You may feel guilty or ashamed about having mental health struggles and try to hide. Sometimes it can be instinctive to want to deny the challenges that you are facing. *I can cope* is an excuse that comes to mind, or here's another one: *it will go away soon*. Sometimes we hope that if we don't face the storms raging within, they might just disappear. A coward and a warrior live within all of us.

Every day we have to be deliberate in making a choice to be the warrior – to face our internal daily battles and allow that warrior to prevail. The coward will tell you that you shouldn't ask for help or that you should pretend everything is fine; that you should go for what seems like the most peaceful road right now. You may ask yourself *why should I leave the mask behind?* After all, it's safe and comfortable. It's convenient if no one knows that you are hiding your pain behind your façade. But to whose detriment? Who comes up with the short straw in the end? You do. You become the hollow tree that is just existing. Barely holding on. As time goes on, you're the one who becomes incapable of giving anyone your best because you robbed yourself first. The truth is, hiding doesn't pay, my friend. It just makes the wound fester. Honestly speaking, I feel that at one stage or another, as we go through life, most of us need support with mental nurture and care. Asking for help doesn't make you inferior or a burden. In fact, you're incredibly brave and strong for asking for the support you need. You'd be surprised at how much help you will receive if you open up.

One of the most invaluable lessons that I have had to learn is that it is incredibly unhelpful to pick and choose when to hide and expose yourself to your husband. Being open is my expression of love and care towards him, even if I don't have all the answers. We live in such close proximity that it's easy for him to notice the little things that give my state of mind away – whether it's something *light* like being lumbered with the duties of the day or something *heavier* like not being able to get out of bed for days.

The truth is that the most beautiful marriages are the ones where the couples are open and in sync, and that requires conscious effort. It means seeing the ugliness and brokenness in the heart of your spouse and loving them through it. I'm not talking about passive and positive emotion. I'm talking about praying, helping them to find the help that they need and being present in the darkest moments of their lives. That's honestly what my husband has been to me. He's held my hand through some of the most difficult moments in my life. He has taught me that my pain hurts him too. The pain that consumes me could kill my husband without touching him, simply because he loves me. When I am hurting, he hurts – and vice versa. Your mental wellbeing has a ripple effect on everything in your life. So, when you work on yourself, for the benefit of yourself, it will benefit your husband and loved ones too.

I have learnt that there is strength in admitting weakness. I love 2 Corinthians 12:9, which says, "my grace is sufficient for you, for my strength is made perfect in weakness." To translate, God can fill all the cracks in our lives, and He makes up for the things that we lack. I can be honest about where I fall short so that God can open all the doors to my healing. Sometimes we don't understand why we struggle, we aren't sure of a way forward, and it can be overwhelming. However, when we can surrender the complexities of our mental challenges to God, then the pressure, anxiety and weight become bearable. Jesus said, "Come to me, all of you who are weary and carry heavy burdens, and I will give you rest."[16] Not only is God able to carry the weight of your burdens, but He can carry you. It is amazing to know that we

---

[16] Matthew 11:28 (NLT)

survived the things that almost destroyed us because we were not alone. I say this to emphasise that God is with you in the hardest, darkest parts of your journey. It is God who will give you the strength and the courage to move past the darkness into the light.

Finding Healing

Healing happens differently for everyone. Some people have miraculous, long-lasting and instantaneous healing, while others have to go through a process many times. God will send you the people and groups you need to unlock the parts of yourself that you never knew were there. The good, the bad and the ugly. See God in all of it. He is shaping you through it all. Some of it will feel amazing, and other parts of it will feel incredibly uncomfortable, but you cannot escape the process. When God is taking you somewhere (and He is determined to get you there), He will give you your own spiritual whale that will spit you out in your own destined Nineveh, just like He did for Jonah (in the Bible). Roll with His Divine tide and let Him wash you to the place that is exactly where He wants you.

That's what He has done with me over and over again. I speak to you from my own life's journey. You are my Nineveh. I have had to go through my own whale experiences that led me to write this book. I can tell you with absolute certainty that God knows what He is doing. Will I get depressed again? We are in the middle of a pandemic as I write this, and there have been moments where that cloud has started to hover. Sometimes, I would be in despair about the pain and confusion that this pandemic has caused. Other times, I would sing a song, and I would think of how amazing God is, and the cloud would lift. My whole life has been about worship, and it has been my healing and escape.

What has God given you that you can escape to? Are you great at painting? Do you love to pray? When the cloud hovers, find that secret place in your spirit with God and escape there. That's when you begin to win. You flip the script and invite your own healing. Don't rush yourself. God is not rushing you into this space, but focus on becoming a professional at escaping into this secret place.

The healing starts in the crevices of your heart. Learn to escape and hide in Him wherever you are. Are you at work? On the school run? Shopping? You can escape to Him right there, and He will never tell you to make an appointment for another date. I can't promise you that you won't have intense moments of mental struggles. I can only say that you have to become so aware of yourself and excellent at knowing exactly how to get to your spiritual physician – that is, our Heavenly Father.

It's also okay to need professional help along the way. When I was stuck in a mental rut or spiritual turmoil, my counsellor was like a mirror for me. It was like her words highlighted that my mental buttons were undone, and my spiritual trousers were inside out. It wasn't always easy to hear her observations, but what she revealed helped me to triumph. I exposed the pain in my soul, and she gave me tools to heal. Tools that are clearly written in the word of God but somehow needed highlighting. That's what the right counsel can do for you, too. Sometimes we need support to handle the weight of it all – someone to see what we don't see. The right GODLY counsel can pull out and amplify aspects of the scripture that you have never noticed before and help you to apply it to your life so that it facilitates radical healing. The impact of having a Christian counsellor was evident in our connection and the implementation of her services. I was at ease, knowing that the counsellor could pray for me and understand the power of faith. So, I talked. It was so good to share whatever was on my heart without holding back. That kind of weight needs a safe space to be released, someone who will listen and be present. To have the person listen and not be invested in the weight of my struggles. It was liberating not to worry about being offensive and knowing that the person listening had one objective – to support my healing. Queen, that's what the right counsellor can do for you. They can remind you of your value and that they are praying for you. Having that kind of support is incredibly powerful. It can pull you from the darkest places and undergird you with impenetrable strength.

Mental health issues are prevalent, and what's absolutely disturbing is that there are so many people under mental strain who haven't been able to put a name on it. According to Mind UK,[17] statistics have shown that mental health problems have increased by 20 per cent in England between 1993 and 2014, and I dread to think what those statistics will look like when this Covid-19 pandemic is over. So many people are roaming different spiritual experiences, drugs and other vices but unable to find the help that they need. With the presence of technology, it's all too easy to hide behind a screen, hoping that someone will reach through that iPhone and quench the loneliness that torments them. I think it is important to emphasise the importance of talking to someone if you are struggling with social media's negative impact. Technology is a modern-day blessing and a curse. We are in a world filled with pain, and if only we could just be a bit more loving and take a little bit more time to spend with others, I am certain that the suicide rate would go down, and the mental state of so many would drastically improve. Jesus does just this when He leaves the 99 to find the one lost sheep. His love isn't prejudiced, and it pays attention to the detail and the pain in our hearts. He looks beyond the sin to the

---

[17] © Mind. This information is published in full at mind.org.uk

roots and the triggers of our pain. We need to have His eyes, His heart and His love. That being said, God lovingly guides us from the place of pain and mediocrity to the place of triumph and freedom that we have never known.

I feel that freedom today and every day in my life. I wouldn't know what living was without Him. He has taught me everything that I know and continues to teach me every day about what it means to be a wife, imperfect but striving to give my all every single day. Flaws and all. I am certain that my family feel that love too. Do I feel sad sometimes? Of course, I do. I just know how to get out of it.

Even so, sometimes, my responsibilities overwhelm me. I have two young boys who depend on me. I am a devoted wife who is dedicated to nurturing my marriage and supporting my husband. To top it all off, I'm radical enough to step out into the business ventures that God has placed in my hands, and that's not just one. I am an author, an influencer, a property manager, a motivational speaker, and so much more! I couldn't possibly write it all here because I do so much. I have found ways to make it all work, but that doesn't mean that I don't have days where I just want to walk away. *What makes me stay? What makes me keep going?*

I am a lioness. I know who I am. I know what it would cost and what would be lost if I gave it all up. So many lives depend upon me to finish my race. There's a scripture that always helps to put things into perspective. It says, "But he that shall endure unto the end, the same shall be saved."[18] The journey can be long and hard, but if you can focus on one thing, that will encourage you to keep going. You will reap the rewards of your perseverance and learn a lot about yourself on the journey. When it gets hard, I keep the end goal in my mind.

---

[18] Matthew 24:13 (KJV)

Pain doesn't always go away. Sometimes we go through things to shape us into the people that God is calling us to be. Sometimes He doesn't take away the pain because He knows that your journey is about giving birth. I wouldn't be resilient if I didn't go through so many painful mental health experiences. Pain comes and goes, but I always turn it into my power. I will always believe that *all things work together for good* regardless of how hard it gets. I will always use my pain to inspire an army of overcomers, super conquerors who may experience the same or even more intense pain levels but will soar above the waves with Jesus. "Yet in all these things, we are more than conquerors through Him who loved us."[19]

You are an overcomer. There will be times when you want to give up, and it may feel unbearable, but you can overcome the weight of your pain and struggles. It's possible to feel low and know that God has got you regardless. Whatever took you to that painful space in your mind may have been a valid trigger, but you don't have to be consumed by the complexities within your mind. Find someone to pray with and speak to. Write it all out in a journal. Look at the words and see yourself. Be patient and forgive yourself. It's so easy to allow guilt, confusion and fear to overwhelm you, but I urge you to understand how much God is *with* you and *for* you and that He absolutely loves you. Whatever you do, don't give up. I believe in you. I can tell you (from the darkest experiences that I have already shared) that you can and will get through this and that you are not alone.

You need the right tools to escape from the maze inside your mind. But first, wholly dedicate yourself to the process of reinforcing every aspect of your mind. Acknowledge that you need to be 100 per cent truthful, evaluating yourself and your journey, and recognising all the

---

[19] Romans 8:37 (NKJV)

things that have led to your current state. Finally, change very rarely happens overnight, so celebrate your certain victory and be patient with yourself. In your journey to heal, bless and encourage yourself. Tenderly and spiritually, nurse yourself through the process of healing.

Be Deliberate

The most invaluable lesson I have learnt about strengthening the mind is that you have to be deliberately aware of what is going into your mind and aware of what is coming out of it. Pay attention to how things around you are making you feel. Is there a conversation that you are having with someone that is making you feel distressed or anxious? Is there a movie that relates too closely to your own painful experiences? If you are having flashbacks, you can redirect your focus by feeding your mind everything that will strengthen it. What also helps is finding something that will inspire the opposite thoughts and feelings; so, if you are feeling anxious, you can watch a comedy that will inspire more positive thoughts and emotions. There are so many beautiful habits that you can create to nurture your mind; connect with nature by going for walks or exercising outdoors, develop a new hobby or even meditate. I love to pray, worship and write in isolation. Nonetheless, it's important to find the things you are passionate about and use them to build.

I have recently been thinking about thriving environments and their value in shifting into a more positive mindset. I am not talking about karate-chopping your best friend because they said something negative. I am talking about developing the habit of gravitating towards positive things and people. Surround yourself with positive things, funny things and inspiring things. Feed your mind all the goodness it craves. One of my favourite scriptures says:

Finally, brethren, whatsoever things are true, whatsoever things are honest, whatsoever things are just, whatsoever things are pure, whatsoever things are lovely, whatsoever things are of good report; if there be any virtue, and if there be any praise, think on these things.

—Philippians 4:8 (KJV)

You can flip the script and become more self-aware. Tell yourself the words that you NEED to hear. I do this all the time. If my husband, mother or my best friends haven't told me how amazing I am for a while, then I will write it to myself. I will remind myself of everything that has made me strong – everything I have overcome. I remind myself that I am a warrior Queen. You have every right to do the same for yourself because no one (other than God) knows you better than you do. If you're even more serious about self-nurture, then you could make a recording to yourself and play it back. Listen to it carefully and feel the words. How does it make you feel to hear what you NEED to hear? I know for a fact that it feels good. Don't wait for someone to save you; be your own heroine and speak good words to yourself.

Writing is another powerful tool in helping you to observe your mental journey. You can look back and assess your state of mind. You can even see if you're improving or deteriorating. It's also surprising what comes out on paper when words are not spoken, and ears cannot hear what is being said. It's a pivotal process that shouldn't be underestimated. There are also questions throughout this section that you can use as prompts to inspire you to write everything that is on your heart.

The final thing that I would like to say on this topic is, when you write, don't hold back; express whatever is on your heart completely. Reservations limit and weaken the process of growth and healing.

If you are worried about someone finding your work, then hide it someplace safe. Always commit to being open in your journaling because that's where you discover the complete truth about your mental, emotional and spiritual state.

Being open and honest says to the world that you are ready to face yourself. It says that you are ready to heal. It is not as hard as it may seem to work towards growth and healing. Just be willing to take the first step. I am fully aware of how complex the mind is, but I dare not presume to have all the answers to its complexities. I will say this though: Jesus is and always will be the ultimate healer and transformer of the mind. It is through the application of biblical principles to our lives that true transformation and resilience take place. Our willingness to yield to the process required to grow will determine whether or not we are triumphant over the challenges that we face in the depths of the mind. The scripture (below) highlights that we reap powerful rewards from nurturing our minds:

> *But [our] delight is in the law of the Lord; and in [our] law doth he meditate day and night. [We] shall be like a tree planted by the rivers of water, that bringeth forth [our] fruit in [our] season, whose leaf also shall not wither; and whatever [we] doeth shall prosper.*
> **—Psalm 1:2-3 (KJV)**

The outcome of a stable mind is that you will be strong enough to accommodate all the blessings you have in your life and the wonders that are on their way. It takes resilience and fortitude to handle the challenges, blessings and ultimately, to prosper. When you are intentional about nurturing your mind, it will strengthen your identity, the direction of your life will become clearer, and you will be assured that your relationships are right for you. Most importantly, you won't settle in any area of your life because you have clarity on the condition of your mind, its potency and its impact on the direction of your life.

> *And do not be conformed to this world, but be transformed by the renewing of your mind.*
> **—Romans 12:2 (NKJV)**

You will no longer try to fit into the thinking of everything around you. Your new mind will be transformative – strong and unbreakable. It is phenomenal to have a stable and rooted mind regardless of the challenges that this life can bring. It is a blessing and a gift to have a mind that isn't swayed, manipulated or pressured by every difficult thing thrown at it. Over and over, the Bible reveals that a transformative and resilient mind is built, exercised and developed. You have to stretch your mind just like you would your body when you exercise. You have to nurture your mind so that it is renewed, refined and powerful. So, how's your mind today?

Prayer and Meditation

Let's pray and reflect using the mirror.

Dear Heavenly Father,

Thank you for the brilliance and wonders of my mind. It can be overwhelming, and I have had it hard, but I know that you are with me in the most difficult parts of my journey. With you by my side, I now have the courage to face all the challenges that I will meet on my journey to a strengthened mind. I open myself to receive all the resources, people and support that you will send to aid my healing. Thank you for hearing my prayer.

In Jesus' name, Amen.

SIX

I HAD A DREAM... ONCE

§

I remember the first year of my eldest son's life. It was difficult because I felt as though I lacked clarity on my dreams. Before I became a mother, I had certainty about what I wanted to do with my life. I knew I wanted to complete my album and that I loved to write songs. Music just didn't seem to take centre stage once my son arrived, and I felt like I was losing myself in a world of changing diapers and cleaning up baby poo. The hardest part of being a first-time mother wasn't sleepless nights, painful breastfeeding, body changes and the like. The most challenging part was overcoming the intense feelings of guilt, loneliness, confusion and... loss. Loss of the person I once was and uncertainty about the woman I was becoming. Everything was changing, and I felt like I was being jolted into it – a bit like an emergency stop when a deer runs in front of a car's headlights. It felt abrupt and uncontrolled.

During this time, I left a familiar and comfortable job while also moving some distance from friends and family. I felt homesick without a home to go back to. In my mind, our new house was strange and alien. All the blessings in my life felt like curses – including being a mother. I was torn between guilt and frustration. Frustration for wanting a sense of purpose and not *just* being a mother. I always knew that my purpose in life was multifaceted and that I had many dreams to fulfil. The reality of motherhood was different from my fantasy of it. I also felt guilty because I should have been enjoying every minute of being a new mother, and I didn't. I wanted more, but I couldn't verbalise why I was feeling discontent.

This swirl of overwhelming emotions and thoughts left me dazed. I felt like I was losing myself and was desperate to know where God was taking me. I remember listening to the business podcast and realising that I wanted to work for myself. It gave me the confidence to understand that anybody could do it, but it was hard work. I wasn't afraid of that, but I was afraid of living without purpose. There was no lightning from the sky, and God's voice didn't boom from the heavens, but He did strategically place resources and people in my path, which ignited my passion for various causes.

So, I began to take a strange and unfamiliar road; I became a Renaissance woman. I didn't think it was possible to juggle so much, but I decided to follow my passion and let my heart be Divinely led to various endeavours that brought intense clarity. God has shown me, over and over again, that this is the right course, and this is all the validation I need to push forward, even when I want to give up. His words, "we shall reap, if we faint not",[20] reverberate in my spirit and fuel me. I remember trying to explain what I wanted to do with my

---

[20] Galatians 6:9 (KJV)

life to my husband, Paul. I was so worried that he would think I was crazy. Thank goodness he believed in me. Not only that, but he partnered with me and invested in my dreams (on every level). To this day, he continues to be my team player in all of my endeavours and vice versa. Over time, I have seen my dreams unfold in unimaginable ways. I have been so empowered that I have chosen to help other women catch that same fire.

What Lies Beneath?

Maybe once upon a time, nothing felt impossible. Your heart's desires and dreams were so tangible that you could almost touch them. Did you have a vision that you thought was so unachievable that you buried it? Were you once told that you were being unrealistic for believing in your dreams? Did life get carried away and consume your ability to pursue your dreams? Was it given prophetically? Did God speak His desires into your life, but they have been left unfulfilled? Has someone said something to make you despise your talent?

Words are so powerful. Before you realise it, your gifts could end up sitting on the shelf for so long that you don't even remember they're there or how to use them. Subtly and gradually, your passion, confidence and dedication dry up. It's hard to know where to start and how to pick up the pieces, especially if there are abandoned spiritual wells of unfulfilled hopes and dreams within you. When did you let your passion fizzle out? When did you lose heart? It probably hurts to think that your passion is now becoming something of the past. In fact, it's something that you may tell yourself – *the season to exercise my passion is now a thing of the past* – as you allow yourself to be carried away with the tide of cares and responsibilities that life has thrust upon you. Perhaps, you have left your dreams in the places that they have gone to die. Maybe you were overwhelmed by doubt, fears and insecurities. Have all the hopes and expectations faded into a whisper as you succumb to the pressures that surround you? Can you hear the overwhelming doubt in the way that you speak? Maybe your speech has changed, and you now replace the words like "one day" with "I coulda…" "I woulda…" "I shoulda…" Trapped in the mundane and the mediocre when God has destined you for the exceptional and the extraordinary.

The truth is that it is all too easy to leave pieces of yourself in the past. It is those gifts that will unlock the beauty of the God-breathed dreams of your future. Was there a moment of realisation that you relinquished the things that you were passionate about? Or did you slowly awaken to the fact that you were leaving something invaluable behind? The pain of losing the dreams that you once treasured is still present. Resentment, inability to celebrate the successes of others and even suffocating the blessings that you currently have in your life may be the many ways that the pain manifests. It's hard to breathe without the dreams that you still long to fulfil. If you are truly honest with yourself, you may even admit that the demands of wifehood have made marriage feel like a stale blessing because of everything you've given up to make it work. Unable to completely express your gifts or live your dreams, it feels like your relationship has choked out all the beautiful possibilities of what could have been. However, deep down, God is telling you that the season of your dreams hasn't arrived yet and isn't over. Now is the time to dig up those wells and polish those dusty dormant dreams.

Missing Your Window

I know what it feels like to wonder if you've missed your window – to question if the dream has died or if you're overreaching. Your passion is the key to your purpose, your contribution to the world. What you're withholding is a fundamental component that will be the reason your marriage will flourish. When you are living your purpose and fulfilling your God-given dreams, it releases a life-invigorating vibrancy that will resonate with everyone you connect with. It's easy to leave yourself behind when you take on married life, even though you do it with all the best intentions. The truth is, leaving yourself behind does everyone around you more of a disservice than you could possibly imagine. How can you give your husband all of you if there are pieces of you missing or left unexpressed? How can your children, family and all those impacted by your life be validated to go for the dreams God has placed within them if they don't see your example?

There is something very telling about feeling frustrated with it all. When life feels overwhelming, come up for air and be all that God has destined you to be. Suppressing your gifts, visions, dreams and sacrificing it all for the people you love is a disaster. They want the best of you, and they won't get it if you don't allow yourself to walk in your God-given calling. Why punish yourself? God has placed those desires in your heart for a purpose that is so great that it will astound you. The funny thing is, I can almost hear you trying to talk yourself out of it by saying, *I haven't got the time. The kids are too young. I have too many responsibilities. I have left it too long. I am too old. I am afraid. What if I fail?* These are all legitimate concerns. Whatever you tell yourself will be your truth.

- I still have time.
- I will find the time.
- I will find a way.
- I will succeed.

When you start asking, *how am I going to do this?* then you begin to open up your spirit to the possibility that it can happen. Then comes strategy. I have been in this space mentally and had these conversations with myself. I had to change my language. Surviving is about living on the sidelines of life and just hoping that you will get by. Thriving is about taking control of your life and your decisions. It's about taking ownership of the times that you allowed yourself not to change the narrative. You are not a victim. You have *allowed* yourself to be the victim. There is a difference. Find a way. Talk to close friends and ask your family to look after the kids. Stop scrolling on the internet or cleaning things that don't need to be cleaned. Then you'll have the time to plan, create, build and execute.

Navigating Your Dreams

It's easy to ask the question, *is God angry with me for burying my dreams?* God isn't angry with you. You haven't missed your window. God knows what you're like. That's why He has compelled me to write this section of the book. You didn't find this by accident. Everything happens for a reason. The piece of you that you thought was dead, God is about to resurrect in this next season of your life. What comes out of your heart, mind and spiritual reservoir will preserve these dreams, passions and visions, but you have to fight for your purpose. Stop making excuses. You are more than capable. You have the time. You're *not* just a wife or mother.

You are a jewel in the hands, eyes and heart of God, and He is about to polish you through your pursuit and execution of the dreams that He has placed in your heart. Don't fight Him on that. Talk to Him and ask Him how to manoeuvre, and He will guide you to your Divinely orchestrated purpose. God will always take the *insignificant, incapable little things* and work wonders. That's His Divine speciality. It's going to seem impossible until it is possible. You just need to step out and watch the ground move before you create a path. His Divine provision will be your most incredible testimony of His greatness in your life.

Build relationships with people that will inspire, encourage and fuel your vision. Expose yourself to resources that will strengthen your faith. Practise and develop the skills you need to achieve your dreams. Make the sacrifices, become more disciplined and seek the materials that you need to grow. Do you need to get a degree to do those things that God has placed within your heart? What additional training do you need to take to be one step closer to your dreams? Take the necessary steps. Don't procrastinate any longer because time doesn't belong to you.

My Husband Doesn't Support My Dreams

What things have you given up for love? When you first made your vows, it was so easy to give up everything that you were passionate about. The euphoria of young love – of discovering someone new and learning about all the beauty you see in them – overrides every other passion. Then the years go by, and you realise that the passion you once had for your dreams was the spark that made you who you were. You start to feel like a version of you that was once so valuable has slipped away. It becomes clear that you are angry with yourself for letting those dreams go, but also frustration towards your husband starts to creep in as you realise that your marriage *doesn't allow* space for those passions.

- Are you in pain because you have given so much to your marriage and feel you receive nothing in return?
- Does it feel like life is robbing you of the things that you once were so excited to do?
- Do you feel like the timing to execute the endeavours that God had laid on your heart has slipped away?
- Does it feel like your husband is fighting you every step of the way?

It's difficult to show love and respect when you're harbouring these weighty feelings. You have to start with *yourself*. As I described earlier, resentment is dangerous. It paralyses and stops you from seeing clearly. It can make it so difficult to follow God's direction because you can become so consumed with what your husband has *robbed* from you that you don't realise that God is trying to restore it. If you could just shift your focus. Don't weigh your husband down with blame, even though he may have had his part to play in your broken dreams. Forgive him and release him from the burden of trying to make you happy and fulfil your dreams. Release yourself from the weight of resentment so that clarity can set in.

If you have to verbally share with him how you feel to purge and move on, then make that time and write down what you want. Make it clear and keep it simple. Put it somewhere that you can visualise regularly. Then work with what you have. What resources do you have in your hands right now that will initiate the steps towards your dreams? Do you have skills? A contact number? Something in the cupboard? Start there. Make time to build on your visions. You have time to build, regardless of how busy you may feel. There is always that time that you use to watch TV, talk on the phone or play dress up in the mirror. Those little moments are crucial. They can take you closer to your goals bit by bit.

One of the people you need to be rooting for you as you pursue your dreams is your husband. Marriage is all about unity and oneness. The success of your dreams and visions heavily depends on your unity as a couple. The strength of your unified vision will be put to the test as you work through your disagreements, prioritise and work out what needs to be compromised. You will have arguments; you will collectively and individually make mistakes. It's all part of the process, but if you truly trust each other, then you'll both learn so much more about each other and grow closer than ever.

I am speaking from experience. This book was written because my husband supported me by giving me time away from the kids to write. It cuts me to the core to be away from my babies, but this is necessary. His wisdom, expertise and encouragement also contributed to making this book what it is today. Without my husband's support, this book would have either taken years to be constructed, or it would never have been written at all. That's the importance of spousal support. How did I get his support? We have a joint perspective that when I write, he writes. When he illustrates, I illustrate. We are a team. There is no competition or rivalry between us. Any endeavour that I pursue is a joint venture. It doesn't matter whose name is in lights or who gets the paycheque. It's about being determined to win together. If I tried to draw like my husband, it would be a disaster because it's not my gift. We know each other well enough to know where our strengths lie.

I am a passionate writer. He would get bored after the first sentence. We know that our individual strengths make us a formidable team.

So, I encourage you to find a way to show your husband that your strengths are also his strengths. Let him see the value in the pursuit of your passions. It may appear meaningless to him, but if he can see that they light up your soul, he would be irrational not to get on board. Be patient with him. It may not happen straight away. You need to pay attention to the Holy Spirit's instructions to know how to proceed. Your husband may need a little inspiration to start rooting for you. If you want to become a doctor, then you may need to get work experience and go to medical school, for example. You will know when the time is right but operate from a place of peace. Don't try to force him into the space of understanding but prayerfully present the benefits.

I've been in a place where I have been afraid to share my vision with my husband. It's sometimes nerve-wracking to share your thoughts, feelings and fears because they're fragile and personal. It's like exposing a piece of your soul. I remember sharing my scarily gigantic visions with my husband and seeing his puzzled look. I thought, *uh-oh, he doesn't understand me!* I learnt to articulate, and my clarity won over his support! It will be incredibly strenuous on your marriage if your husband is resistant to your endeavours. Your resources can drain quite quickly without his support. From simply lacking in energy to needing an extra pair of hands to help build your dreams. There's no doubt that his contribution will make a difference. Work out what you want from him and communicate it to him. Unite and agree on a way forward. Be decisive as you move forward. Your confident actions will show that you mean business. There's no doubt that it can be tough to push for your dreams together but persevere. Offer your plans to God, and He will give you all the clarity you need to move forward. Have faith that *all* things, including the fulfilment of your dreams, will work together for your good.

You may have more of a fight on your hands than you bargained for, and your husband may completely go against your dreams (for whatever reason). It takes resilience to pursue your visions in the face of adversity, but if you don't let go, then there is a chance that your grit will speak to him. If that doesn't seem to unite your purpose, visions and collective ministry, then there may be other underlying issues to address. Some of those complex aspects of your marriage may be in Chapter 9, *Strained Relationships and Family Feuds* or Chapter 12, *When Marriage Is Killing You*, so evaluate other aspects of your relationship. Sometimes you just need to sit and talk it out. Work out whether there are fears, lack of clarity or frustration about your vision. Having someone to pray for you through this challenging situation is invaluable. Also, make time to write in a journal and spend time speaking with God about your own marriage if you want to get complete clarity on what you want from your husband.

Faith, Favour, Fire!

One of the most powerful gifts that you can give yourself is to work on the unseen things to manifest the things that you want to see. This isn't hocus pocus and has worked phenomenally in my life. When you partner with God, trust His word and depend on the promises of His word, then you provoke the overflow of blessings into your life. It isn't simple or easy, but it's worth it. Observe, apply wisdom; work diligently, and you will reap boundless rewards. There must be an exchange – your unshakable faith for your dream. Faith is expressed through actions. For example, if you believe that it's going to rain, then you would open your umbrella as a sign of expectancy. Your dreams go to die in the places where this level of faith is absent. You have to be deliberate about working, protecting and stretching your faith. When you act upon your faith, it calls what you're expecting to receive into being. In other words, your action causes a *faith* reaction. When you start to pursue your vision, faith is always the first place to begin.

Your belief in that dream will be the fuel behind all the hard work that goes into seeing your vision come to pass. It's your faith that you must work hard to protect and nurture. Faith is what will anchor you when things seem to go wrong or when the naysayers challenge your truth. I love the Amplified version of the Bible's definition of what faith is. It says:

> *Now faith is the assurance (**title deed**, confirmation) of things hoped for (Divinely guaranteed), and the evidence of things not seen [the conviction of their reality—faith comprehends as fact what cannot be experienced by the physical senses].*
> **—Hebrews 11:1 (AMP)**

This quote gets me every time! That means that you can taste it even when you can't taste it, you can see it even when you can't see it, you can feel it even when you can't feel it. It is an indisputable fact, even though it isn't visible *yet*. The fire must burn within your soul before it sets the world alight. Let the fire burn greater than your fear. This will give you the grit, determination and strength to push through the hardship of your journey. You can chant your mantras till you're blue in the face, but if you lack passion, discipline and *active faith*, it won't become tangible. Faith is your entitlement to seeing what you believe turns into a reality. It should burn so strong that your husband should feel it, and not only should he feel it, but it should ignite his soul.

If you've ever bought a property, then you'll know you need a title deed before you have the authority to gain access to it. It's the same with faith. Faith is why your hopes will come to pass. It gives you the authority to call those visions into existence. When you believe in your vision, then you will act upon that belief. You will sacrifice for that belief, and you will invest in that belief. *Faith is dead without works.* I urge you to genuinely seek the heart of God and His investment into your dreams; make Him the centre of it all. Manifestation doesn't happen without favour. Your vision has to be in God's heart and mind before it comes into your hands. The Bible reveals that there are laws and a process to seeing the things that we hope for come into fruition. To ignore the laws and the process is futile to our progression. Sure, some will receive what they want, but illegally, and won't be able to handle it because they didn't go through the process. The process says, *I'm entitled to this thing because I have sacrificed; I have earned my stripes.*

The disappointments, loss and pain are all a part of the process. They build and shape you. They equip you to handle the blessings of what you are hoping for. We live in a society that wants everything fast, but it means the power of process is often overlooked and under-valued, and that's where all the learning and growth happen. When you are challenged by your husband about whether this dream works for you both, you are being processed. When the project fails, and you have to start again, the failure is part of the process. The process isn't fluffy and pretty. It hurts, stings and burns out anything unnecessary. It is also God's seal of approval on your destiny. Stand in the confidence that no one will walk in your power, vision and destiny like *you*. God's favour on your life is unique to you, and when you execute your vision, there isn't a person on the planet that will be able to imitate you; it's as unique as your fingerprint.

Joseph the Dreamer... Offers Invaluable Truths

Genesis[21] tells the story of Joseph having a dream and sharing it with his brothers. I believe that he wouldn't have told his brothers if he knew what would happen next. His brothers were jealous and even discussed killing him before throwing him into a pit then selling him into slavery. What's interesting is his life still revolved around his dreams. Joseph dreamt, and his future was forged and sealed based on the Divinely instigated dreams imparted to him. Dreaming led him before the most formidable ruler of that time. Dreaming made him the second greatest ruler in the land. Dreaming saved the people that wanted to kill him and left a legacy for generations and nations. That's the power of a dream.

What will your dream save you from? Whose life will be impacted and transformed forever because you believed in it? Don't bury your dreams because you assume that they are just for you. God is strategic. Someone else's freedom may be tied up in your dreams. You owe it to yourself *and to them* to pursue your dreams.

Let me be honest: your dream has a price, regardless of its size. Just like Joseph, you will face adversity. It could be the haters and naysayers, and they could be living in the same house. They could even be wearing the ring you gave to them. Whether it's closed doors or disappointment, you may fail over and over again. It's a part of the process, and it cannot be avoided. The harder you sweat, the sweeter your success will be. Don't allow the price to deter you from stepping into all those things that God has prepared for you. The rewards will always outweigh the cost. Stay focused on the end goal. Don't kill the dream because of the journey. Every single person that God gives a success story worth telling has to go through something to get it.

---

[21] Genesis 37–45 (KJV)

Honestly evaluate yourself and assess the areas of your character that are holding you back. Is it chatting on the phone with Janet for three hours? Do you overlook details and think, *it will all come together*? Do you quit every time it gets too hard?

Get a little tougher on yourself and build your resilience. Push through. These will be invaluable lessons for the next phase of your life – lessons that will transform you into the person that God wants you to be to accommodate the blessings that He has waiting for you. Just like the story of Joseph. When his brothers saw him again, Joseph was so different that they didn't even recognise him. He ordered them to visit him multiple times, and he even convinced them to leave the "youngest and most precious" brother behind! He became unrecognisable. That's the power of the process. The process toughens you and builds you into a more resilient person because you know your *power*. Joseph's story teaches us invaluable lessons about the power of dreams and what they can reveal about our nature. There is power in the pain of our experiences; it's not all in vain. We look at our pain as a problem, but in reality, pain is transformational. Pain is the reason that you will be able to handle the blessings that are coming your way. Pain is your *spiritual workout regime*. It is like when you are in the gym, and the pressure of your workout results in tiny tears in your muscles, but when they reform, they are much more durable and stronger than before.

I deliberately wrote Chapter 3, *Who Am I… Again?*, before this one because it takes a strong sense of self-identity to run with and bring into fruition every aspect of your dreams. Your heart's vision, dreams and desires have been placed there by God. It's His way of speaking to creation through you. You are the steward of a unique message that He intends to bring to the world. But you have to partner with God. Can He trust you to be all that is required to bring His dreams, His voice, into this realm? Can you fight vehemently to see the vision come into fruition? Waiting for vision isn't passive. Sometimes we see waiting as a stagnant and inactive position. It is really an active and preparation position – like using an umbrella while waiting for rain. Expectancy is potency.

I remember when I was at the beginning stages of building TWIRL (my women's movement). Everyone I shared the vision with said, "It will happen in God's time" or "Don't rush God's timing!" or even "Be patient." It confused me and threw me off. I would think, *should I just sit here and wait?* I felt like a duck without direction. I took their words to mean stop researching, praying, planning this vision. Then everything slowed down, and that confused and frustrated me even more. Then it hit me that writing the vision is a part of the wait. Expectancy is a part of the wait. Giving birth to the vision is a part of the wait. "Decree a thing, and it shall be established unto thee."[22] Give birth to the vision within your heart before it becomes a reality in this realm.

I will let you in on a secret. Whenever I want to give birth to my visions, I look for similarities within my environment. So, if I want to get a new building for my office, I visualise space size, the number of desks required, layout for customers and so on. I would then visit buildings similar to the type of office style that I have in my mind. I feel it with my hands and walk around the building. I imagine all the possibilities for that office space. My heart and mind have to feel and live out that vision before it reaches this realm. I ensure that it feels like it is within my reach *first*. Eventually, when the opportunity presents itself to physically build, then everything has a clear direction.

If I am leading the project and am asked questions, then everyone working with me can have confidence in my leadership. It's something

---

[22] Job 22:28 (KJV)

that may initially make you look crazy to others, but it has been an amazing trigger for me. It has helped me to overcome many obstacles when building my visions. It has reassured me that it is possible to attain my goals, and it has provoked me to continue to pursue those things that I am aspiring to. I still use this visualisation method to conceptualise my visions to this very day. No, this isn't manifesting. I am not clicking my fingers like Dorothy and hoping for something to drop out of the sky! I am provoking myself to believe in the possibility that I can achieve something if I am willing to build. Of course, prayer and faith make all the difference, but the Bible says: "So too, faith, if it does not have works [to back it up], is by itself dead [inoperative and ineffective]."[23]

Please don't get pulled into this manifestation rubbish, because it breaks a lot of hearts. The universe provides resources, but God provides opportunities. It is only God who opens doors and closes them. It is to Him that you must bring the petition to fulfil your heart's desires. He does make dreams come true (I can attest to that), but there is a clause. Ultimately, it is for His Divine purpose. It is always because there is a message that your life must bring to the world. When you value His mission, then He will value yours. So, it's more of an exchange than a *magic manifestation*. Also, be prepared to get a version of what you want, but it is almost always different to, and better than what you asked for.

He can give you "exceedingly abundantly above all that we ask or think, according to the power that works in us."[24] And great is our Heavenly Father's power that works within us. Take the limits off. Start dreaming globally like your universal God. Your little dreaming

---

[23] James 2:17 (AMP)
[24] Ephesians 3:20 (NKJV)

is playing it way too safe. He wants to move so greatly in you that you know that it was Him and only Him that could've transformed your life in this way – so much so that even those who closely witness your journey will "rise and call you blessed". I'm sure that there will be challenges on the journey, but when you partner with God:

> *Eye has not seen, nor ear heard,*
> *Nor have entered into the heart of man*
> *The things which God has prepared for those who love Him.*
> **—1 Corinthians 2:9 (NKJV)**

God wants to blow your mind through the fulfilment of your dreams. Dreams will reveal the dormant greatness within you and your immeasurable value. It will be amazing in the end when you can attest to the fact that it was only God that could work such wonders in your life. So, don't allow your life to be gripped by fear, reluctance, hesitation and wishful thinking. Direct your focus on the One who can make you achieve ten thousand times more than the things that you dreamed of, and be brave enough to go on this adventure with Him.

Breathing Life into Your Dreams

You are never too old. It's never too late. You are not underqualified. You are not stupid. The kids are not too young. It's not too hard to learn. Allow your mind to explore the possibilities of what your life could look like if you stepped into your dreams. Expose yourself to the wonders that God so desperately, *yes desperately*, wants to pour out into your life. Trust that your path will light up before you and that you will gain the clarity that you need as a result of partnering with God. He says, "Delight yourself also in the Lord, And He shall give you the desires of your heart."[25] One of the most powerful statements that I have heard concerning the fulfilment of dreams is:

> *The grave is the richest place because it is filled with so many people who had the potential to bring that wealth into this realm. However, they, unfortunately, allowed the grave to rob them of their dreams.*
>
> *Les Brown, American motivational speaker*

How many of those people put their dreams off until tomorrow, but tomorrow has never come? Time ran out. Those last moments of their lives will forever be haunted by a strong sense of unfulfillment. Unable to verbalise their regrets. As the course of their lives *flashed before their eyes*, so did the gravity of their lack of action. Knowing that they refused so many opportunities to act upon the things that their hearts yearned for. The brutal truth is that they gave up early and buried their dreams. In complete contrast, those who choose to *dream with their eyes wide open* are not somehow immune to adversity. No one is above the process of birthing a dream. We all have to go through these things. The truth is that those who succeed simply refuse to give up. Were there the same distractions or obstacles? Do they have the same disappointments? Was there someone else who could have executed their visions better than them?

Of course! All these things are true. They weren't somehow luckier. Life's hurdles don't have favourites. They will fail a thousand different times, and they treasure the vision like their life depends on it. Sure, they may achieve the trophy of fulfilling their dreams, but what you don't see is the myriad of invisible scars that they have received during

---

[25] Psalm 37:4 (NKJV)

the process. They were reshaped and rebuilt during the journey. They understand that the process is the real trophy. What you don't see is that they have been shaped by pushing for their dreams to come to pass. The lessons that they have learnt have transformed them, simply because they believed in the power of their dream. They were shaped in the trauma and forged in the pain of the process. Their reward? Their life and life's purpose make sense. They were not incomplete books with missing chapters.

Have you ever read a book and been really excited about it initially but been disappointed to discover that *this book just doesn't make any sense!* You tossed it aside and forgot about it. This example is parallel with an unfulfilled life with unfinished dreams. *Think I'm harsh? I haven't even started yet!*

Just imagine your gravestone with a big question mark over it with the words: *She was so capable, equipped with so much potential but never followed through.* Your life equates to one big question mark, an unfinished book. Impacted little to no one. Left behind no legacy worth holding onto, remembering or passing down through the generations. Just like the book that I mentioned in my earlier example. We would all toss aside a book that didn't make any sense – even this one. If that sounds harsh, it's because I want to do everything within my power to get you to value every aspect of your life in the same way that God does, no matter how insignificant some parts may seem. Everything about you matters. Take your life seriously because you will only travel this path once. There are no replays, rewinds or retries, so let it make sense and make it count.

JOURNAL

- If your life was summed up in one statement, what would it be?
- Are there any essential dreams or visions that you have achieved?
- How did it make you feel?
- What lessons can you learn from the process?

Don't overlook any achievements, regardless of how small. The lessons that you discovered from the small accomplishments will now be the principles that you will use to attain more remarkable achievements. They will be the catalyst for a shift in your mindset.

Fulfilling Dreams

One of the dreams that I recall fulfilling was passing my driving test. It may seem like a small accomplishment, but it meant so much. I was never very confident with exams when I was younger, but I was stunned when I finally held my driving certificate. I will always remember the sense of accomplishment. It taught me that all I needed to do was to believe in myself. I also learnt that if I had confidence, discipline and focus, I could do anything. I took those lessons and applied them to so many other achievements. As I became more confident, I scaled up until I was confident enough to write this book, run seminars, events, companies, you name it! It all started with the little things. So, my encouragement to you is to don't despise small things. There are so many lessons to be learnt from the small and seemingly insignificant achievements. The small achievements give you the strategy required to slay your giants.

You'll have taller mountains to climb, but the principles of discipline, perseverance and resilience will always remain the same. One of the most noticeable changes as you scale up is that you have to find strategies that prevent you from being broken in spirit by the weight of it all. Knowing that greater responsibility and greater risk with every choice can be overwhelming if you're not skilled at shifting the weight onto the person who can handle it – God! After all, He is the One who establishes kings, builds companies, is so innovative that He created worlds out of nothing! He can definitely handle the weight of our dreams. There is great peace in knowing that "I can do all things through Christ who strengthens me."[26]

That's where our confidence needs to come from. Every other foundation will crumble under the pressure of sustaining our dreams. You just have to partner with God to carry your dreams to fruition. That means a shift in mentality. It means letting go of all the excuses that have stopped you from streamlining your focus. It also means that you don't wait another minute but that you start right now. You start believing that the fulfilment of your dreams is a possibility. You start replacing *if* with *how*. You start looking for methods, resources and people who can teach you how to execute your vision better.

Not everyone is going to understand. Why bother pulling your hair out to make everyone understand the burning vision that God has given to you and ONLY you? You have been entrusted to carry the vision and unleash your life's unique assignment on this planet. Your vision will be absolute gibberish to everyone else until you step out and allow it to unfold and make sense. Your actions, not your words, are

---

[26] Philippians 4:13 (NKJV)

going to open their eyes. Trust me, I've been that girl. Constantly telling my husband, mum, social media, the birds and the insects in my garden all the things I was going to do. Then you see the puzzled look or a bewildered "Eeh?!" escapes from their lips, and you know they didn't understand the vision. I was that girl dragging every horse that I could find to water, and guess what? No one was drinking. I learnt to lead with action and not with words. The only words I am now sharing at length are the ones written in books. The ability to take action is my noise. To be known as *the woman who does what she says* is of paramount importance. It saves a lot of energy too. The world is full of people screaming, but the ones who are heard are the ones that take action. Are you yearning for your voice to be amplified and heard? Stop talking, start walking! Don't get me wrong, I love a good chit chat, but I am so much more in the doer category than I have ever been in my whole life.

I talk, but I don't share my dreams with everybody. What's the point if they can't help me make things happen and make the visions come to fruition? I may share parts of my dreams with those who can contribute to achieving the end goal, but I am careful. Not everyone is *for* me. You'd be surprised who the professional dream killers are. I have learnt to shut my mouth around those who might crush a dream at the flicker of hope. It is easy to become jaded, discouraged or disheartened about your vision on the worst of days. Most of us have to coach ourselves into stepping out and fulfilling those things that we were born to do. It becomes even more challenging if you have outside voices saying you are incapable of executing your vision. You don't need that kind of negativity in your life. You need people who can coach, mentor or pray for you, cheer you on or help you streamline your vision. Those kinds of people are worth fighting for.

We can't eradicate people from our lives because they don't catch the vision. Sometimes dream killers are our siblings, parents and even husbands. So, what do we do? *Behave wisely.* They can have their opinion, but it's up to you to guard the vision and your heart. The contention, strife and struggle can drain the soul and your energy. It's so much healthier for your relationships to just grind in silence and let success be your noise. There's really no need to try to explain or justify your vision to everybody.

The only time I believe that agreements need to be made is if your vision impacts others around you. For example, some of your visions may cost money, so it may be necessary to work out whether they affect your family and work around the hurdles. It may not always be an easy process, but you have to ask yourself if that vision is worth fighting for or sacrificing for. If it's worth pursuing, then you will push through and work it all out. It can be difficult to agree on moving forward with your husband, because you could have completely different perspectives and agendas. Let me be completely honest with you: every pioneering couple has these struggles. It may not be concerning dreams and visions, but it may be concerning other aspects of life. One of the things that Paul and I do within our marriage is that we won't make major decisions unless we agree. If I wanted to start a company and my husband did not, we wouldn't start a company until we were on the same page. There's nothing worse than making life-changing decisions with one of us being resentful. If the issue is incredibly complex and we can't talk about it without getting angry, then we keep taking breaks and coming back to it when we have calmed down. If that's not how it works in your relationship, then there's nothing wrong with getting someone to help you both work through it. It is wise to find a mediator that isn't closely connected to you both. It's also not easy for both of you to open up to someone you think may judge you.

Words can't describe how painful it feels to be underestimated. There is nothing worse than having a burning passion for fulfilling a dream, but everyone around you undervalues it. You can feel like you're going crazy. Maybe there are many times where you have put your dreams aside because you have listened to them. Have you ever said to yourself, *Maybe they're right?* It can be hard to tell where your fear begins and where their doubt ends. It's part of the process.

I have been there. It's incredibly painful. It took me years to nurse my wounds and grow in confidence. Give birth to a new focus. Be driven by the greater plan and let it make you unrecognisable. Clap for yourself. Celebrate your own personal bests. That's exactly what I had to do to grow. It's going to be hard, and you are going to cry. There are times when I still do. Giving birth is a painful process. No one can carry your dream baby for you. No one can push that baby into the world for you. That struggle, that weight and that sacrifice are yours, but the prize is seeing that dream baby outgrow you. Seeing that dream baby send ripples through the world (no matter how big or how small). You will take delight in seeing your vision become more than you ever dreamed that it could be. You have what it takes, and you were born to do this.

I'm so excited for you! I just know that your life is about to change as you take your power back. Unapologetically show the world your brilliance and shine like the Queen you are!

Prayer and Meditation

Let's pray and reflect using the mirror.

Dear Heavenly Father,

Thank you that you are the author and creator of my dreams. Please orchestrate the resurrection of all the dreams that I have loved and lost. Bring life to all those visions that were destroyed by all the negative words or actions of myself and others. Open the doors and opportunities for me to develop gifts and expertise that contribute to the development of my dreams. Restore my passion and confidence for my visions. Give me the boldness to go after those dreams that you have given to me.

In Jesus' name, Amen.

SEVEN

WHAT'S YOUR FANTASY?

§

She opened her mouth to speak, but the words wouldn't come out. She felt the heat rise as she tried to resist the raging inner conflict. She knew that there would be a price to pay for following her fantasy. The days and nights that she spent hiding the secret that would become her demise. She clung to the hope that no one would find out. The reality that she had so much more to lose due to her indulgence weighed heavily upon her conscience. She wished that she could go back and undo the mess, but it was too late. She knew she had to pay the price, but what would it be? Divorce? Separation from a life she had become accustomed to? Death?

Execution seemed likely, now more than ever. Her secret was exposed, and as a result, she was vilified and dragged before a crowd of accusers. I can almost hear the slanderous words being hurled as she hung her head in shame. "Whore!" "Slut!" "Dog!" She was starting to believe they were right. She thought as she dared not to look up, *was he there? Was he about to throw a stone? Partner or husband? Accomplice or victim…* It didn't matter. All she could see were her mistakes and the pain she had caused, regardless of who had joined her in inflicting the pain. They continued to talk about her mistakes and publicly ridicule her, and she refused to defend herself. Everything they said was true, and she refused to refute it. They continued in the hope that their claims would be justified and approved by the Son of God. Instead, He convicted them. Silently listening to their accusations while kneeling on the ground, head bowed in what appeared to be deep thought. Was He even aware of what was happening around Him? Then, after what felt like forever, He stood up and spoke: "He who is without sin among you, let him throw a stone at her first."[27] Then He turned to her and said, "…where are those accusers of yours? Has no one condemned you?" She said, "No one, Lord." And Jesus said to her, "Neither do I condemn you; go and sin no more."[28]

It is no mystery that our actions exist as a result of our thoughts. It is difficult for me to believe that this woman decided to cheat on her husband without a moment's thought. Maybe the affair developed gradually or rapidly, but there is no doubt that it started as a fantasy. Maybe the adulterous woman realised when it was too late, or maybe she knew that there would be a price to pay from the beginning. She realised that there was nothing left – when it was too late. She abandoned every blessing that she had in exchange for false promises. Nothing she had and nothing she hoped for was in her reach.

---

[27] John 8:7 (NKJV)
[28] John 8:11 (NKJV)

Could the attraction of her love interest have caused her to believe that the fantasy could be her new reality? Only she would know the answer to that. Some say that the mind is a terrible thing to waste. I say that if your fantasies consume you – then the mind simply becomes a terrible thing. When the world inside your mind becomes the only thing that you desire, then you will suffocate the blessings that you already have. The torture intensifies when you pursue a fairy tale that has no basis in reality. Some dreams are meant to fade. What's true, deep, rich and real is what really matters. The fantasy is a honeytrap that tries to lure you away from all the blessings in your life.

Weighed Down by Fantasy

What is your fantasy? Have you indulged in sexually immoral acts that makes *Fifty Shades of Grey* look pearlescent? Or has your addiction to drugs held you ransom? Maybe all you can think about is him? Or is it subtler? They all lead to the same place. The destruction of your marriage, your family, your faith, your identity. Everything you have worked so hard to build. You clearly feel like there is no way out because of the weight of it all. Consumed by your flaws and the entrapment of your mistakes. Your husband sees one side of you, but there is something much more sinister simmering on the inside. Like the woman (in the story above) caught in adultery, you're consumed and alienated by your shame. Expecting God to execute a judgement that is somehow worse than everyone else's. Just like her. No doubt the woman's wrongful act started as a thought – a fantasy – before it became an action. The thoughts festered in the depths of her mind before she made a decision to act upon them. That's the danger of allowing yourself to become trapped in immoral fantasies. They lead to immoral actions.

Maybe like her, you have been wrestling with the conflict between your conscience and urges. It can weigh you down so much that your eyes are constantly heavy from the lack of sleep and your cheeks are sore from the pretence of trying to keep up the happy façade. GOD sees you. He sees the flaws and struggle. He sees your desire to change and heal. He sees your intense need to be free and become a woman that is no longer overwhelmed by condemnation and shame. You want to be honourable and sincere; trustworthy. It takes sacrifice to become this person. It takes strength to expose every crevice of the shadows lurking in the corners of your soul. Don't give your shame a place to hide; begin by admitting the truth to yourself. You're struggling. You made a mistake. There is a price to pay for the decisions that are made on impulse and urge. Look ahead to the outcome, weigh up the cost and make wise decisions. Decisions that are not based on your urges but on what is true, right and good. While you are alive, you can change the trajectory of your life. Become the person that you have always been destined to be. Change your situation so that your life can be overwhelmed by a torrent of joy, peace and happiness. You will be able to look at yourself in the mirror and be proud that you broke free of the deception of the fantasy.

"For all have sinned and come short of the glory of God."[29] Your mistakes are not worse than mine in the eyes of God. We are all on this journey of growth and called to evolve into the Divine Queens God has called us to be. It means paying our dues regardless of who's watching or the consequences that we may have to endure. Let them whisper of the shame that you once carried while you shed it like old skin. Become the breath-taking butterfly that they never knew that you had the potential to be. That's the person that God is looking at in the

---

[29] Romans 3:23 (KJV)

depths of your soul. The butterfly that wants to break free from the ugly cocoon that has imprisoned it for so long. Transformed, full of wonder and beauty. Ultimately, be weightless as you free yourself from the secrets that have trapped you for so long.

The Fantasy Illusion

I became aware that I placed a high value on my own fantasies within my marriage when my relationship began with my husband. Many years before I got married, I subconsciously signed up for a fantasy of what I wanted my marriage and my husband to be. I had a list of what I wanted and how he would fit into this unrealistic vision that I had pieced together in my mind. Throughout my life, I built up expectations that were unrealistic for any man to uphold – including my husband. I expected him to fit those criteria and not to deviate from the plan that I had for our marriage. In my mind, the future was bright – only if he didn't disrupt my fantasy of what a marriage should be.

As our marriage progressed, the fantasy created fractures in our relationship, and I applied unnecessary pressure for him to *perform* a role that he did not sign up for. It was nonsensical for me to have a long-lasting relationship with the fantasy in exchange for losing my husband. I had to let it go. I have learnt to love my husband for *who he is*, not who I *think* he should be. I had to distinguish the lines between reality, fantasy and the reasons that I instinctively craved those fantasies. *Was there something that was missing? Something that I craved? Was that why I was putting unnecessary pressure on my husband?* Only I had the answers to those questions. I had to find ways to get support and find a way to address those needs without damaging my marriage.

Fantasies always have a grass-is-greener effect. It's so easy to be deceived into believing that *if you could just…* then life would be better. If your husband was more like so and so. If your marriage was more like your friends' marriages on social media. If you could just have your cake, chop it up and slice it *your way*, then all will be well. It's an illusion to believe that somewhere over *there* is your happiness. You can find your happiness right where you are if you can just see how green it is. Listen to yourself and pay attention to the illusions that crowd your mind. Those deceptions try to rob you of the blessings that you already have. The dictionary describes the word fantasy (in other words) as *a concept with no foundation in truth*. It's when we succumb to the deception that things are better over there. The better we become at identifying the lies, the easier it becomes to forge a clear path to be liberated for the road ahead.

> *Casting down imaginations, and every high thing that exalteth itself against the knowledge of God, and bringing into captivity every thought to the obedience of Christ…*
> **—2 Corinthians 10:5 (KJV)**

I've learnt how important it is to strip dangerous fantasies of their grip by clinging to the beauty of truth. While fantasies lie to us by telling us that God has not provided everything that we need, truth is what grounds and stabilises us. The truth isn't always flattering and pretty and it usually isn't what we *think* that we want. Truth exposes painful aspects of who we are. Truth is progressive, and it will take us to places that fantasy *cannot*. The truth is scary. Sometimes, if we are truly honest, we just want to hide from it. There can be so much beauty in reality, and you can enjoy it if you open yourself up to embrace it. If you could look more closely at the challenges that you are trying to hide from, then you will see that they are trying to speak to you. They draw out the beauty and strength that is hidden within you. Give yourself a chance to recognise that you didn't need the fantasy after all. Maybe your husband doesn't take on the role of a husband the way that you wanted him to. Perhaps your marriage hasn't evolved into the fairy-tale vision that you once hoped that it would be. If you could just look a little closer, you'll be astounded to realise that God gave you something that surpassed the expectations of your fantasy. Open your mind to seeking those treasures in your life that are waiting to be found.

The Origin of Your Fantasies

It is wise to assess the birthplace and roots of your fantasies. We do this by asking this simple question: are my fantasies the outcome of a *need* or a *seed*? If there is an unfulfilled *need*, then you are likely to feel like something is missing in your life. It becomes so easy to believe that the fantasy will compensate for the things that you have lost. Maybe you thought that your husband would heal your insecurities? Or could it be that you believed that marriage would satiate the feeling of loneliness that has been present in your life?

Whereas fantasy seeds are a lot more subtle. They are the things that have appealed to us. They are in the movies, books, connections, environment and conversations that surround us. They suggest to us that what we have is not enough. They tell us that we should always want more than what we have. They try to rob us of our peace and leave us with discontentment. It's subtle and slow torture to always want what the Joneses have. Could it be that the frustration that you feel is because of the suggestions of outside forces? Become efficiently skilled at filtering out those seeds. Kill them on sight by shifting your attention to the blessings that you *already* have. See all the beauty in that wonderful man that you married. Be keen to understand him better. Create a space that is safe enough for you to share your pain, anxiety and fears. The journey to happiness and contentment is an individual one, and only *you* can choose to be happy. Be proactive in nurturing your blessings; resist the temptation to indulge in the deception of fantasy traps.

Defining Blurred Lines

There are unique distinctions between the reality that we live in and the fantasies that appeal to us. Fantasies are embedded in our wants. Our realities are grounded in what we already have; they exist and are indisputable.

- Could it be that fantasies captivated your focus as a result of your yearning for the things that you do not have?
- What is it about life that just makes you want to escape?
- What is it about your fantasy that appeals to you?
- What is missing?
- What is your inner person trying to tell you?

For example, it may be a fantasy to expect your husband to become more extravagant in expressing his affections towards you. The fantasy may be your husband's lack of affection, but the need could be unresolved issues or loneliness. Address the root issue — your needs. Listen to the sound of your soul, and the answers will emerge. Start by distinguishing the lines between fantasy and reality. If you are struggling with working through this on your own, find someone who can journey with you to help you find the clarity you need. An exercise that I highly recommend that you try during your reflection time is making a table like the one below.

Fantasy	Need
I can make my husband express his love towards me in a more extravagant manner.	I need more affection, and I am lonely within my marriage.
I want to be in a relationship with someone else.	I feel unfulfilled within my marriage. It's lost its spark.

Writing this down in a table form will help you create distinct lines and work towards finding the solutions that your spirit craves.

In Dangerous Territory

Thoughts, ideas and fantasies present themselves all the time, but when does it become dangerous? When you fantasise about another man while you're making love to your husband? When you practise a habit that you are using to compensate for a more devastating urge? When you start to plan ways to fulfil your fantasy? Where are the lines, and how do you know when you have crossed them? We head into dangerous territory when our imaginations become wildfires, and we do not exercise control over what we let in. It takes self-evaluation, nurture and temperance to protect the mind. Whatever you feed the mind will grow. If you feel like you are struggling with uncontrollable dark urges, it's important to get support. Nurture and strengthen your mind in the water of the scriptures. Let its truth invigorate the soil of your spirit. It's always easier to kill the thought when it's a seed instead of when the weeds of corruption choke all the blessings out of your life. "Guard your heart above all else, for it determines the course of your life."[30] It seems harmless until you can't sleep, think or breathe without doing that thing. That's when life begins to spiral out of control. It's easy to think that the situation isn't as extreme until consumed by those fantasies.

I can't help it may frequently resound in your mind. When you feel like you're just going for a ride to the places that your fantasy takes you, then it becomes hard to find healing. You can easily go round and round on the fantasy trail until it becomes an addiction and a compulsion. What's worse is the feeling of being trapped and not being able to talk to anyone about it. *They will judge me. They will laugh at me. Who can really help me without making me feel condemned?* These are all valid thoughts but not more important than being liberated from the weight of your secrets.

When you feel trapped in dark spaces, it is so easy to condemn yourself instead of cry out for help. Maybe you tell yourself all the negative things you think God is saying to you: *I'm going to hell. I'm not forgiven. God doesn't love me.* Far from it! God is waiting for you to partner with Him through this journey. Relinquish the weight of condemnation and trust God to guide you to freedom: "Where the Spirit of the Lord is, there is liberty."[31] Maybe you're like the woman in the opening story. Waiting for judgement and unable to claim the redemption that you so desperately crave. Suffering in silence and hoping that someone will free you from your invisible prison.

---

[30] Proverbs 4:23 (NLT)
[31] 2 Corinthians 3:17 (NKJV)

Journey to Healing

Everyone has a unique process to go through to strengthen their mind. Let me share some prolific and transformational truths about the process. It all starts with a strong awareness of your mind and your ability to reposition your focus. Let's agree to stop focusing on the fantasy, the addiction and the struggle. No more condemning yourself about all the flaws and shortcomings. Be serious about your growth and transformation. "Be transformed by the renewing of your mind."[32] Let's become more aware of the triggers, overwhelming emotions and negative circumstances. Let's work every day on becoming more self-aware through secluded time in meditation and prayer. Talk to yourself about all the things that you are doing so well. Celebrate yourself and your journey. Focus more on who you want to be rather than where you were. Ask yourself questions that would help you to explore how you're wired. Like *why do I have this struggle?* And *what's making this so difficult to let go of?* Immerse yourself in the promises of God and really believe that you are the person that God's word says that you are:

> *But you are a chosen race, a royal priesthood, a consecrated nation, a [special] people for God's own possession, so that you may proclaim the excellencies [the wonderful deeds and virtues and perfections] of Him who called you out of darkness into His marvellous light.*
> **—1 Peter 2:9 (AMP)**

On my own personal journey from the fantasy trap, God revealed that my emotions were key to unlocking my freedom. Instead of allowing shame to hold me in a position of condemnation, I clung to the words,

---

[32] Romans 12:2 (NKJV)

"There is therefore now no condemnation to them which are in Christ Jesus, who walk not after the flesh, but after the Spirit."[33] I had no desire to stay in the delusions of my fantasies. When I shifted my focus from my broken state to what God was able to do, it became easier to let go. I clung to the truth that with God, "all things are possible".[34]

The fantasy dissipated as I shifted my focus. That doesn't mean that it was always easy. I had to resist the urge to control my life's appearance and how it looked to everyone else; their opinions lost value. Speaking about the weight of my struggles took away its power over me. God is phenomenal because He sees our struggles, but He also sees our desires to get past them. He is strategic and put people in my path that would inspire me to push past my failures.

Some people will have to claw their way out of the consequences of acting upon their fantasies. I believe that if the conditions are right and support is available, anyone can move past their struggles. Have a space to talk about why you have struggled and how you came to be in that position. How do you feel when you are in that space? Why do you crave that space? These are all questions that you have to evaluate to be liberated, progress and heal. Be brutally honest with yourself. Was it something that began when you were younger? Is it the need to escape?

The only way to take power and control away from your struggle is to identify why you needed it in the first place. Fantasies and addictions are crutches. They're crutches that you may feel like you have control over, but the truth is that they have control over you. It doesn't matter how many times you say, "Just one last time…" or "I can quit

---

[33] Romans 8:1 (KJV)
[34] Matthew 19:26 (KJV)

whenever I want to…" They are the lies that you tell yourself so that you can go on depending on your vices. Denial of weaknesses keeps you in chains. Your freedom is in your ability to address your struggles and work through them.

I know. I had to do it. I had to rip the band-aid off and take a good look at myself. To me, it was equally as painful as going cold turkey. Ultimately, there is nothing more liberating than throwing away that crutch and standing in your power. That is what God is calling you to. The power to look at the old version of yourself and not recognise her in any way, shape or form. The person that you are about to become has bigger giants to slay and greater battles to win, but you must start with the hardest battle of them all – the battle of conquering yourself.

Be Honest with Yourself…

Is your fantasy *killing* you? Maybe your vice excites you, but you have to see beyond how it makes you feel. There is nothing that we can do to stop ourselves from being *tempted*. Even Jesus was tempted, but giving into it is a failure. Failure is giving into the mindset *I've already made this mistake, and God doesn't forgive me, so I will continue doing this*. Condemnation will keep you tied to your addiction and fantasy. The Bible also shows us that we should not exploit the grace of God: "What shall we say then? Shall we continue in sin that grace may abound? Certainly not! How shall we who died to sin live any longer in it?"[35]

There is a greater and more powerful version of you waiting for you to overcome this illusion. This fantasy trap is only as strong as your belief, so shift your focus to the person who is greater than any deception. Jesus Christ heals addictions, obliterates fantasies and gives us the desire and will to do better. Without Him, everything in this life

---

[35] Romans 6:1 (NKJV)

is harder and more painful. When you shift your focus to His strength, He will blow you away with the transformation that He can do in you. I should know. I no longer recognise the lost and enslaved girl that I was. I was a slave to my fantasies and had no idea, but I had to start being honest with myself and trust that as I began my journey to freedom, the strength to overcome it would be drawn to me like a neodymium magnet. It didn't happen overnight, but when it did, I didn't look back and rarely have the urge to turn back. It may not be the same for you. If you stumble, pick yourself up and keep trying.

Don't allow shame or guilt to paralyse you. Let your desire to overcome intensify your determination to break free. Learn your triggers. Recognise the traps. Don't deceive yourself into thinking that you can go down that route and win. Only you can get a grip on your own mind and prevent it from going to dark places by doing something as simple as shifting your focus. I can tell you that every time I win, it's because I am dependent on Christ, and it is my faith in Him that anchors me.

What Are You Good At?

Having a hobby as a distraction in the early days may be a great means of shifting your focus. Music and songwriting have always been great outlets throughout the toughest points of my journey.

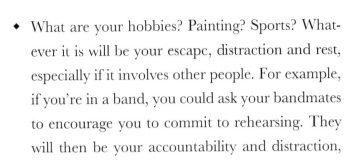

- What are your hobbies? Painting? Sports? Whatever it is will be your escape, distraction and rest, especially if it involves other people. For example, if you're in a band, you could ask your bandmates to encourage you to commit to rehearsing. They will then be your accountability and distraction, whether they realise it or not.
- What makes your heart sing?
- What activities do you totally lose yourself in?

But what happens when fighting the urges, mental challenges and addictions gets hard? How do you deal with lapses or situations where you fail to resist temptations? Don't hide in the shame of it all. It can paralyse you and stop you from moving forward. Be willing to own up to your mistakes and ask yourself fundamental questions like, *how do I break free from this cycle?* Ask someone to support you and hold you accountable in a supportive and loving way. We all need support to grow and heal. When I had someone to talk to, I felt less stuck and able to make the necessary steps to grow. Understand that you are not a failure because you failed in that situation – there is a difference. We don't deliberately go out of our way to fail, but when we do, we just get up and do better. Don't allow it to take over your whole life. That's a trap of the enemy. You can move forward, and you can get past this.

Draw strength from the promises that overflow from the word of God. They speak of your value and of your potential. They will be your fuel. There are so many verses, and here are a few:

- "I will praise thee; for I am fearfully and wonderfully made: marvellous are thy works; and that my soul knoweth right well."[36]
- "Therefore if the Son makes you free, you shall be free indeed."[37]
- "But God clearly shows and proves His own love for us, by the fact that while we were still sinners, Christ died for us."[38]

I hope that these scriptures encourage you, but never just take mine or anyone's word for it – get to know God for yourself. He is best at guiding you out of the sticky, murky mental places that immoral fantasies try to trick you into.

There is something earnest about a heart that says, *I want to change, and I have genuine remorse for what I have done or how I have lived.* The desire to change speaks volumes about the direction that you want to head in. Moreover, it speaks of the nature of our love for God. It is out of that love that we honour Him through our lifestyle. Yes, we have the grace of God, and He is loving and forgiving, but our approach towards His grace says everything about who we are. When my eldest son does something that he knows he shouldn't have, I am less likely to deal harshly with him if he shows penitence. However, if his attitude is shrugged shoulders, lack of remorse, and "so what?" I will become enraged. I believe that it is important that we do not frustrate the grace of God. "A broken and a contrite heart, O God, thou wilt not despise."[39] Your heart's condition is the true sign that you want to change direction and that you want to do better.

---

[36] Psalm 139:14 (KJV)
[37] John 8:36 (NKJV)
[38] Romans 5:8 (AMP)
[39] Psalm 51:17 (KJV)

Committing Crimes

If the weight of your secret is destructive enough to be considered a crime punishable by law, then you will have considerable ground to cover. There's no way to put it lightly. You have to pay your debt. I can imagine that this will make the feeling of dread wash over you, but I want you to consider this. One prison is much worse than the other. It's up to you to choose whether you want a short or long-term one. The prison in your mind will last a lifetime, if not an eternity. But when you pay the price you owe to those that you have wronged, then you begin the process of becoming debt-free in your mind, spirit and to the world. The journey to change is never easy, but I believe that you will be relieved when you no longer have to look over your shoulder and worry about what repercussions are coming.

At the opening of this chapter, I wrote about the woman who was caught in the act of adultery. She had committed a crime within her society and against her husband. When she was brought to be judged, it was God who vindicated her. In the same way, when you go through the proper channels within society and pay your dues, you are saying to God, "I want to change. I want to do better." You are now allowing God to take the driving seat. Trust Him to be a great driver. Never think that your silence means that you have escaped. You will *always* reap what you sow. You may pay it forward now or pay it forward later, but you *will* pay it forward.

There are consequences for sin. That's why it's always important to weigh up life's choices wisely. So, be your own catalyst for the change that you want to happen. Yes, it will get hard before it gets better, but you are initiating a transformative process in your life. I know that you're tired of hiding and running. Tired of looking over your shoulder; the sleepless nights and the dreams of terror that have plagued your mind. Rest is waiting. The kind of rest that your body, mind and soul crave. It only comes through the process that I have just shared. Pay your debt and be free.

One of the most damaging effects that addiction can have on marriage is deceit. I started this chapter by speaking to you as an individual because you have to see yourself first. See your areas of weakness, identify and conquer your enemies; the devil, your addiction and yourself. Deception can kill marriage quicker than a speeding bullet. You may already know this, or you may not, but if your marriage is built on lies, then it will only be a matter of time before your marriage crumbles. Your secret is a threat to your marriage, whether your husband knows it or not. That's why it is important to share the weight and truth of your secret so that you can work through it and heal with your husband.

Let's Talk About Sex

Growing up in church, the perspective that I was taught was that, as a single woman, you can't do *it*, don't talk about *it*, or, if you do, *it* is spoken about in a negative light. I remember how taboo the word *sex* was. However, I believe this approach towards the topic of sex was a car crash waiting to happen. While, on the one hand, trying to emphasise the importance of waiting until marriage to be sexually intimate, on the other hand, sex became a dirty word. We so easily forget that God invented sex and that in its purest form, with love as the foundation, it is a beautiful thing. It is one of the highest expressions of love within marriage. I waited to get married to have sex with my husband because I wanted to honour my commitment to God. I also wanted to make sure that I was giving something that I highly valued to the right person. Many guys tried and failed to usurp me of the experience of sharing something that I valued highly with someone who would treasure it and my heart in the process. Honestly, I am so glad that I did because when I got married, I was ready for that level of intimacy, and I am honoured to be open, intimate and vulnerable with someone that I trust so deeply. The absolute and unfiltered truth is that courting was hard for me because I wanted to be as close as possible to the man I loved, but we tried to respect the boundaries until we were married. There were times when we failed miserably. However, when we married, we were glad that we set the boundaries and focused more on the other areas of our relationship. We learnt so much about each other when we were dating and engaged.

That being said, when I finally was able to be intimate with my husband, the fantasies I had about my marital sex life were shattered by reality. I found it difficult to adjust and painful. It took a while for me to honestly say that SEX IS GOOD. I learnt not to shy away from conversations about how we could have the best sex life. We worked together to find our sexual stride. We had conversations about what we like and what we don't. We learnt and still learn so much about each other through sexual intimacy. Stuff that no one knows, because of course, it's NOYB (none of your business). Haha! But seriously, no one told me that sexual intimacy is a journey, and if you both want to be happy with your sex life, then you've got to be honest and have the conversations. No more pretending you are on your period or have a headache. Stop leaving that man in sexual flames of yearning and desire. Tell him the sex is horrific, and it does your head in! Sex is a crucial underlying thread for many areas of intimacy between wife and husband.

I am not saying that every few minutes hump like bunny rabbits, but the absence of sex in marriage generally spells trouble. Obviously, some couples are unable to be sexually intimate because of health issues etc. However, health complexities aside, sex is why you are recognised as a married couple and not flatmates. In the eyes of the law, government, God and everybody, your marriage is sealed when you consummate it. There is generally a lot of onus put on the act of sex itself within marriage.

- How's your sex life?
- Do you enjoy it?
- Is it non-existent?
- Can you trust your husband with your body and heart? (If uncertain about the level of trust towards your husband, then you may want to have a look at Chapter 11, *Cheated and Broken*).
- Is it a quickie in the bathroom because you can't be bothered or just want to get on with your responsibilities? Or is it an intense explosion after a slow, simmering build-up and a great date?
- What about your physical connection?
- Do you still look each other in the eyes or hold hands?
- Do you still talk about what you both generally enjoy other than the kids and your other responsibilities?
- Are you interested in the *person* that is your spouse?

Intimacy Matters

It is so easy to take each other for granted as the years go by. You learn their characteristics, routine, buttons to push, and even their bodies can become oh so familiar. How do you keep the spark and yearning to be with each other... alive? How do you remind him that he has the best person for him and vice versa? How do you keep each other coming back for more? Especially when you have been having more and more and more.

There are thousands of questions where relationships and intimacy are concerned, but I don't think they're as complicated as they seem. Firstly, you both have to want to please each other and have an interest in each other. When that interest goes, then that's where the trouble starts. Putting everything aside to connect has to be a deliberate thing; date nights, walks, alone time are all crucial. Even when I was pregnant with the second baby and sick as a dog, we sat on the bed with a Chinese takeaway and watched a movie. Honestly, it was one of the best anniversaries that we've had to date. Connection is so much more important than flamboyance. Don't be afraid to try new things – play! Pay attention to what your spouse likes and go with it (even if it's just once). Be spontaneous. Be full of surprises. Talk! Ask each other, "Do you still like...?" or "Why don't we try...?" Marital sex is your playground, honey! Have fun!

Of course, logic dictates that you simply can't play alone. If your partner has lost the appetite for sex, then it's important to find out why. It's incredibly difficult for a marriage to survive without sex (except for the previously mentioned complexities). The marriages that have complex issues regarding sexual intimacy tend to connect in other ways. Love is expressed through nurture and care. But healthy, young, red-blooded couples? No excuse! Am I saying that if your husband is not sexually intimate with you, you should march up to him, strip him down to his birthday suit and pounce?! Goodness no! I am saying that you should pay attention and be available to have the conversations that need to be had. Whatever you do going forward, please don't argue about the lack of sexual intimacy. Sex is supposed to be fun and enticing, not obligatory and stressful. Relax, talk to God about your sex life. Work on your own personal journey by yourself and with a counsellor. Observe how the lack of intimacy is making you feel. Are you feeling insecure? Isolated? Lonely? Having unfulfilled sexual urges? Be honest about it, so that you know how to build yourself up. Obviously, it's hard to deal with the sexual urges aspect alone, but the rest?

There are other ways to build confidence and eradicate loneliness. Spoil yourself. Go on retreats and pamper days. Build connections and keep your spirit strong. Don't allow yourself to break down about the things you have no control over or don't understand. Draw strength from the wells of your community. Don't be desperate to force him into being attracted to you. Operate from the space of heightened awareness of your value. Act, walk, talk and live like you are gold. Let your confidence show that you will not be broken by the lack of connection. Trust God to reveal the answers in time. Trust me: in time, everything is revealed.

You will know why things have been the way they have been, but you have to be patient. There is a Divine timing in place that will eventually unlock the truth you have been waiting for. Don't try to rush ahead of that timing. Don't feel like you have to withhold the fact that you are aware of your decline in sexual intimacy. There is nothing wrong with letting him know. Speak to him with kindness, without agitation or aggression. Let him know that you are available to talk about it whenever he is ready. Invite him to share what is on his heart rather than dragging it out of him kicking and screaming. You may be surprised at his response. Listen closely and pay attention to what he doesn't say (his body language, for example). I understand that this may be a distressing time, and you may have been crying secretly for a while now, but it will get better. Focus on building yourself up and strengthening yourself for the journey ahead.

Every couple's sex life fluctuates. Regardless of how much love is in our marriages, life happens. It's not some strange thing that only happens if someone is cheating. Sometimes it is not possible to be intimate, and there could be various reasons for it. There may be times where you simply just don't want to do it. That's okay. Having an increased workload, stress, children, lacking body confidence can also be some of the reasons that your sexual intimacy takes a nosedive. It's wise not to jump to conclusions about why your spouse isn't as active in that department as he was. The idea of marriage and the unity of two people coming together is great (especially where sex is concerned); however, we must never forget that we are individuals also. We have individual needs, challenges, journeys, complexities, struggles, desires, and we should always work towards flourishing individually. In the same sense, our individuality has to harmonise with our relationship's marital requirements to thrive. This principle applies to the sexual relationships within marriage.

Does He Know Your Sexuality Has Changed?

Alternatively, it may be you no longer have an appetite for intimacy with your husband, and it has made you question your sexual orientation. Or it could be something that you have been struggling with all along. Do you feel conflicted about sharing the truth about your preferences or burying it in the cloak of your marriage? I just want to say that you don't have to hide your secret. It's too much to bear alone.

The weight will cripple you over time. I believe that it is important to purge your mind, heart and spirit of the secrets that weigh you down to thrive. It's necessary to delve deeper into why you feel the way that you do. Especially if you feel like you have changed. There are parts of your soul that need to be unlocked and unpacked so that you can discover the roots as to why you feel the way that you do. I would encourage you to find a Christian counsellor and a safe space to open up, even if it's just to listen to yourself speak about your struggles out loud.

Take one step at a time. Be honest. Don't think about what will happen to your marriage and what will change all at once because you will become overwhelmed. Just start with unpacking the complexities of your soul. Work towards having the conversations with your husband and a confidante that will be able to hear your voice, fears, struggles and navigate you to the clarity that you need. What if the complexity of your sexual orientation presents the risk that your marriage will deteriorate even further? Honestly, put on your big girl boots and get to work. You will have to have the discussion at some point, and you will have to decide how to move forward. You can still navigate through this difficult season with grace and love. Present your feelings about your sexuality before God and be honest about the pain and struggle of it all. He honestly cares about you, regardless of how you may feel about Him right now. You can still pour out your heart to Him and ask Him to enlighten, guide and direct your life. This journey will not be easy for you because you will have to work through a lot of hurt between yourself and your husband. I pray that you will find your way through the turbulence of this season and receive the clarity that you need to thrive. However, while you're on this journey, hold onto the truth that things *have to* get better because eventually, they really will.

Does He Know Your Fantasies Would Terrify Him?

No thought becomes this crippling overnight. The destructive nature of your thoughts has taken time to build. There's a moment when the thought entered your mind, and you ignored the option of casting that thought out. Instead, you slowly digested those dangerous ideologies, concepts and notions. Those thoughts took root within the depths of your mind. You allowed them to grow to the point that they became like wildfires, and now you find yourself desperate for a way to quench the raging and uncontrollable thoughts within your mind. To kill the appetite that you have for those things that you have been desperate to overcome. Where did those thoughts come from? Why did those thoughts appeal to you? Have honest conversations with yourself about their origins. Like anything with roots, if you deny it sustenance, it will die. You have to starve those thoughts of anything that will fuel them. You cast down those imaginations by feeding yourself the things that are not destructive.

Set your thoughts on "whatsoever things are true, whatsoever things are honest, whatsoever things are just, whatsoever things are pure, whatsoever things are lovely, whatsoever things are of good report; if there be any virtue, and if there be any praise, think on these things."[40] Shift your focus onto anything that will strengthen your mind. Shut out the darkness and embrace the light. If you find this too difficult to achieve, then find help. Don't suffer in silence because, again, there are counsellors that will support you as you work through the dark places in your soul. You are not strange, weird or odd. Everyone has something that they need to work through, but I believe that when you find a confidante – someone who is patient, non-judgemental and not condescending – you will be free enough to do the work

---

[40] Philippians 4:8 (KJV)

necessary to heal and flourish. Don't hold back. Share the depths and complexities of your mind and allow them to journey through it with you. For many, the transformation isn't instantaneous. It may be long, difficult and frustrating, but persevere. Temptation is inevitable, but the Bible tells us to resist. Don't allow those thoughts to take root in the depths of your mind. Be aware of the seeds that are being sown and cut them off before they become difficult to control.

Do you feel like you can tell your husband about your struggles? Maybe he already knows. Or maybe you haven't felt strong enough to share the difficulties that you are having with him. I believe that it is important to be open with your husband regardless of whether he will like the truth or not. After all, if you can't be honest with your husband, then who can you be honest with, right? However, if you feel like you can't be that open with him straight away, find someone that you do not know and build the confidence to share your challenges with them first. Make openness with your husband the goal and build up to it. Pray about the journey, and journal to express your thoughts, prayers and desires for the path ahead.

God Is with You on Your Healing Journey

God is for you. It's easy to feel that you have been abandoned and are undeserving of God's love when you struggle. I am certain from experience that God sees more value in your desire to grow and become a better person than in the mistakes and struggles you have. Now, I am not justifying anything. Let me make that clear. I am saying He is on your side and absolutely rooting for your win. He knows exactly what led you to this place and how you got so stuck, and He is passionate about your growth. Carry this understanding throughout the tough times in your journey. When your voice shakes as you speak to your counsellor or when you have to look your husband in the eye and tell him all the things that you know that he will not be happy to hear. You have a Divine cheerleader in your corner, and He will always be with you through it all.

Whether your thoughts and feelings were triggered by pain, loss or dysfunction. Something that you have not given much attention to. Something that has slipped under the radar all this time. Can you identify what it was? What triggered this spiral? That's the place where you begin the work and your journey to healing. Go back within the depths of your mind to the places, the things and the people that made you feel those triggers. This may be difficult if those feelings come flooding back but keep pushing through. Write it all down. What one word sums up how you feel? Is it rejected? Belittled? Robbed? Forgotten? Write down the one word that comes to mind and circle it. Ask yourself, *why?* Now think about something, somewhere or someone that makes you feel the opposite. Write the one word that you feel and write "why?" The opposite things are the things that will be your support for healing and growth. Maybe you love to sing, and it makes you feel the love and acceptance that you have so desperately craved or maybe you have always been passionate about running. Make the time to do those things that will build and encourage you.

Prayer and Meditation

Let's pray and reflect using the mirror.

Dear Heavenly Father,

Please forgive me of my sin offences and free me from the prison of a troubled mind. Thank you for seeing me in all my flaws, struggles and imperfection. Thank you for being my friend, loving and supporting me throughout the darkest parts of my life. Show me how to be strong and to make the right choices for my wellbeing and the wellbeing of those I love. I thank you and trust you to continue to guide my journey.

In Jesus' name, Amen.

EIGHT

I Don't Love My Husband

§

A touch that once used to arouse her now made her skin crawl.
She may or may not remember when it happened, but some-
where along the line…
She fell out of love.
She no longer wanted to be attached to him in any way.
How would she be able to admit the truth about the fact that…
She wanted out.

Don't believe the deceptions that married couples put out. If you are
determined to stay married for the long haul, then you are bound to
have difficult seasons. There will be tears, the silent treatment or gap-
ing holes where everyone is desperate for the right words to be spoken.
Marriage can be tough. You're not alone. There are emotional waves,
the highs and the lows. Sometimes growth feels slow.

But what happens when you no longer have a desire to be in that marriage? How do you navigate through those feelings? How do you work out whether or not your marriage can survive? Should you allow your feelings to take the driving wheel? Making the right choices for yourself and loved ones become harder when feelings are involved (or, in this case, the lack thereof). If you are married, then you will understand the weight of wanting to close such a life-changing chapter in your life. It is not as simple as packing a bag and walking away, even if you have some valid reasons for doing so. I want to explore this subject's complexities, hoping that you are empowered to make the best choices. It's the worst thing to walk away from something that could've been salvaged. It will be even more painful if you look back at this moment and realise that you threw away something you could have worked out. That is, of course, if you could've worked it out! I believe that it helps if you can weigh it all up, and that's why this chapter has been written.

Happily Ever After

"And they lived happily ever after…"

The most dangerous phrase that fairy tales have ever coined. It implies that marriage equates to that feeling of being happy. This marriage isn't making me happy. I don't feel in love with him anymore. The sex and chemistry are rubbish. We've just grown apart.

Maybe you've fallen out of love. Or maybe you realised that you were never in love in the first place. It could've been that he did something that you have struggled to forgive him for. Crushed by the resentment of what he did or didn't do. Or it could be nothing at all. You just know for sure that you aren't in love with him anymore. Is it a feeling of numbness? A lack of butterflies? Something that just isn't the same as it used to be?

There are so many reasons that couples fall out of love. There has been a damaging dominant perspective in the air that marriage has to serve our feelings. If it doesn't serve your feelings, then there's no way that it can be right. Right? Wrong. The secret in the heart of most long-married wives is that there are times that they have fallen completely out of love with their beloveds. There's no way that the euphoria of young love is sustainable long term. A very wise woman (who has been married for over 60 years) has shared the secret to her marriage's success. "You make it work," she once said. This woman has seen two of her children die, silently suffered through unimaginable losses and still holds on to this value.

The reality is that a long-term, sustained marriage takes work and dedication. Truthfully, I don't *feel* in love with my husband all the time, but I would fight you if you touched him! He would say the same because we both know that marriage is a choice. He is more than my lover. He's my confidante and life partner. He's my champion, and I am his cheerleader. He's my business partner and such an amazing father to our children. I am not just in love with him, but I respect, am loyal to, and value him. I choose him every day.

We deliberately take time to be exclusive to one another so we stay connected. Whether it's quick dates with an ice cream in the park or a relaxing weekend away, we have fun. Marriage isn't some drab and dreary thing. I don't believe in keeping up appearances or saving face, but I believe it's necessary to have the hard conversations that will push you on to better days. Effective and clear communication without ego or offence allows your partner space to say what's on his heart without a filter. He doesn't need to worry about your tantrum or quick-witted response. He can just be honest and know that his truth is being respected and appreciated regardless of how wrong it is. When he speaks, look at his mouth, listen. Don't think about your response.

Just watch him and his body language. It's all going to tell you more about who he is and how he feels than your words ever will.

You already know how you are feeling, and you will have your time to share how you feel, but for that moment, make him feel like his words are the only words that matter. You will be surprised at how much that takes the angst out of the situation you face. That moment shows him that you respect him regardless of your differences. Regardless of the outcome of the conversation, your gift to him at that moment. I'm sure I have mentioned before that marriage is more about *us* than *me*. How you feel is very telling about what you may need at that moment, but what you actually need may be locked within your husband. For it to be released, a dialogue is necessary. Having the necessary conversations can transform your marriage.

There have been a countless number of times when I have started a sentence with, "Babe, I feel like we are getting out of touch and I don't feel like… you love me? I love you? We are disconnected somehow?" We may say it with shaky voices, and we may even cry, but we say what needs to be said because the end goal is our joint healing. He can't support a need that he doesn't know is there and vice versa. It's great when you take the fear of these difficult conversations off the table. No one needs to get offended or angry, but everyone within the relationship needs to be ready and willing to understand. Is he a man with good intentions? If your answer to this question is yes, you should also bear that in mind when having the necessary conversations.

Always Learning

The following advice was shared with me by my friends (who happened to also be a married couple) before I was married: "When you've been married a long time, then the things that you once found appealing about your spouse can start to become annoying."

I was a bit surprised because (as a young single woman) I thought that marriage would mean living in eternal pleasure. Now, being a married woman with two children, I don't think it's possible to be married for years and NOT annoy each other. I used to panic and think, *does that mean that our marriage is in danger?* Of course not! It's the nature of relationships. The number of times I've clashed with my mother about things that annoy me about her. Yet I couldn't live without her. It's the same with my husband, if not even more so. I consider that it shows we are on the right track. We are different and united in our difference. We are always learning something new about each other. We are also always learning something new about ourselves. We are always growing and changing. When we give each other the space to grow, marriage can flourish into something more brilliant than we could've ever conceived.

Just like a plant we've nurtured from a seed, it grows and blooms into something stronger than we ever imagined. That takes time. It doesn't just happen, and it isn't dependent on how we feel. We will reap what we sow, we will reap more than we sow, and we will reap later than we sow. That is a law to a thriving and successful lifestyle that we can never escape. We have been misled by society into believing that there are shortcuts, but the reality is that anything worth getting takes dedication and work. EVERY marriage will have hard times. If you leave this marriage and go into another marriage, I guarantee you will have hard times within that marriage. So what if he doesn't do the chores or he snores too loudly? Weigh up the cost against the value and recognise that things could be a lot worse. Pick your battles. Can you work around the difficulties that you are having in your marriage at the moment? This is a crucial question because there are so many out there who would never tell you that they wished they'd worked it out and didn't act on impulse. The hurt could increase if you let a good one slip away. Remind yourself of the qualities in your husband that you once fell in love with.

Sexual Intimacy

Great sex comes from understanding each other. Not just on a physical level but much deeper than that. For instance, sex will be the last thing on my mind if my husband watched me slave away all day and burn all my energy. That attentiveness, sensitivity and support are so appealing. Energy affects our mood and how we feel about our circumstances. There are a thousand and one things that can affect sexual intimacy. The marital sexual journey is a winding road as the years go by. Anyone who says the contrary is lying!

I believe that it helps to have conversations that will bring about positive change. Take a break. Get to know each other again. Date. Tease. Play. Tell him what you like. If you don't know, then try new things. Make it kinky; spice things up. Be spontaneous. Be cheeky and wild. You've earned your stripes to make your marriage as vibrant as it can possibly be. If you feel like he needs a map, let him know what you need to have a fulfilling sex life. If your bits don't fit together in a pleasurable way, then you can always find other ways to make sexual intimacy more enjoyable. I will not use this book to go into it, but you can always use the internet for inspiration. He might just be guessing that everything is fine because you haven't spelt it out. Start slow if you need to. Don't put pressure on yourself to feel things that you don't feel. What do you have in common? What's so annoying about him all of a sudden? Leave the kids with the grandparents while you go away and reconnect. Although marriage should not revolve around sex, great sex is a fundamental part of married life. For some, it's really natural to have great chemistry and intimacy, and for others, it isn't.

So many people adapt to sexual intimacy with ease when they get married. My story was much more difficult. When I first got married, I struggled with it, and I was in excruciating pain. My body fought to adjust to this unfamiliar experience. As I described in the previous chapter, I had never had intercourse before marriage, but I assumed that the earth would move beneath me, and it would be the best experience of my life. Young love is euphoric, and we craved connection and intimacy as young married couples usually do, but it felt like my body was betraying me. This was no Hollywood experience and nothing short of traumatic. What did I do? I talked – or should I say, cried, to my husband about it. It was a shock to the system and the new norm, but it was overwhelming that our intimacy wasn't anything like I had expected it to be. It made me value the friendship aspect of our relationship so much more than I ever had before. He wasn't just thinking about his needs, but we took our time and worked through the complicated aspects of intimacy together.

Sometimes the sexual aspect of marriage doesn't come together as easily as others, and that's okay. It doesn't mean that you've married the wrong person. It doesn't mean that you are sexually incompatible, and it doesn't mean that your sex life is doomed. Take your time. Be kind to yourself and to him. Work it out together. Bear in mind that it may not change overnight, and it may get harder before it gets better. Pull back and explore other ways of intimacy. Date? Foreplay? Whatever works for you both. You will find common ground if you are patient with one another.

Talk about what aspects of sex you enjoy. Don't lie and don't be shy, because it's a long life to be married and unsatisfied or frustrated sexually within your marriage. I truly believe that more marriages would survive if people had the necessary conversations early on in their marriage instead of having *enough*. Bottling up your emotions and frustrations is a recipe for disaster and can have a devastating effect on your marriage long term. Pray for your sex life. Pray for inspiration, connection, creativity and... fun! Sex is a beautiful thing within its proper function, and you are deserving of great intimacy between yourself and your husband. God isn't trying to withhold that from you, so if you ask for His support and creativity, then expect to receive it. After all, God is the inventor of sex and marriage, so His wisdom will be of great value.

Changes and Life Cycles

Taking the prospect of divorce off the table is a game-changer when hoping to have a marriage that lasts decades. Marriages go through many seasons. There will be times when we feel an erotic kind of love for our spouses. There will be times where that person will infuriate us on sight. There will be times when they will feel like a flatmate. Let's be real. Even if you marry your best friend, there will be times where you just feel worlds apart. It's okay. Don't trivialise how you feel because there may be reasons for it, but ask yourself this question: will you ever find anyone better?

If the person is abusive in any way, shape or form, maybe your answer is yes. However, love in the everyday is not a fairy tale. Love can be bitter, yet sweet. Sometimes more bitter than sweet. It's not easy, but it's worth it. Understandably, you would get to a point where you feel like walking away. Everybody goes through challenging seasons. My encouragement to you is always find the friend in your spouse, and the lover will appear. When you make your husband the first person that you want to talk to when something great happens or the first shoulder that you turn to when something painful happens, then your love is reinforced. Everything out there is coming for your marriage because marriage is God-inspired, designed and implemented.

What's out there is not going to be better than what you have right now. Bar abuse, I'm sure that most marital complications can be worked through IF both parties want to work them through.

Get Your Fight Back

Sometimes we underestimate how overwhelming the mundane aspects of marriage can be. Those little things can make you wish that you never walked down the aisle. The daily things that can have you choking back tears, feeling overlooked, under-appreciated and even unloved. The daily things that can wear you out. They can have you feeling more like a servant than a loved and cherished wife. They're the things that may make you secretly wish you could go back in time and shake yourself out of the insatiable desire to fulfil your urge to be a wife. I bet you could see yourself slapping the younger version of yourself in the face and saying, "Don't do it!" Maybe you are far from impressed with the reality of what marriage really entails. Maybe all the unforeseen aspects of your responsibilities crept upon you like a thief in the night. Where you were once filled with wonder and expectancy, you now are overwhelmed with frustration and regret. When did you lose your voice? Do you find it difficult to speak your truth, your pain, and address the weight of your oppression? It's easy to let the escalating bills, working all the hours that exist, and chaotic lifestyle weigh you DOWN!

* He snores too loud when he sleeps.
* He doesn't help out with the kids!
* He never buys me flowers.
* He dumps his clothes around the house.

I get it. As a mother and wife, things can easily feel like they're going at a hundred miles an hour. I understand your desire to want to run and never return. When you are burnt out, you will naturally want to quit everything. Your vision becomes blurred, and it's hard to see the blessings from the unnecessary challenges that you just don't feel like you need to take on in your life. Especially if your husband is unsupportive and like a grown, lazy baby! I completely understand that he doesn't feel like a blessing in your life right now, just dead weight. You're snowed under by carrying everyone else's needs, weight and responsibilities. When will it be your turn to be taken care of? When will you have the opportunity to thoroughly enjoy everyday life? It may not come out of your mouth, but it's obvious that you feel like your marriage is sucking the life out of you.

JOURNAL

- Are you void of the dreams that you once had?
- Are you too overwhelmed by responsibility to pursue your dreams?
- Do you feel like you are losing yourself as a result of not being able to pursue your dreams?
- Do you envy the girl that you used to be?

Sometimes she seems so far away from the person that you have become. Sometimes you envy the blessings that you once had and the blessings that you took for granted. She's hidden somewhere deep within you – suppressed but waiting, hidden but hopeful.

The weight of this season will one day pass away. A new version of the girl that lies dormant within you will emerge. You will find her because of the lessons that your marriage has taught you. You will learn to be free-spirited within the responsibilities that your marriage may bring. Applied pressure will cause you to speak out on the things you are no longer willing to tolerate. Having time, vision, financial or relationship constraints, and priorities will demand the version of you that sets boundaries. Becoming more resilient will require you to change your outlook, to recognise that even the most perfect version of your husband would annoy you from time to time. You vowed to commit to every aspect of who he is regardless of how insufferable he may sometimes seem. Your change of mindset is going to add blessings, strength and beauty to your marriage. The wisdom within you reveals to you that your husband is still a blessing in so many respects. I am sure that you both love each other and could have chosen so much worse where spouses are concerned. The most beautiful marriages are not served up on a silver platter. They are actually built from the ground up. Nothing worth getting is going to come easy. It doesn't matter how the sparks flew in the beginning. It doesn't matter how many times you used to have sex per day when you first married. The real test of what you are made of is shown when everyone's ugly is exposed. When no one walks away, then that will tell you whether or not your marriage will stand the test of time.

Nowadays, marriages disintegrate at the peep of a bit of ugly, only to find that there were so much worse uglies in the world. We need to learn how to fight for the right things. Put your fight in the right direction. Lose the quitter mentality. Become a professional in extracting greatness from everything and everyone around you. It starts with you. It starts with your mentality. See your marriage as something that has boundless potential. Stop looking at everything else to save you. Besides heavenly intervention, this book is as good as it gets, and even I will not let you off the hook. A true test of your character is your ability to push through the difficult aspects of your marriage. Every single marriage is tested. You have to find a strong sense of teamwork and unity to get through the difficult seasons.

Identify the real enemy. Your husband is not your enemy. Whatever divides you is your enemy. Find common ground. Worship God together. Pray together. Make time to reconnect. Give the kids to someone that you trust and spend some time with each other. Make your marriage a priority again.

It's the Principle...

Sometimes the little things are not the problem... Sometimes they are the symptoms of a much bigger problem (or a few). My mum always used to say, "It's the principle..." The underlying issue may be a lack of care, foresight or observation. So, let's say you've spent 45 minutes scrubbing the hallway floor and your husband walks in. Firstly, he doesn't notice your hard work (*strike one*). Secondly, he walks all over it with his muddy boots (*strike two*). Thirdly, he leaves his muddy boots in the middle of the hallway (*strike three*). You're bound to explode with levels of anger that you have never reached before. Why? Because of the principle. The care you've put into your labour of love had been overlooked and trampled on without an afterthought.

I know there are days where this feeling overwhelms you. It may not be as a result of the same scenario, but you're not alone. There are a lot of these circumstances in marriage, for wives and for husbands. That's why self-control is so important. We can't do it without the fruits and characteristics that the Holy Spirit gives us when we yield to Him. Self-control is a fruit of the Holy Spirit. "But the fruit of the Spirit is love, joy, peace, longsuffering, gentleness, goodness, faith. Meekness, *temperance*: against such, there is no law."[41]

---

[41] Galatians 5:22 (KJV)

Without total dependence on God, we can't have thriving marriages. It is God who promises to act as our Counsellor and Helper. He is of great help whenever my marriage goes through bumpy twists and turns. It is through God that we can embody the attributes that contribute to a thriving marriage. The Bible is our spiritual mirror; it shows our flaws, beauty and even the aspects of our character that we need to develop to thrive in every part of our lives, including our marriages. It's definitely a daily process, but we all get weary from time to time. You are not alone. There are a lot of valleys in marriage, and it comes with the territory. Every day I work on communicating better, loving deeper, and seeing things from God's perspective. I am not saying that you should be a doormat! The Lord and my husband know that I am proud that I can speak up for myself. That's equally as important. But over the years, I have learnt to hesitate a lot more, ask more questions and verbalise how I feel. So many marriages die because of the simple fact that couples don't know how to communicate.

Just before I got married, I worked in divorce court (*ironic right!*). I was dizzyingly in love with Paul but spending most of the days (leading up to my wedding) watching many marriages fall apart. Before a case one day, I was sitting next to one of the judges, and I asked her, "What do you think is the single cause of breakups in most of the cases that you've seen?"

Her answer was simple: "Lack of communication." Please understand that she had been married 15 to 25 years at that time. She highlighted that because the couples could not communicate, she would have to have the final say on fundamental decisions, which effectively put them in the children's position. "Trust me, a lot of them behave just like children!" I remember her saying. Simply because they didn't want to work it out. Simply because they refused to reconcile or communicate, they became like babies.

Consequently, the government told them who would have the children and who would have the house. The court told the divorcees how to split the money, even who would get the car. Every fundamental and life-changing decision was taken out of their hands. Simply because everyone wanted to win at each other's expense. In reality, everybody lost. Particularly the innocent children! Nobody benefits when the family fights. So, if there's any chance of saving your marriage, don't stop until you find a resolution. If you're a hothead (like me), go cool off. Then have the necessary conversations. If you have to visit painful topics until you find clarity, then do that. Whatever you do, don't let the dialogue come to an end. Once dialogue dies, then everything spirals out of control. Dialogue is everything.

This also applies to our relationship with God. Two-way conversations actually work! I have to work double-time to ensure that my husband is heard when we have the necessary conversations. He's a man of few words, so I know that it's important for me to zip up my mouth, open my ears and pay attention when he speaks. It's easy to miss a phrase or misinterpret a sentence while we communicate. "Can you say that again, babe?" or "That doesn't make any sense" or "What do you actually mean?" are sentences that I will liberally use before I come to any conclusions. As much as I'm a bold, fiery and extrovert kind of woman, I know the importance of listening to understand. Not just hearing. There actually is a difference. It's easy to think about my next line of defence, but sometimes misinterpretation and lack of attention to the conversation's details are a ticking time bomb.

Communication Breakdown

With regards to lack of communication, marriages often break down for the following reasons:

He's Caused Me So Much Pain

Being resentful while staying in a marriage is next-level torture. Nobody's leaving, but nobody is happy. Everybody suffers. Resentment does happen, but honestly, there is something absurd about staying in limbo. You do, or you don't. Be sure about committing. Live life free without the weight of resentment and unforgiveness. Maybe you need a second to recover from the sting of the hurt that your husband has caused you. All that time and energy that you are wasting on being resentful is holding you back. You could both have moved forward into bigger and better things. So, my encouragement to you is... be sure. Know where you are going and do the work to take those steps in the right direction. I for sure know you'll be happier about it.

I Don't Want to Fix It

If you are certain that you no longer want to work through your marriage, stop reading this chapter of the book. I'm serious. I am not here to convince you to make decisions that you don't want to make. Head over to Chapter 12, *When Marriage Is Killing You* or Chapter 13, *Life After Marriage*. Hopefully, you will find more direction for the next stage in God discovery, your relationship and self-discovery there.

I Want My Old Life Back

What is it about the previous lifestyle that appeals to you? Is it freedom? Is it being alone? I accept that there may be aspects of your single life that you may yearn for, or maybe it's just the whole thing. The truth is that marriage is non-reversible experience-wise. You can't erase your marital journey or experience. You can't be that young singleton again. You can't unmeet your husband. You have tasted the sweet acacia honey of marriage, and now you know the flavour, even though it has gone as sour as the taste of a bag of lemons. It's unforgettable, isn't it?! You will never be what you once were because, in reality, you are better than you once were. That being said, I would never ignore this yearning because it signifies that there is something that you are looking for that you do not have right now. Make the time to hear what your heart is trying to tell you. If you are thirsting for something that you used to have in your former lifestyle, then it's worth gaining clarity and working out with your husband on how to work towards it.

I Love Someone Else

While I was working within divorce court, I witnessed lives destroyed by divorce. I will never forget the pain on the faces of former couples as they fought to break apart everything that they had built. Going back and forth as they took to the stand to explain why they were right and why the other was wrong. It seemed evident that everybody had lost. Not only did they lose houses, cars, land, money and the quality of life, but their children, families, friends and community were torn between the two. That, to me, is the greatest robbery. Close up, you may see the thrill of what you're doing and feeling, but step back and weigh up the cost.

Marriage is more than just *feeling* in love. You are building and strengthening that love with roots that go beyond your relationship. People only see the tree, but they don't see the roots that make a healthy relationship what it is. YOU know your relationship. Ask God to reveal to you the impact that your relationship has. You may not realise how powerful and impactful your relationship is on everything and everyone around you. You may not see the dormant potential of what your marriage could become. It takes wisdom and foresight to see ahead. It takes a wise woman to push past the hard parts until a shift takes your marriage to new levels. You have to be incredibly strong to be the catalyst for change that your marriage needs. If there is any way that you can preserve and nurture what you already have with your husband, then please don't hesitate to do so. I am sure that many of the divorcees sitting in my courtrooms wished that they had read a book like this before setting down that path. Please don't be like them and realise the value of what you lost when it is too late.

I Want to Work Out How I Really Feel

Sometimes things can get a little bit hazy along the way. I understand that. Especially in strenuous and contentious relationships. It's okay to say, "I need space." Go and rediscover yourself if you really need time to listen to the sound of your own inner person. Don't apologise for that. There have been so many times when I, too, have said to Paul, "I just need to rediscover me" (and vice versa). I don't believe that he ever thought I wanted to end our relationship, but he was loving and courteous enough to give me space. Life can become so overwhelming at times. It's easy to get so caught up in the hustle and bustle of it all that we can't hear. Hearing the most important voices for direction in life can seem like a trivial thing until you get lost. When you start to wonder where you are going in life – hit reset. Make time for your own growth and build your own relationship with God, and you will never go wrong. There is nothing worse than feeling like you are being dragged through life and that you are not being heard. Hear yourself first and defend your voice and the instructions that you hear from God. He will always guide your path if you invite Him to.

Nah Sal, I Actually Love Him, But I Can't Make Him Stay

Let him go. Never fight someone to see you for what you're worth. You cannot make anyone do what they *don't* want to do. They will resent you for it. Work on your own heart and believe in your value. Act like you're a rare jewel. He will never find another like you. Be okay with him taking the time to work that out. Don't wait around or look for him. Just build on your relationship with God and surround yourself with those who appreciate your value. Oh, and Queen, if no one has told you lately, then I'm telling you that you're going to be alright!

***

You are doing so well! Pushing through all the difficult aspects in this book and finding your own personal brave. You should celebrate yourself and all the strides that you are making to make your life *better*.

Prayer and Meditation

Let's pray and reflect using the mirror.

Dear Abba,

Thank you for the beauty of sacrificial love. Show me how to express this kind of love in my marriage and relationships. Give me supernatural resilience and strength to push for the blessings buried in the complexities of my marriage. Free me from the chains of resentment and pour out an abundance of joy into my life.

In Jesus' name, Amen.

NINE

STRAINED FRIENDSHIPS AND FAMILY FEUDS

§

Tears streamed down her face as she thought about everything she had already given up to preserve her marriage.

She had already made so many sacrifices to preserve her relationship.

What once meant everything to her was now suffocating her and her marriage.

She was sick and tired of fighting and desperate for the conflict not to penetrate the walls of her home.

She just wanted peace.

If she had to walk away from her marriage to get it, then she was willing to pay the price.

Not everyone will want you to have a peaceful, happy, flourishing marriage. Sometimes, the people closest to you won't wish you well. Even worse, they may be the reason that your marriage is under strain. It is easier than you may think to be driven to the edge by those who are supposed to support your marriage. How many times have you felt like walking away from it all because of them?

I've had so many moments like the woman in the story (above) where I have wondered… *is it all worth it?* Especially during the times when I have forgotten the value of our marriage and the importance of fighting the right battles. Honestly, family dynamics and changing relationships can be some of the most difficult aspects of marriage. Undoubtedly, you were hopeful, excited and expectant of a bright future when you met your partner's friends and family. Maybe there was instantaneous friction, or maybe it developed over time? However, those relationships' value is inconsequential when they leave you with strain, pressure or strife. Increased pressure over a long period can leave you regretting the decision to marry this man. It doesn't matter how perfect or handsome he is. The thought, *I didn't sign up for them* may gleam in the spotlight of your mind. You are right. You didn't sign up for it, but they come as a part of your husband's life anyway. They were foundational components of his journey to you and are a part of *his* story… even if it's history.

Grafting for Love

Relationships usually don't work themselves out all on their own. The best ones take graft, disagreements, agreements, falling apart and coming together again. It can be draining, but conflict is inevitable. Disagreements happen when discord becomes so venomous or toxic that it affects your marriage. So, how do you navigate your way back to thriving relationships?

It's commonplace for couples to get married without giving thought to conflict brewing on the horizon. Even worse situations can weigh heavy on your soul, like marrying into one side of a bitter family feud and being forced to take sides in a fight that you had no involvement in. *We don't have to live with them* might cross your mind when reflecting on your situation. You've married your husband, not his family. The fact that there is bad blood with relatives or close friends has nothing to do with you. In other words, it's **NOYB** (none of your business).

I used to believe the same thing when our love was young. The truth is if my husband is losing sleep over it, and if we are arguing about it, then it's a problem. Sometimes complex relationships stay with us like a stain. We hope they will go away, but instead, the contention grows. Whether the person in question knows it or not, they impact our marriage. Like a lingering smell, the issue just doesn't seem to go away. In reality, it's both yourself and your husband that allow outside influences to take hold and instigate strife. What you allow beyond the doors of your home into your union and family life will continue to take hold. It all comes down to putting your fight in the right place. Identifying potential threats to your marriage may shift your relationship with your husband into a better position to heal. Is it a family member? Is it yourself? Is it a combination of things? Identify what issues need to be dealt with, work out what threat needs to be eliminated and unite against it, **NOT** each other.

I remember thinking that I had the marriage of my dreams, yet it seemed like there was a cloud hovering over it. I always had this image of my friends and family championing my marriage throughout my life. "Isn't it amazing that they have such a beautiful and thriving relationship?! What a special couple!" is the conversation that I had always imagined them having. The reality of how challenging it can be to sustain relationships with people that want you to stay the same after you have had such a life-changing experience is disappointing, to say the least. The truth is that, whether we like it or not…

Marriage Changes Us

Marriage changes your mentality, priorities and your lifestyle. Family life causes a shift from the singular, self-centred mindset to a team-focused mentality. This shift is necessary because teamwork has to be the pulse of any successful marriage. There has to be unity that changes the details of your life. It shifts the focus from yourself to your family unit. Marriage has a way of changing the way that you think if you want it to be healthy. I used to spare no thought for others when I had to do grocery shopping, but whenever I shop nowadays, I don't just buy what I want. I think about what my husband and my children want. They come first. If I go for coffee with a friend, I make sure that my family have whatever they need before leaving the house. A fundamental principle that I have adopted to this day is "never leave your house undone". I don't go and do any endeavours for myself without making sure my family are provided for first. I ensure that they are supported so well that it's like I've never left the house. It is my expression and labour of love as a wife and mother. It tells my family that they are my priority, and my exploits don't take precedence. That includes friends and extended members of our families. It's the nature of prioritising. I have learnt that as a wife and mother it is important to support my family.

There was a point where I was trying to figure out where the boundaries were and how I would establish them to become the best wife and mother that I could possibly be. When I started to learn where these boundaries were needed, I began to lose friends and alienate people. Relationships with friends and family became strained.

Growing Pains

She's changed. She's become cold. Who does she think she is? I would shudder as I imagined the conversations in response to my realigned priorities. Marriage forced me to change lanes, shift my focus and priorities. I became more disciplined with my time, energy and how I would use it. My shifted focus meant that I would say, "I'm not available on that date." "No, I won't be there because it doesn't work for my priorities." Or "I'm really sorry, but that's no longer worth my time." I became shameless about where I put my time and energy. I would say that this principle is even more important to me today, but it caused turbulence and even disconnection within a lot of my relationships. I needed to embrace my new priorities. Were there teething problems when working out what to give my attention and time to? Of course. It wasn't easy, and there were a lot of damaged relationships. Friends that were in different stages of life distanced themselves and stopped calling.

There were many fractured relationships (not just for myself but for my husband), and we had to work through it together. Growing pains. Transitional discomfort. Together and individually, we have been growing through our pain and loss. The death of some relationships left me shell shocked. I constantly wondered if there was anything that I could've done to make those relationships last. Transition is a blessing, but sometimes it can be extremely hard – especially with friends, family and relationships. It's a journey that can be extremely damaging to marriage if there is no dialogue. I say that because marriage is between a man and a woman. Still, some relationships are pivotal in making that man and woman into the people that they evolve into – those relationships can't be ignored. Those relationships, whether we like them or not, have an indirect impact on our marriages. To ignore them would be detrimental. It can be the building of the marriage or, as the building blocks of strain increase, cause pressure and take its toll in the long run. Anyone that has consistently instilled principles into you from the time you were a baby is a fundamental relation. Their principles and lessons are consciously and subconsciously etched into your character. It takes deliberate effort to undo their principles and establish new ones.

I have had to redefine and assess these foundational principles repeatedly since getting married. It comes from a place of being determined to break new ground, personally and within my marriage. I've had to learn to listen more, to pay attention to detail, to prioritise, to budget harder, to be more patient and to exercise restraint. It is still difficult, and I have to remind myself of the irreplaceable lessons that marriage has taught me, but, ultimately, I couldn't do it without God. It takes His Divine insight and foresight to look at situations and know that what I used to do won't work.

Marriage requires a different mentality. It requires dialogue and exposure. It requires sincerity. I shared with my husband that the loss of relationships (that I thought would last for a lifetime) almost broke me; it was painful. We had to talk about it so that he could understand the effect it was having on my view of all relationships and people. The dialogue brought us closer because we would talk to each other about the relationships we missed and work out what we needed from external relationships. Some of those relationships wither like old flowers and are never revived. Over time, new relationships bloom, and it feels like we have broken new ground. New birth. Beauty comes out of the pain. Healing will always triumph over grief.

Sometimes God allows us to go through these difficult chapters in our relationships because we are always changing and discovering who we are. I never trivialise the entrance or exit of people from my life because they all teach me something. God is strategic, and I try to pay attention to what He tries to teach me through all of my relationships. We learn so much about ourselves from the relationships that we have and the relationships that we lose. We learn who we have to live without, and we learn what someone may have provided for us within the season that they were present in our lives.

Looking back is not as painful as when I was on this journey. I recognise how transformative marriage is, and I embrace it because it has taught me some of the biggest lessons of all. When friends and family were distant, I was bitter. I cried and wondered what I had done to deserve this. I know that it wasn't always anything that I had done or anything they had done particularly; sometimes life changes force us to grow apart. Honestly, though, maybe in some situations, I had done something wrong, but I have learnt not to overthink things I can't answer. There is no peace in that. I have learnt so much about what I needed and what I could do without. I learnt about what was seasonal and what I could not carry into my marriage. I learnt to be okay with change. I learnt that I would never have to beg the people who were meant to be in my life to stay. That being said, I've learnt it is okay to mourn what was but celebrate what now is. I always hope for the best for others, regardless of whether we connect or not.

Heart response and condition is so important. Let me clarify further: how we feel towards those who mistreat us and our journey through next level pain speaks a lot about who we are. If we retaliate by seeking revenge, then it shows that we don't truly understand and embrace our Queendom. Queens depend on God to fight every battle, hold our heads high and push through adversity until we reach our win. I speak from the pain of my own journey and seeing God come through so many times. These lessons are all chapters in the book of a life well-lived. We are all just travelling through, and I hold no one hostage that is no longer in the same space as me. It's not some vindictive message, *if you leave my life, you will suffer for eternity!* No. It's having a mature enough outlook to recognise that not everyone can continue on the journey with me throughout my life and marriage. If we have long-lasting friendships that last the span of our lives and marriage, then that's great. Therefore, it's wise to enjoy the beauty in every relationship that blesses and strengthens our marriage and leave the rest to God. My heart's desire is to impact the lives of all in the best and most positive way that I can, while trusting that each relationship's outcome will work out for the best. We must have peace knowing that "all things work together for good to them that love God, to them who are the called according to his purpose."[42] Whoever comes works out for your good. Whoever goes works out for your good. So, it's all good!

That being said, I believe that fundamental relationships need the most nurture. It's dangerous to adopt a flippant approach to those relationships because they are the most personal and impactful. Hence, cutting off your father-in-law may be the worst thing that you could ever do, for example. So, it's all about identifying crucial relationships worth fighting for and investing your energy into.

Having the Necessary Conversations

Candid conversations are important. By this, I mean those conversations that make-or-break relationships. Those heart-to-heart discussions leave your hands sweaty and your mouth dry. Those conversations you are forced to have while your voice shakes and tears roll down your face. Many relationships die because of silence where the right and necessary words needed to be said, such as, "I'm sorry." Maybe even, "I love you." Or even, "I made a mistake, but I didn't mean to hurt you." Sometimes, just sometimes, silence operates as the

---

[42] Romans 8:28 (KJV)

most vicious killer of relationships. Then there's the lifetime of regret of living with what could have been.

It's all about having the courage to sacrifice your fear, pride and shame to save those things that are most valuable. To break new ground and to learn something new about the people we love. The truth is that we are all flawed, imperfect, and a work in progress. We all need someone to forgive us and love us through our mess, no matter how wise and *together* we may seem. We are all on our unique journeys of growth, but at the same time, we also have to work together and build the most flourishing relationships. The best and most beautiful relationships are born out of a place of "I see your ugly, but I still love you anyway."

Yes, boundaries are needed, and sometimes it's difficult to love someone past their ugly, but something speaks about the durability of those relationships that come out of the darkest places. A love that survives pain. I have learnt from pushing through the most fragmented relationships in my life that *some things are worth fighting for.* When having necessary conversations, I believe it is important to learn the right time to approach that person to discuss sensitive issues. I cannot discuss anything stressful in the morning or evening because I am putting the children to bed or waking them up. My attention is split, so I am more likely to be agitated. Lunchtime is the best time to talk to me because I'm not tired or groggy or thinking about a thousand things that I need to do that day. My husband also has times that are not best for me to discuss stressful topics with him. Planning an outline of what I want to talk about (or get answers from) is also really helpful. I'm a waffler, and Paul is not, so he gets really agitated when I spend a thousand years trying to talk about one subject. Having an outline really sorts this problem out. Trying to understand things from his perspective also helps ease the tension in any conflict that we tend to have. Most of the time, no one is wrong, and no one is right. We just have different views. Compromise and reconciliation are all about learning the other person's perspective and respecting their entitlement to that perspective, even if we still cannot agree that it is the right view to have. Listen to hear, not just to *get your word in.*

This is something that I have had to learn over the years. I am from a family of talkers, and Paul is from a family of introverts, so I would just be itching to tell my side of the story. I still revert sometimes, but more and more, I have learnt to listen and ask, "Why do you think such and such...?"

Sometimes his answers have made me realise that I have misinterpreted his initial statements, and I am relieved I didn't interrupt him. Paul has taught me the importance of a compliment sandwich. Highlight the amazing things that have been done right, bring in the things that need to be worked on and close with the things that you love about them. "A soft answer turneth away wrath: but grievous words stir up anger."[43] When we communicate our frustrations and disagreements correctly, we make it easier for our offender to receive them. I know for sure that if someone came to me shouting, flailing, pointing in my face and not allowing me to respond, I would be less likely to think about whether there was any validity in whatever it was that they were saying. Why? Because their delivery was wrong. Lead with love and respect regardless of how painful it may be to do so. It reflects strength on your part and knowing that you did your utmost to bring about a positive outcome. Also, be prepared to take ownership of the mistakes that you have made. This is the hard part if you believe that you are perfect, but it stops your husband from feeling attacked.

---

[43] Proverbs 15:1 (KJV)

So, how do you know what relationships are worth fighting for and which relationships have well and truly passed their expiration date? Most of the time, we can feel when a relationship comes to an end. Even if it's just on pause for a season. I have learnt the hard way to let people go if their season has come to an end. I am deliberate about not begging people to stay longer. It's amazing when relationships last for a lifetime, but some relationships are only destined to deposit lessons for a season. I have even experienced healing and enlightenment about my own journey from temporary relationships. Even though it's sad to see them go, I have learnt to trust God's Divine timing and continue to embrace what's ahead.

You may have seen one of those *God will pay all my haters back* posts on social media. I am a believer that such a perspective is incredibly unhelpful for our growth, healing and transformation. Whether we like it or not, God loves our enemies too! Those people that send our temperatures through the roof on sight. Yeah, those people! God made, cares for and wants the best for them too. Even if we don't! So, even if we can't make them like or get along with us, we instantly bless our own lives with peace, sanity and healing by genuinely and irrevocably wishing our enemies well. Even removing the terminology "enemies" from our minds subconsciously removes a lot of weight. Just let them go, wish them well and condition your heart to focus on the good. I literally live by this truth and have seen the wonders that having a good heart has unleashed.

Don't get me wrong, I am fully aware that some people are addicted to chaos and contention. In those situations, I personally would encourage you to avoid them at all costs. However, it may become increasingly difficult to avoid them if they happen to be the person you are married to! Honestly speaking, it can drastically affect your peace if you remain in this kind of circumstance for a long time. I would always encourage you to protect your wellbeing. Once you make this your priority, the rest will eventually fall into place, and clarity will come. That being said, I implore you never to make drastic decisions about your marriage without taking those issues to God first. That may sound a little cliché like "Oh, just pray about it!"

Honestly, it's not a haphazard suggestion. I mean, really, take the time to find the answers that you need about the complexities of your situation. Talk to someone who can support, encourage and pray for you. I find that writing gives me clarity. I have been known to occasionally write my prayers in a book and look back at them. I reflect on what is going on inside of me and what I have written on the paper. I allow scriptural principles to be the basis of my decisions. If things are just overwhelmingly difficult, I find solace in confiding in my husband or a close friend. I process my feelings and the situation, I hesitate, I pray. There is nothing more detrimental than making a life-changing decision on impulse. Some actions leave immeasurably deep scars that, for some, may be irreversible. The closer in proximity you are to a person, the more deeply you can inflict scars. It is so easy to hurt your spouse because you are both exposed and vulnerable to one another. All the vulnerable aspects of your nature are revealed in marriage. You know where all the buttons are. This is all the more reason to prayerfully make drastic decisions.

Life is so short, so I find it helpful to ask myself, *if my husband or I was about to die, would this conflict actually matter?* It sounds a bit morbid, but the truth is that our focus shifts onto what is most important when we recognise that we live on limited and borrowed time. In a lot of ways, life is *too* good. So good that we forget that we won't be here forever. Maybe if we started to focus on the things that we loved about each other when we first met. It may be difficult and painful, but when the hard times roll, I picture us holding hands and watching our grandchildren running on a beach somewhere. There is something so beautiful about love developed and strengthened through decades of learning about each other. This is the kind of love God has created marriage for, not the rubbish we see on TV. I believe that patience, dedication and growth develop a love that transcends the ages, just like the love of Jesus Christ for us. That's the kind of love that I encourage you to continue to build and to fight for.

JOURNAL

- Could it be possible that you wish that you had never married your husband because of his toxic family or friends?
- Do you wish that you had waited longer? That you got a clearer picture of what marrying him would entail?
- Do you feel that you rushed into marriage without knowing his family or friends better? Do you wish that you realised how much impact his relationships would have on you?
- Do you feel like your husband changes around family or friends?
- What steps do you need to take to improve your situation.

Avoiding the Marital Minefields

The minefields that marriages can have can easily weigh heavy on the soul. Not knowing whether the next step you take will cause an explosion. The worst thing you could do is grin and bear it. The next worst thing you could do is live with it for the rest of your life. It will certainly be short-lived. Sometimes you can talk about something so much that it wears you down because there is no conclusion.

The first thing I want to say about these issues is that respect is a fundamental component of a successful marriage. Without respect, it becomes toxic and difficult for both parties to live in extreme and volatile situations. It may be down to you to change the narrative. This may be slow, painful and take time, but I believe that pointing at all the things that he needs to fix just stokes the fire. Transform the atmosphere with your conduct. Text him randomly in the day. Compliment him. Pray for him. Encourage him. Make him your best friend. Avoid being in the company of people that will stir conflict between you both.

Don't micromanage who he is around. Completely let it go. When I say "let it go", I mean get it out of your system. Don't roll your eyes, don't tense up when he hugs you, just give up fighting. When you stop fighting, God has the opportunity to take over. Surround yourself with people who will uplift you. Draw from things that will strengthen your mind. Don't half try and then give up when it seems difficult. You married your amazing husband, and you vowed to embrace him flaws and all. You can work through this. Take care of yourself and love yourself. Build yourself up so that you can be a pillar of strength in the relationship. I'm not saying to allow him to berate you in public. You have a voice, and you have a right to set boundaries on how you would like to be treated. I do believe that couples nowadays need to fight a bit more for their marriage rather than against it. I know that having a bit of perseverance has made a difference in ours.

I remember my mum saying, "Sal, you know I've never heard you and Paul argue." My response was, "That's because we have agreed to privately discuss our disagreements." It's one of the ways we have agreed to honour each other. Is it easy? Not always. Especially when emotions are high. The good thing is that by the time we get some privacy to discuss some of the issues, we have had time to cool off. One of the things my husband and I don't do is work through serious disagreements publicly. Are we always harmonious when we argue privately? No. I'm a hothead. I have to say sorry to God and to Paul, over and over. Sometimes even when I don't want to. It's humbling, but that's marriage!

I need to add that marriage should shift your allegiance to your husband above all others. Anyone or anything that gets through the cracks can have a devastating impact. It's also written in the Bible in black-and-white. Then again in red and white! "For this cause shall a man **leave** his father and mother, and **cleave** to his wife; And they twain shall be one flesh: so then they are no more twain, but one flesh."[44] This scripture then goes on to say, "let no one split apart what God has joined together."[45] It's deliberately in the Bible on more than one occasion that marriage is designed to separate (outsiders) as much as it is designed to unite the marriage. That truth is not for the faint-hearted. It doesn't matter whether it's your husband preferring his family over you or vice versa; if the principle of "leave to cleave" is not honoured, it will have damaging long-term effects.

Marriage is sacred to God. So sacred that He issued this warning to those surrounding married couples. Don't try to split them up. Mind your own business and let them work it out. The most beautiful relationships blossom as a result of our ability to respect the boundaries.

---

[44] Mark 10:7-8 (KJV)
[45] Mark 10:9 (NLT)

Best Friends and Boundaries

One of my biggest regrets was not having the necessary conversations with my best friends in the early stages of my relationship with Paul. I remember thinking, *am I imagining this? Is this all in my head?* Things start changing in your friendships when the calls become less frequent. Those long conversations are a thing of the past, and everybody is *too busy* to have those coffee dates. There is nothing that you can do to make those friendships what they once were. The truth is that a drastic shift happens in both the relationship with the best friend and the husband. So many things become sacred within marriage and cannot be shared with best friends. This is out of respect for the husband and boundaries. It's not called the *sanctity* of marriage for nothing! Bestie no longer has priority over your husband, and the change could easily be a hard pill to swallow. If I could have changed one thing, it would have been to give my best friends more clarity about my boundaries. Check-in and have those difficult chats, and be a bit more patient with the turbulence that comes with the territory. It isn't easy to verbalise some of the adjustments that happen in the early stages and speak about what it means for those close relationships. It is tough, but the reality is that there should never be a space between me and my husband that is big enough for anyone else to fit in.

Discern when a friendship is putting pressure on your marriage or causing you and your husband to drift apart. This can easily and unintentionally happen because of misaligned priorities. We all want to be accepted, which sometimes means that we give our power, focus and energy to the wrong people. Take a minute and reset. If those priorities aren't clear, then write it out. Who takes primary priority in your life? Your husband? Your kids? Your siblings? Don't be apologetic about what you want to give your resources to. You're preserving and protecting your resources by becoming more astute.

Friends are important and add value to my life, but my husband should never feel like they are his competition. When the bestie's opinion carries more value than your husband's, or you're more enthused about spending time with your best friend, you have to ask yourself, *who are you married to?* Use wisdom with relationships and let your king stay *king*. It does wonders for marriage to know where your priorities and allegiances lie. That being said, never feel like you can't or shouldn't have friends; they enrich the soul. Ultimately, the best friendships are built on understanding boundaries and clarity.

When Kids Are the Problem

Having children can change everything about your relationship – maybe it already has? Lazy weekends in bed, date nights and even dialogue can become incredibly difficult when parenting responsibilities take centre stage. It can be even more complicated if you have stepchildren in your family unit. Especially if the children are difficult to get along with. No one would want to admit that they think their kids are brats. Children can take you right to the edge of your control but are also lovable enough to stop you from falling over it. Having to bite your tongue so that you don't say the wrong thing. Working together with other parents to find the best parenting techniques. Just balancing being a parent with being a wife can be incredibly difficult. If your authority is constantly usurped or your children play one parent against the other, then it's bound to have damaging long-term effects. The guilt that comes with admitting that you actually don't like the kids can overwhelm you with shame.

Is it wrong not to want to be a mum? is a thought that may cross your mind. Admitting it to yourself is difficult, but what if it's subconsciously expressed in your actions? Maybe you lack engagement or always seem agitated around them. Can they feel it? The lines can seem so blurred. One thing is for sure: your voice is valid, and if your heart is speaking, then it behoves you to listen. What is it about your children that you just don't like? How is it affecting your relationship with your husband? What are the things that you *really* want to say but cannot? Journey through your feelings so that you can build on your relationship with your family. I will tell you a secret… there is no parent on the planet that (at one point or another) doesn't wonder why they signed up to be a parent. On the toughest of days, always remember your advantage. You have been in existence for a lot longer than the kids. You know so much more than they do (even if they don't seem to agree).

I always make a point of looking for the good in my children and speaking that out loud. No matter how we feel, it's important to deliberately lavish love on them – not just words but with our expression and actions. Uniting and solidifying teamwork with your husband is crucial to the improvement of your relationship with the kids. If there are cracks in your relationship, then the children *will* find them. Make it a priority to work on closing those cracks with your husband, even if it means involving a mediator. I cannot stress enough how important it is to involve God in your parenting journey. Pray, ask Him for discernment into the perspectives and life experiences of your family. They may be fighting battles that you know nothing about.

There are so many times that God has opened my eyes to the struggles that each member of my family has endured. Even with regards to the behavioural changes that my baby has gone through. God wants to be involved in the little things and will speak to us through those details. An astounded, "how did you know?" is a response that I have become accustomed to when it comes to my family. Discernment has enabled me to respond completely differently to their actions than I originally intended. See each member of your family as unique individuals and meet their needs in this manner. See them for who they are, not who you *think* that they should be. Respond to them from that place. You'll be surprised how much impact this has on your relationship. Look harder. Listen closer. Slow down. Let them know that they are respected and heard. I am in no way saying to be a pushover. Keep boundaries and structure because children need them. Have the conversations that need to be had. Show children the value of dialogue by saying, "I am not trying to replace your mother. I am here if you need to talk. I value and appreciate you." All these words have an impact. Don't slander other parents involved in co-parenting the children. Encourage a culture of respect. Hold onto your integrity. All these details will have a great impact on your relationship. They say a lot about the Queen that you are. When it's all too much, then find a network or support group that you can join as an outlet or to express how you are feeling. You'll be surprised how many people are going through the same challenges. Ultimately, remind yourself of the investment that you are making into their lives. You are doing an awesome job, whether it feels like it or not. You've got this, Queen!

Let's Talk About... Mother-in-laws

The infamous mother and daughter-in-law relationship struggle is a real thing. I only realised that this was extremely common when I went to an intensive course for pre-marriage counselling one weekend with my (then) fiancé. I sat in a room with a bunch of female strangers. "What do you think that the hardest part of marriage is going to be?" I asked them curiously, thinking about other aspects of marriage that were far away from their collective response of "the mother-in-law!"

"Really?" I responded, wanting to know more. "She does [this]" and "She does [that]," they continued.

At the time, our love was young, but I affectionately referred to my mother-in-law as "Mum", and we were cool. I honestly have to admit that there have been many arguments with my husband about boundaries with my mother-in-law. We come from different worlds and have different approaches to so many aspects of life. Sure, we come from different racial backgrounds, but we needed to understand each other's cultural differences – for instance, things like how we ran our homes and how we raise our kids. I am flamboyant and bold. Somehow, I just don't believe that she would describe herself in the same way! If we were of the same race, then we would still have our differences because our homes' culture would not be the same. When I use the word "culture", I am referring to our domestic traditions and procedures. The nature of most relationships is that there will be clashes, and I'm sure that the future will hold fireworks for us both.

However, there were times that I would complain to my husband, and he would feel like he was stuck in the middle of the two women that he loves the most on this planet. It went this way over and over. At the beginning of our marriage, I wanted my mother-in-law to be like my second mother – another best friend I could confide in and journey through family life with. There were times that I would try so hard to prove myself to her, but we would always clash. There were so many situations where boundaries would be a point of tension and discussion between me and my husband. I wanted him to be our collective voice, and he wasn't always clear about what I wanted him to represent. We weren't sure how to move forwards as a couple, and it was a counsellor that helped me gain clarity about my relationships (including the relationship with my mother-in-law). I can honestly say that she was the best thing that ever happened to our marriage in this regard. She never counselled us jointly, but what she shared with me transformed my perspective of all my relationships. "You are in control of you, only you and no one else but you," she said. Whatever reasons for my need for acceptance, approval, and to fit in were inconsequential.

This advice was transformative for my perspective on my relationship with my mother-in-law. I stopped trying to prove my value to her and focused on being more welcoming. I love her, and she is a part of my family. We are both valued parts of our family unit. We contribute to the legacy of our children and our children's children. That being said, we don't always have to sing *kumbaya* by the fire every night. I am not always easy to understand, and we are both strong personalities. As time goes on, I have stopped fighting for approval or feeling the need to be understood by anyone – including my mother-in-law. It took counselling to realise that I was operating from this space, and it was damaging me. I approve of myself. I am comfortable with myself. I've come to welcome and appreciate my mother-in-law because she has unconsciously shown me myself. She (along with many other relationships) has challenged my growth in so many ways. She created this incredible man and taught him all the principles that make him the amazing husband he is today.

Having a change of heart and perspective has also impacted my marriage in such a positive way. It's the matters of my heart that God is looking at after all. One of the things that has helped is the ability to see things from her perspective. Especially now that I am a mother of two sons. They, too, will grow up and have their own lives. Will it break my heart? It sure will. Why? Because I love them more than I love my own life. I am sure that she had the same perspective regarding her own son. It's a painful thought to think that the children that you have invested so much of your love, time and energy in will one day grow up and leave home. They may even leave the country, and I will have absolutely no control over it. Neither did she.

A mother's love and bond don't dissipate as the children get older, and I'm sure that the love that I have for my children will equally remain as passionate as it is today. I share this knowing that she may read it, and her face may change to the colour of a tomato as a result. It is necessary to share my experience because you may have a much more complex relationship with your mother-in-law. Maybe there are painful things that have happened? Or maybe nothing is happening, and you don't understand why the relationship has not progressed to what you would like it to be. I believe that women steer the directions of their homes. When two women enter the same space, then there's a chance that they want to steer in opposite directions. That can cause friction, especially if Mama has been steering all her life, and now you're at the helm.

Don't get me wrong; I have seen and heard it all. Intimidating and manipulative tactics, putting pressure on the husband to take sides, interference in the matters that only concern the husband and wife. Some mothers-in-law act like a loud or quiet poison, crippling the marriage sometimes closely and other times, from a distance. Some cause the death of the marriage without lifting a visible finger. It can be a difficult experience which a lot of marriages do not survive. One of the most meaningful lessons that I would like to impart is to be aware of your heart's response to your mother-in-law. As a wise woman aptly put it, "If they go low, you go high." To respond with wisdom, you will need to have foresight. By this, I mean you ask yourself the question, "What will be the consequences of my response to any behaviour that I consider vindictive?" Will it distress your husband? Lead to a fractured relationship with other members of your family? Your children's confusion and despair?

Other essential questions to ask yourself are:

◆ Can this relationship with my mother-in-law work?
◆ Is there any way that I can contribute to its success?
◆ Is there any value in the relationship?

These are crucial questions that you need to answer to work out how to move forward with the relationship. These were questions that I asked myself. There are also strong biblical principles that influenced how I navigated through the relationship that I have with my mother-in-law, such as scriptures like, "If it be possible, as much as lieth in you, live peaceably with all men."[46] Be a peacemaker if it is at all possible. I don't mean being weak or insincere. I don't mean hiding how you feel and not allowing your voice and decisions to be heard. I mean to express the essence of the love you have within. Be kind if you can. Support and encourage where you can. Be your true self. It took me a while to learn this, and I impart it to you for your own peace and joy. As much as possible, *try your best* – war in the right places. You can choose war or peace. That choice belongs to you.

I felt that it was important that insight into the in-law transition was not one-sided. Consequently, I invited my mother-in-law to kindly contribute her perspective on her journey. Here is her insight in her own words:

> *Family illness has prevented us from spending time with each other. You know you've lost your child when they find love, and that's not easy – you have to start to get to know them again. Mothers have to let go and talk to children about that kind of grief. If both sides can bring the walls down and leave the defences*

---

46 Romans 12:18 (KJV)

behind, then it will help strengthen the relationship between mother and daughter-in-law. Sal is the daughter that I have never had, but our relationship has progressed and become stronger over time. We have had to learn to see things from each other's perspective. It's important to spend (one-on-one) time together and get to know each other. Be deliberate about doing it away from the husband or son. That helps improve relationships and communication. We have had to be intentional about working on becoming less like strangers and more like family.

What if That's Not Enough?

I've also seen mothers-in-law totally and effortlessly destroy relationships. What's tragic is that it's been totally deliberate. So many women have disclosed to me how overwhelmed they are by the relationship struggles that they have with their mothers-in-law. Some have refused to allow their mothers-in-law to have contact with their grandchildren. Some have allowed their mothers-in-law limited contact with their grandchildren, which is a tragic state of affairs. I can see how the situation has escalated to this level of chaos. Sometimes it's the lack of boundaries. Sometimes it's cultural and life differences. Sometimes people just don't get along. I believe that if it reaches those extremes then the mother-in-law and daughter-in-law should go their separate ways, but what I don't agree with is forcing a son not to see his mother. That is a marital death trap if I haven't seen one. It may not happen straightaway, but over time those resentments resurface, and it may get very ugly for the marriage. Remember I said that the ability to have foresight and to strategically war for your marriage is necessary. If negative things are being said to the children and it is causing them distress, you may need to take them out of the situation for a season to provide some stability, but your husband is his own man. Let him make his own decisions about his family.

I love how these two scriptures deal with the issue of irreconcilable differences with friends and family. Abram said to Lot:

> *Let's not allow this conflict to come between us or our herdsmen. After all, we are close relatives! The whole countryside is open to you. Take your choice of any section of the land you want, and we will separate. If you want the land to the left, then I'll take the land on the right. If you prefer the land on the right, then I'll go to the left.*[47]

Abram had to agree to separate from his own nephew to keep the peace. Again, you will find that Paul and Barnabas could not agree or work together and concluded that they would have to go their own separate ways. Specifically, "And the contention was so sharp between them, that they departed asunder one from the other."[48] Both these men were Christians and good people, but they had to agree to keep their distance to have peace. Sometimes, just sometimes, distance is a good thing. I believe that when there is no other choice, then distance may be necessary. The objective is peace and not a vendetta. You're not trying to punish your mother-in-law. That is not the heart of God. You're trying to establish peace within the walls of your home and marriage. Sometimes distance is necessary.

There is a question that I believe is pivotal to the direction of your relationship with your mother-in-law. It is a question that will determine whether you have a relationship worth building or whether you

---

[47] Genesis 13:8-9 (NLT)
[48] Acts 15:36-39 (KJV)

should walk away. *Does your mother-in-law view you as a daughter? Or someone who is attached to her son?* If you genuinely believe that she views you as the daughter that she never had, then you have a relationship that you can build upon. You can now have these discussions with her to see if there are opportunities for growth in your relationship.

Other Family Members

Sometimes the mother-in-law is the least of your worries. It could be siblings or your family that cause applied pressure on your marriage. Maybe your marriage is worn down by the constant conflict about a particular family member or friend and their effect on your marriage.

Set the boundaries that work for the harmony of your own family. Stake your territory and be unapologetic. Protect your peace by exercising your strength. I have heard so many women being held ransom by their family-in-laws. They anguish over the pressure of being connected to stifling relationships. There is no way that I could write this book and not speak to the situation when it is so common. The vibrancy that you bring to your role as a wife and mother is pivotal to how your environment feels. Don't underestimate the value of your position. You are the keeper of your home. You pray over your home. You work with your husband to establish the boundaries that protect your family.

Don't let anyone come into your space and intimidate you. Be like the watchman that sees far ahead and around the corner. You can prepare for trouble, and by the time it reaches your door, you can say, "Baby, I was ready for you last year!" Your actions should speak of your greatness within your marriage and family. You won't be surprised by the challenges that come your way if you are connected to our Heavenly Father. He will show you so much ahead of time.

Your spirit should follow your children and their growth. I knew both of my children before I gave birth to them. Even though I suffered so much when I was carrying them, I remember telling my family their characteristics to the most minute details. Their responses to my revelations would always be, "Yeah, right." Then they were astonished when the kiddies' personalities matched my predictions to the letter. I wasn't. My spirit followed them as they grew in my womb. I prayed, and I listened. I observed their nature. To this day, I still talk to God about my children and ask Him what they will become. How to help them grow into God-fearing men of excellence and thrive due to the principles that I instil in them.

Are You the Problem?

We should never be afraid to question our part in the division that is caused by relationships. I don't believe in condemning yourself or driving yourself into a deep state of depression for past mistakes, but I believe in learning lessons. Self-observation is necessary to prevent perpetuating cycles. Sometimes the family-in-laws are only partially the problem, and we are the other half. Sometimes we are the instigators of the chaos and contention due to our inability to evaluate our wrongdoings and to say, "I'm so very sorry." To say those words from the bottom of our heart and genuinely have a desire to move forward isn't easy. It's humbling and soul-crushing, but on the other side of that apology is a beautiful relationship. Maybe there will be a time where you both laugh at the people that you once were in the early stages of your marriage. Sometimes it takes a catalyst for change and improvement. Maybe, just maybe, you are that catalyst. Remember my earlier advice was to war for your marriage in the right places. Change the narrative. Again, assuming this is even possible. I'm not encouraging you to feed the antics of narcissists (or the like), but I encourage you to find avenues towards a thriving relationship with your in-laws.

It's the little steps that make the biggest difference. Are you nagging your husband to pick a side? Are you complaining to him all the time? Are you heckling your mother-in-law or stopping her from seeing the grandchildren without good cause? Question yourself. The worst thing you could do is complain to your husband repeatedly, as it drastically wears down the relationship. Talk to God about it over and over. He won't get tired of hearing from you. He's not biased. He will direct you on approaching your in-laws in an honourable way and without contempt. You may never get the best out of your relationship with your in-laws, and you should be okay with that as long as you are not deliberately making yourself the problem – still your heart, your worries and your complaining. Leave your cares at the feet of our Heavenly Father and trust that the situation will improve.

If the situation doesn't change then you have to get wiser and stronger. Love fierce. I'm not saying that this should be a guessing game, but if you recognised all the ways that you have contributed to the problem, then you will be able to identify where you need to move forward.

When you identify that you are not the problem, then you can go on to evaluate what your core family values are. For example, one of the values that we have as a couple is being discrete with our disagreements. Some discussions shouldn't be privy to other ears for the sake of their perception of one of us. It's our way of protecting one another. If there is an issue that we can't conclude or make an agreement on, then we are extremely selective on who we go to for help and advice. Marriage can become fragile and broken within an instant. It is wise to carefully select who has the power to speak into or advise your marriage. We only embrace advice that is right for our marriage based on our core values.

Breaking New Ground

I remember the first Christmas that I spent with my husband's family. It was lovely to feel so welcomed, but as I sat quietly eating dinner at the Christmas table, smiling on the outside, I was in pieces on the inside. This felt like the end of crucial aspects of my single life that I had come to love. That night I lay in the bed of a house belonging to a woman I barely knew with a lump in my throat. Is this the end of the things that came as naturally as family traditions? My family is loud and busy, and there were so many of us at Christmas celebrations. We would get together, sing loudly and laugh. Then Granny or Grandad would finish the night with words of wisdom and a prayer, "You all must stick together!"

I recall Grandma saying one Christmas, "Don't let nobody separate you!" She would continue as we would subordinately reply, "Yes, Gran." Others said, "Yes, Mum." Then Grandad would pray for what felt like hours: "Thaaaaaaank you, Lord. Thaaaaaaank you, Lord. Thaaaaaaank you, Lord. I just want to thaaaaaaank you, Lord."

We would all sing in our unique harmonies with a melodic sound that I'm sure would make heaven stand still and listen. Music was a massive part of our family legacy and heritage and another aspect of Christmas that I had come to love so much. Within a year and a half, I was catapulted into this new way of life. Don't get me wrong, no one held a shotgun to my head and forced me to get married, and yes, I was happily married, but I was almost shocked by how quickly things were changing. To be honest, I was not 100 per cent sure that I liked the changes. I didn't want to admit it, but I was lonely. Believe it or not, you can be in a room full of people and be lonely. The truth is you can be married to the love of your life and still be lonely.

Fundamentally, it's the feeling of displacement and not being fully understood that can isolate anyone. It felt disconcerting to be welcomed by many people who were almost strangers and feel so alienated from people that I had known all my life. It was like tectonic plates were shifting beneath me, and I just couldn't find my footing. It was even harder to verbalise how I was feeling. I remember wanting to call my mum one evening after watching a TV programme, silently nodding reassuringly at my new husband when he would repeatedly ask if I was alright. I had such a mixture of feelings because I was so happy to have found the love of my life. Beginning a new chapter in my life was dizzyingly exciting. Everyone was so welcoming, yet everything was unfamiliar – the Christmas music, the games, the films, the environment – and there were points when it was overwhelming. I was celebrating and mourning at the same time. Celebrating new love and new life. Mourning leaving my old one. It's a secret that is sometimes difficult for new wives to share because there are so many expecting nothing but overwhelming joy. I've had the occasional, "You should be grateful that you have a husband! Marriage must be sweet!" And so on. It puts an unspoken pressure that we must ignore the turbulence. Sometimes the hardest part of it all is strained friendships and family feuds. You smile and enjoy your marriage but are conflicted by the loss of the ones that you love. The ones that were with you from the beginning and impacted your life greatly. It's difficult to accept that those relationships might change, and that change may be forever.

Traditions: Finding the Balance

There was a time when I felt that I had a duty to leave my past behind to embrace my husband's life. I felt like I was just being a team player and honouring my husband by following his traditions, but the truth was that they were not working for me. He was so happy, but I was miserable. His family was so welcoming and hospitable, but I was homesick. I couldn't verbalise it at the risk of sounding ungrateful or unappreciative of their kindness. So, I suppressed my feelings and went with the traditions that everyone had already set within his family. As time went on, and I shared my angst with my husband, we started to break the invisible rule book we were conforming to and decided to make new traditions. We were, after all, a family of our own, leaving our single life and cleaving to one another. We had to start to think about what was best for our family unit and for our collective happiness as a couple. We decided to rotate Christmases between our families, which worked beautifully when we didn't have children, but now that we have our children, we have had to re-evaluate what works for our family "on the whole". As time has gone by, we have realised that it's okay to keep reassessing our boundaries and traditions as our situation changes.

The most beautiful marriages flourish because both people are given space to express themselves in a way that only they authentically know how to express themselves. I am an extrovert, and I love to be surrounded by people. My husband is an introvert and is most fulfilled by having time to himself. I don't try to make him into someone he is not and vice versa. We've had to learn that we even gravitate to different types of personalities. We're okay with having our own friends, but we're not okay with those outside personalities harming our marriage. So, it's all about wisdom and balance.

He who walks [as a companion] with wise men will be wise,
But the companions of [conceited, dull-witted] fools [are fools
themselves and] will experience harm.
—Proverbs 13:20 (AMP)

Marriage is our blessing, and we are wise and selective about who has access to our blessings. The best friends are the ones that respect and value our boundaries. Although, part of having boundaries recognises that not everyone has your best intentions at heart. Ask God to heighten the gift of discernment in your life so that you can be aware of who is meant to have access and who is not. You need company that will bless and enrich your marriage with wisdom, prayer, support and genuine love. Anything that is the opposite does not deserve access.

Everything Changes

In many instances, change means growth, and it is something that we should embrace in our marriages. I've previously shared examples of marriages where change can be damaging, but I now want to talk about instances where changes are necessary. As the years go by, you both will inevitably change. Your desires change. Your visions change, and your needs change. When you first get married, it's just the two of you, and all you can think about is how amazing, good looking, talented and loving your husband is. Then responsibility kicks in. You get mortgages, houses, bills, routines, chores, careers, ministry and babies. It changes you. It changes your priorities and what you are willing to give your energy and time to. With these changes, your perspective on what is needed in life changes. It's no longer important that your husband is good looking or even talented. Having a best friend and team player, a loyal and supportive husband takes more of a front seat. You may not even care whether or not he's good in bed as long as he can help you in the house and with the children. If he doesn't grow with you in these respects, then the marriage struggles, and you could literally be in different worlds. Even though marriage's obvious objective is to grow together, it is easy to be married and be worlds apart. One of the things that has helped my marriage tremendously is dialogue. Trust me: sometimes men and women do not speak the same language. We have to break it DOWN! Never suffer in silence, because if you want your marriage to last forever, then eternal silence will be a heavy price to pay.

Sometimes revisiting complex growth spurt issues over and over is not easy. Especially if one partner doesn't like changes while the other changes all the time. It takes grit to push through those complex areas of the relationship. Not all change is good. Maybe you've looked at your partner and thought, *I don't know you anymore.* Marriage isn't for the feeble, and it doesn't always bring out the best in everyone. Some changes can be soul-crushing. It can leave you feeling robbed, like you didn't get what you signed up for. Sometimes people change for the worst and not for the better. When this happens, shock, disbelief, fear, worry, confusion, pain and resentment could overwhelm you. Anchor your mind on building your identity and total dependence on God throughout the trying aspects of your relationship. Remind yourself who you are even in the midst of uncertainty. Work through difficult aspects with a counsellor and be open to new ways of nurturing your relationship with your husband.

It's so easy to become so consumed by it all that you allow it to damage your marriage and family unit. Becoming overwhelmed by worry will suffocate the gifts and blessings that are still remaining in your life. Wait on God for change. Pray for conflicts to be healed. Keep being a blessing to those around you regardless of the pain.

Shifting the focus from yourself can lead to your healing, especially when you know that you're making a difference to someone else. Even though you may feel drained, spiritually limp and broken, love harder than you did before. You will reap in due season if you don't give up. Shine brighter regardless of the pain. It is a testament to the strength endowed on you as a result of your dependence on God. That being said, I don't believe in being disconnected from the pain that you're feeling. Sugar-coating never works for anyone because it comes out in other ways. The anguish that you may feel about relationships that are damaged needs a place to go.

You need to let it out. Listen to your thoughts and be aware of how you are feeling. Give your emotions an outlet. Some of my outlets are writing, driving, walking, singing or even writing songs. The release is euphoric. I find peace, and it's my way of connecting with God and saying to Him, "Here's my pain, Lord."

Sometimes I forget, and I want to take that pain up again, but I know that it's unbearable, so I have to keep coaching myself into handing it over. Then, over time, the pain doesn't hit me the way that it used to. I have seen people that I have felt damaged by in the past, and nothing has happened. Simply because I have gotten them out of my system. I have shifted the weight of the pain onto the One who knows what to do with it – God!

I also don't underestimate the power of new blessings. There have been so many new blessings in the form of life experiences and new people that have been the antidote to my spiritual ailments. They have brought such life and light into my life, and it has healed me in ways that I never knew possible. Don't underestimate the power of new growth. Surround yourself with fertile ground. Don't just expect your husband to hold you up or fix the pain, because he might be weighed down by his own. Sometimes you just need to be in an environment that will allow you to flourish as the best version of yourself. Open yourself up to the possibility that the person who can unlock your healing is waiting on the path ahead. God knows what He is doing. Trust Him.

Boundaries Promote Structure

Boundaries and structure are necessary. The wildfire of tragic relationships spreads when there are no boundaries. It can also go the other way. Tragic relationships can happen because there are so many restrictions that it sucks the life out of everyone. Boundaries are needed regardless, but there has to be balance. Knowing what works for your family, for yourself, for your friendships etc., takes strong self-awareness.

JOURNAL

- Make a list of your priorities (1 greatest, 10 least).
- What is robbing you of fulfilling your priorities?
- What 3 steps will you take to eradicate those obstacles.

These things change as you go along, and you will want to change the goal post from time to time. Again, it's all about how self-aware you are. I have quite a few boundaries for myself, my relationships, family, friends and even my church because of the many hats that I wear.

I want to excel at the many things that I consider most important in my life. Hence, they require boundaries. Sometimes I want to hang out with my friends, or I need family time, or I have business demands or just want to spend time with God. Right now, I have set a boundary with my family, and they are gracious enough to accept the terms. I need an hour or so (a day) to write this book. I am disciplined with the time that I dedicate to this book, and then I have to go and fully complete the other duties that I am committed to with my family. However, if I take the whole day to write, leaving the kids in chaos, no food on the table, snotty noses running, no bedtime routine, everybody suffers. It comes down to something that seems so simple but has a great impact on everything: lack of structure and discipline. Sometimes it means that someone will be upset. Sometimes it means that I may be upset. I don't want to be away from my babies for a minute, but sometimes it is necessary. I can see the vision and the full picture. I don't always explain that fully. Sometimes I just say, "No, that doesn't align with my priorities." Or, "No, that's not going to work for me." Or, "I've got to go." Or, "I'm not available on that day."

I mentally have to look down the road and see what impact today's decisions have on the future. Boundaries create momentum in the most amazing ways when implemented strategically. What boundaries do you need to set to improve your quality of life and relationships? What simply needs to change? Know how to speak up for yourself even if your voice trembles. Be okay with not being liked and be more focused on the vision ahead. What is the goal? More family time? A happier family? Opportunities to improve your quality of life? A stronger and richer relationship with God? You know the outcome that you are trying to achieve. If you have to close your eyes to say "no", then do that. Eventually, they will understand that you value your boundaries and your vision. Persevere.

Forgiveness Is a Heart Business

Forgiveness doesn't always mean that the person needs to have the position that they once had in your life. You may have discovered reasons why they don't deserve to be in the position that they once held within your relationship. Guard your heart. Guard your mind. Guard your sanity. If you give some people a chance, they will drive you insane and keep going. It's up to you to have the wisdom to know that it isn't safe to let a snake come back for seconds when you barely survived the first bite. Always be kind, always show love, but always be wise.

Forgiveness is heart business. Do you wish that the person was dead? Do you hate the person? Do they make your heart beat faster when they walk into a room? Why? What about them makes you so angry? Ask yourself these questions. Assess your heart's response. It's okay to say, "God, I need to work on this forgiveness thing." Or, "It hurts." Or, "I'm not sure that I can forgive this person." There's no point lying to God. Plus, there's somewhat of a great release that comes with saying, "This person makes me want to punch through bricks and barbed wire!" Truth is your mirror. It's your way of saying, "I have some spiritual blotches on my spiritual clothes that need serious cleaning." Take your time with yourself and work through them. God is right there, working through it all with you. You know yourself better than anyone.

If unforgiveness weighs you down, then be deliberate about purging your soul from all that toxicity. Sometimes, there can be such fear about dealing with the issues of unforgiveness for so many reasons. Does unforgiveness make you look bitter? Do I have to forget what they did to me? Do I have to restore them to the position that they once had? So many questions surround this issue. Look at it this way:

you're doing your mind, body, spirit, heart and soul justice by letting it all go. Weightlessness and liberation come with forgiveness. You deserve to experience every ounce of the benefits that come with forgiving others. Don't be afraid to push past the difficult parts so that you can reap the benefits of the best parts of letting go. Your unforgiveness was like a spiritual knee jerk reaction to the pain that you suffered and the trauma that it caused, but honey, you really have to purge. Clean house. Unforgiveness cannot stay. Unforgiveness will kill everything good and Godly in your life. You aren't weak for letting go. You're fighting that good fight and winning. You win when you let it go.

Give Birth to Something New

Whatever your resentment, it will be passed down, around, upside down – you get it. It will spread. Maybe your children will see it, and it will affect their relationships and outlook. Maybe your parents will see it and start to carry resentment for those that hurt you. It's not wise to pass your pain around; I mean, talking about your offender with everyone that will listen and trying to get them on your side. Let's be real. If they're not qualified to help you work through the difficult aspects of your conflict, then the chances of them sharing your information or hating your offender are quite high.

What's worse is that when you have healed and moved on, others may still hold onto it. I would never say to suppress it but always find ways to channel it into the right places. Let your territory (and home) be the place for fertile ground. Let the pain give birth to something new, something stronger than the things that unforgiveness tried to take away. *Let go of the former things* and focus on the things that give birth to new growth. I say this from my own personal experience. This *labour of love* (book) allows all the pain to give birth to something so much better. Allow yourself to come to the stage in your life where you are unbreakable. Every brick they throw at you will be used to build you. That's the beauty of a winner mentality. No more space for the vengeful mindset: *I'm going to get you back*. We push through. We get stronger. We overcome because Christ has shown us what unbreakable looks like.

Prayer and Meditation

Let's pray and reflect using the mirror.

My Abba,

Thank you for the gift of family and friends. I pray for the wisdom to know how to keep us all together. I pray for the opportunities to have productive, fruitful conversations that lead to healthier relationships. I pray that you heal the wounds caused by broken relationships within my family. Open my eyes to see the people that you have brought into my life for the purpose of growth and healing. In times of confusion and conflict, Lord, let your resolute strength, peace and wisdom take the driving seat.

In Jesus' name, Amen.

TEN

MONEY MATTERS

§

Money is the elephant in the room.

Every time a bill comes through the door.

Every time the children ask for an extra couple of pounds to fund their endeavours, she cringes inside. She hoped that this problem would go away, but instead, it seems to get increasingly worse.

Their finances have been crippling their relationship for a while now, but how do they work it out without someone walking out?

If only she'd known the impact that money would have on her marriage before she said, "I do," then maybe things would be different now.

The truth is that it's taken her all these years to realise that…

Money matters.

Most of the world doesn't like to talk about money, which is a great indication of how much it matters. Silence speaks. If anyone tells you that money has not had a positive or negative impact on their relationship, then they're lying. Money can highlight the health of your marriage (or lack thereof). It's easy to say that marriage is just a piece of paper, but its significance is much more than that. Some would sell their mother to have it, while others are genuinely happy with very little money. Even in my own marriage, money matters. We've been on an educational journey when it comes to tackling our financial development. Especially me. When I first met Paul, I was £15,000 in debt and used to seeing the minus sign in my bank account. Overdraft was my best friend! I was an emotional spender. I knew that I needed to do better, but it was incredibly stressful to think about my finances. I remember thinking, *what have I done?*

When I started to talk about the magnitude of my debt and started negotiating to make payments to claw my way out of it, the financial mountain seemed so great, and the journey to financial freedom seemed so far away. The feeling of anxiety would wash over me every time I talked about the stupid decision that I made. I was 21 years old when I bought a new car, and I hadn't even passed my driving test. I had to be chaperoned every time that I drove, so the enjoyment of it was very limited. When I finally passed my driving test, I got into a car accident and damaged the rear left side! It was an absolute nightmare.

When I met Paul, I was as upfront as ever. When we started to talk about getting married, I explained the weight of my debt, and I was amazed that he didn't run a mile. It was pretty obvious to him that I was an emotional spender. What was helpful, and still is, is we were both transparent – about our fears, our hopes and our goals. We talked about what the future looked like for both of us and were fully aware that we had to work together to achieve the required financial objectives. Small money, large money and even someone else's money! It's called borrowing and loans, folks.

What's essential is we didn't make each other feel inferior because of our financial shortcomings. We united as a team, humbled ourselves because we had so much to learn and found the resources that we needed to grow in understanding how to manage our finances. Needless to say, we were able to clear off a massive amount of my debt. We then moved in with our parents and saved our hard-earned money for a deposit on a house. We built slowly and sometimes, painstakingly. We missed out on events, holidays and other luxuries. We sought out and bought cheaper versions of things. I have always been skilled at making cheap things look good, and that's what we did. We also spoke to financial advisers, accountants and read books about finances. There is so much free help available, and we made sure to access it. The biggest lesson we have learnt is to "be transparent and united about your financial growth".

What Does Money Mean to You?

Money is personal, and it's important. It's important because it affects your quality of life and your relationship. It reveals your character's strengths and weaknesses and can also be very telling about the state of your relationship. Do you trust your husband? Your money will speak. Are you competing with your husband? How you jointly handle your money will speak. Money will tell you if you are disciplined, selfish, focused, irresponsible, faithful or strategic. Whether or not you wish to discuss your financial values with others, your money management will inevitably impact your marriage. Money is arguably one of the biggest reasons that couples separate. Even if there are other reasons for the breakdown of many marriages today, somewhere in the mix is divided financial perspectives. Don't tell me the lie that all you need is love and that money doesn't matter because once you have a few babies, a car, that beautiful house with the picket fence, then you'll need money for your mortgage, bills, insurance, savings, etc. It will certainly matter if either of you is frivolous. Money will matter if the bailiffs come knocking or if there is no roof over your heads. Money is necessary. Money speaks, and money matters.

In a sense, money has been given too much power. It lurks in the crevices of the minds of most of society — a web woven throughout fundamental aspects of our lives. That anxiety you feel because you can't pay your bills. The excitement of buying a new car. The significance of paying your tithes. All have the underlying factor of money. What about in the context of your marriage? How does money affect your relationship? Is it something that you cannot seem to agree on? Or is it something that is never discussed? Whether it's a silent or dominant factor, it's something that you're not going to escape.

Money Changes People

Money can be a blessing or a curse. It can distract from your relationship with your spouse and even with God. It can contribute to effective ministry and change lives for the better. It takes wisdom to handle money in a way that will bring a blessing to your life and honour to God. Your financial status can fluctuate as you journey through your marital lives, individually and as a couple. You may appreciate the positive impact on your marriage of having money, or it could have quite the opposite effect. I want to strip it of its ability to grip you as we discuss its effect on your life in this segment.

As always, honestly examine your heart and how it is impacted by money. How does it make you feel? Do you feel like you have to work 27 hours a day to make sure you have lots of it? Are you obsessed with its benefits? Or do you have so little that you are worried that one day it will all catch up with you? Does it make you anxious? Do you lose sleep at night? Do you feel like there are so many unanswered prayers concerning your financial situation? Be honest. God is looking at the condition of your heart and how you are affected by money. "Guard your heart above all else, for it determines the course of your life."[49]

Money should never be in control of you. However, you've got to be in control of it. Start by examining how money makes you feel. Then, evaluate what you know or need to learn about money. Then, pay attention to how you handle the money that you have. If you apply wisdom, discipline, humility and strategy towards how you approach your finances, then you will be able to see it work in your life for the better.

Naturally, I inherited my perspective about money from my mum. She would hate to admit this, but her spending habits are uninhibited, to put it lightly. Like dear mumsy, if I saw something I liked, then I bought it! Who cares if it would send me into overdraft, and I wouldn't be able to get to college the next day?

My husband was taught quite a different approach. He would happily wear holes in his clothes while his bank account flourished. It never occurred to us, in our much younger years, that our approach to money would either contribute to the success or the downfall of our marriage one day. We would have to work together to find a financial approach that would work harmoniously with our family ideals and, of course, our bank account!

There have been many stressful discussions about our financial direction and the impact that our individual financial decisions were having on our collective financial success. I had to become more aware of my spending. It's honestly a struggle for me not to just buy something

---

[49] Proverbs 4:23 (NLT)

that I want. Sometimes I have done well with managing my finances, and other times it's been a catastrophe. I am always learning new strategies for my personal money management. If I wanted to buy something, then I would have to become more creative about how and when I would purchase that thing. I would have to ask myself questions that I was too reckless to ask myself in the past, like, *do I actually need this?* If the answer was an honest "no", then I would slowly and in some ways excruciatingly return the product or service.

My husband, on the other hand, had to lighten up a bit. Sometimes we need shoes, clothes, food etc. We had to agree to find the balance. Also, unity is a theme in our united approach to money as it is to everything else. We don't hide money from each other. Most of our accounts are shared. You'll hardly ever hear us say "my money" or "your money" unless it's in our pockets. We set financial goals, talk about our fears and pray over our financial endeavours. We educate ourselves and compare what we have learnt. We share our fears and celebrate our successes. We coach, inspire and encourage each other to develop our money management.

"Love of Money Is the Root of All Evil"[50]

I really believe that there has to be a healthy balance between our need for money and the love of money. We need money to live, but the love of money can alienate us from blessings and completely destroy character. Is money an obsession for you? Is it something you think about and deliberately manage, or is it something you give very little thought to? To make money an obsession is to allow evil to take root within you. As in, you would sell your mother, husband or soul for it. To care too little is to make someone else suffer because of your neglect.

---

[50] 1 Timothy 6:10 (KJV)

Take a lesson from the ants, you lazybones.
Learn from their ways and become wise!
Though they have no prince
or governor or ruler to make them work,
they labour hard all summer,
gathering food for the winter.
But you, lazybones, how long will you sleep?
When will you wake up?
A little extra sleep, a little more slumber,
a little folding of the hands to rest—
then poverty will pounce on you like a bandit;
scarcity will attack you like an armed robber.
—Proverbs 6:6 (NLT)

Sounds a bit harsh, right? Having a lackadaisical approach to money also has an effect on everyone around you. Being meticulous and disciplined with whatever finances that God places in your hands is the height of wisdom. I cannot emphasise enough the value of a united strategy where marriage and money are concerned. If you're spending faster than your husband is saving, then guess what? You're never going to have any money! I remember having to change my financial habits to work harmoniously with my husband. We had to be completely honest with each other: no hiding money or debt. No competition. No belittling or patronising because not everybody is financially literate. No lying about where, when or how we got our money. Just completely trusting and completely open to change. It takes teamwork.

You have to want to see each other win. There can be so much fear, intimidation, worry and anxiety around these numbers or pieces of paper that seem to have a massive impact on our everyday lives.

If you can have open discussions about where you stand, what is important, how you should spend or how you have spent your money, then situations within your lives could completely turn around. We have had to have these discussions over and over. We have had to go to financial advisers, move in with parents to save money, work in jobs that we didn't like, cut down on extravagant spending that we once thought that we couldn't live without. There's no shame in that. We are so proud of the journey because we've always had the future in mind. We had you in mind. We had our family in mind. Over and over again, we have chosen to lose now to gain later. It felt like we were failing in those seasons, but we knew we would win in the long run.

The nature of vision is to have the foresight and see the long-term impact of our immediate decisions on our future. The skill of foresight is invaluable and necessary for us to thrive. To be honest, we still have to make sacrifices now, and I'm sure that we will continue to have to make sacrifices when we achieve our financial targets. There is no shame in taking two steps back to move four steps forwards. Who cares if they laugh at your odd (home-styled) haircut? Who cares if you have to live in a little box room for a while? It's part of the process. Have fun and celebrate in the box room. You might just miss those days later on.

For Richer for Poorer

I passionately believe that unified financial wealth depends on your unified growth strategies and the level of trust that you have as a couple. The improvement of your finances doesn't magically happen; it takes teamwork, dedication and nurture. The growth may be slow, but once you have established strong foundations, then you are bound to see a turnaround as you progress. Be transparent and patient with each other because sometimes change takes time. You are not protecting your spouse by withholding information about any financial straits. While you're worried about your financial situation, your partner could be oblivious to the gravity of their financial situation and be spending money that they don't have. Speak the truth even if your voice quivers. Then, work through it together.

It's not possible to say that you trust your partner while hiding money from them. Transparency will save and nourish your marriage. It's all about being open to trying new strategies and new perspectives. Always be willing to find financial systems that work for your household. Be adaptable if what you're doing isn't working for you. You might argue a few times before you work it all out, or you may just have it all together but be okay with that. It's the nature of two people with two different perspectives coming together and working it all out (as with most things in marriage).

"Where There Is No Vision, the People Perish"[51]

Nothing sticks without a clear, written vision. In the financial form, that would be recognised as a budget! We are always using ours to build and grow financially. We assess our budget whenever necessary and make the required changes to ensure that we stay on track for financial growth. We also have multiple accounts to help us monitor our expenses and income in greater detail. It has made it infinitely easier to manage our finances.

[51] Proverbs 29:18 (KJV)

Here's how we have distributed our finances:

* Account number one: wages, bills and benefits
* Account number two: savings
* Account number three: shopping
* Additional accounts: credit, businesses, self-maintenance

We also ensure that we save for our children's future, for emergencies and giving to charitable causes. It also makes it so much easier when we have to work through our finances with our accountant. So, there you have it! Our secret sauce! Are we where we want to be? No. Regardless, once we achieve a financial target, then we set new ones. We are always pushing ourselves and working towards new financial challenges.

Another golden nugget that I am willing to share with you is that we are always reading financial books, listening to podcasts, or finding communities that will teach us new ways of managing our finances. We have an open mind to try new financial systems that may be better than what we have already learnt. That being said, we are incredibly careful because we know that there are a lot of wolves out there who pretend that they are financial experts when really all they want is to take our money. There are so many resources out there that can benefit your financial growth, individually and collectively as a couple. Make the time to invest in your own growth, and you will reap the rewards. We are always filtering what works for us and what does not. Sometimes it simply comes down to trial and error. Some financial strategies only worked for us for a season, and we have to be paying close enough attention to know when to switch gears.

What Financial Character Do You Have?

I've identified five key traits that the majority of us have towards money. These may not apply to everyone, and some people are a combination of a few personalities. This should give you more clarity on your financial perspectives and help you have a more harmonious financial relationship with your spouse.

Penny pincher: This individual doesn't miss a penny. They won't spend money unless it is absolutely necessary. They would happily allow you to believe that they don't have any money instead of flashing cash they would have to part with. (My husband fits into this category.)

Frivolous spender: If you are an emotional spender, spend for fun or just throw money to the wind, then you would definitely fit this category. Other traits include reluctance to save, wearing money on clothes (i.e., designer etc.); this person basically has holes in their pockets. (Guilty as charged!)

Hogger: To this individual, money is personal. They don't like to share it. Your money is yours, and their money is theirs. They won't talk to you about yours so that you won't talk to them about theirs. (A dangerous perspective to have when jointly managing finances.)

Controller: They will happily give you money but with conditions. They will tell you how and when to spend it. They will withhold it if they don't feel like you deserve it. In other words, it's a tool for control. (Another dangerous perspective in marriage.)

Pious spender: They use religion to cover up their fears, put pressure on or control how money is spent. For example, they won't save too much because they may believe that "money is the root of all evil". They usually have extreme perspectives on money. They don't make the effort of finding a productive and balanced approach towards money.

There are definitely other personality types out there, but I am determined to share the relevant types to financial progression within marriage. If left unidentified and untended to, these financial personalities can be dangerous to progressive finances within marriage. Discord and collective mismanagement say, *I don't trust you*. Trust is absolutely necessary for progressive finances within marriage. Don't be afraid to share information, strategies, failures and successes with your spouse when it comes to the state of your finances. Do you remember the vows: "All that I am I give to you, all that I have I share with you"? Allow those vows to apply to your finances too. Open up, discuss your fears and agree on a strategy to progress. The biggest risk you took, secondary only to the moment that you said, "I do", was revealing another layer by sharing your financial state with him. That being said, I have highlighted that there are dangerous financial personalities and that they can harm a marriage. It may be necessary not to declare aspects of your financial situation to protect yourself.

Are You Being Financially Abused?

You may be wondering if you fit into the criteria of being financially abused. I would like to share a very helpful definition of financial abuse:

Financial exploitation includes restricting the ability of a victim to access, use and retain financial resources. Many that are financially victimised can be prohibited from working. They can even have their own money limited by the abuser or robbed by him. And they seldom get full access to money and other tools.

You may find yourself being overwhelmingly nervous, afraid, unwilling or even depressed to move ahead with financial planning. I've heard of women being driven thousands of pounds into debt when their relationships ended, and one of the women who shared her story even spoke about her desire to commit suicide because of it. Financial abuse can have a serious effect on your mental, spiritual and physical wellbeing. If you feel like you are financially manipulated or abused, I encourage you to seek help. You don't deserve to be driven into debt financially, pressured into spending whatever should not be spent or financially abused.

There are so many organisations and charities that are available to help you. I understand how financial straits could easily apply stress, anxiety or pressure to your life and marriage. Don't suffer in silence. Speak to a counsellor and financial adviser. Start to write down what you want to happen and the steps that you would like to make to improve your financial situation, even if you have to do it without the support of your spouse. Again, it does not benefit your marriage to sneak around making these decisions on your own, so I would encourage you to have the necessary conversations while trying to work out a way forward at the same time. If you find it difficult to have these conversations, then do not hesitate to include a reputable third party to mediate.

The hardest aspect of trying to progress financially with a spouse is if they withhold information or lie about their financial situation. Especially if you are financially connected to them. God must always be involved in all your decisions. It may sound cliché, but He sees and is completely aware of the distress and pain that you are under. Let Him carry the weight of your pain. Prayerfully create opportunities for dialogue. Again, if there is no success, speak to a financial adviser and start making plans to salvage your financial state. Don't underestimate the help of financial advisers and counsellors. Learn as much as you can about money. Look for ideas to make more money. What skills do you have? How can you use your skills to generate income? Start there. Community is also important. You are not alone; so many women are going through exactly the same thing, and they will be able to laugh, cry, encourage and support you.

There have been so many people in the Bible that God has entrusted with financial wealth: Abraham, Joseph, Esther, Job, Boaz and Ruth, to name a few. Every time that God entrusted anyone with money, it was the heart that He looked at. How did they handle it? Did it take His place? Could they leave it behind? So many were trustworthy with an abundance of wealth. While I don't believe that everyone is destined to handle being financially wealthy, I believe that we can master our approach towards managing it. My perspective on why I don't believe that being rich is for everyone is for another book. However, this scripture epitomises the correct approach that we should have towards money: "If riches increase, Do not set your heart on them."[52]

This scripture is absolutely the right approach. We will inevitably leave it all behind one day, so we set our hearts on heaven. We must also use whatever God places within our reach to bless Him through the lives of those we are fortunate to touch and in whatever way that honours Him. That means His wisdom in our lives and in our financial situations is extremely important. We mustn't use the wisdom to grow financially through His word as a way to fuel our own fears, insecurities, shortcomings, laziness etc. As Proverbs 6:6 says, "we will use the ants' wisdom, and we will build wisely." It is incredibly difficult to progress financially with someone who misinterprets the Bible for their own financial endeavours. If you encounter this kind of personality, use wisdom and silence. Focus on developing strategies to increase income flow. Use your skills. Learn about money and be a part of a

---

[52] Psalm 62:10 (NKJV)

community that will support your growth. It can be very difficult to have a dialogue with this mindset, so hold onto focus, prayer and all the wisdom that you can get to grow.

Fighting for Your Money

Sometimes it can be difficult to be confident enough to ask for what you want, but it's more painful to suffer because you kept your mouth shut. Walking away from a deal without fighting for what you want stings far longer than the few minutes it takes to speak up. Try adding being female and from the UK into the mix, and it gets even more difficult to talk about money.

* Give me my money.
* I deserve a pay rise.
* I'm not going to pay that much for…

JOURNAL

* What would happen if you had the necessary conversations about money? How drastically would your life change?
* What if you were to discuss, plan and strategise your own financial success with your spouse?
* What impact would it have on your peace of mind concerning your quality of life, ministries, children's lives and future, and even marriage as a whole?

It can easily be the fundamentals that are paralysing the financial aspect of your life. You can feel the changes that you need to make to change the direction of your life, but you hesitate. Why? Is it fear of being disliked that grips you? Or does it just make you feel uncomfortable and out of your comfort zone? Weigh up what's more important: the need to be liked or the desire to make a difference in your life and the lives of those around you. It takes a few seconds to make a lifetime of change.

So, where do you need to start? Is it the conversation that you need to have with your husband about his frivolous spending habits? Do you need to cancel that holiday and put the money in a savings account? You know the areas that you need to work on and the areas that God is trying to change. Move forward, boldly. The first time is the hardest, but once you dare to speak, you won't stop. I should know. I have been that girl. I felt like it was un-Christian and rude to ask for money. I felt like needing money was a sin. I lacked the courage to say what I needed; then, I started to suffer because of it.

I started to realise how many people in the Bible were provided for by God financially. It didn't affect their integrity. They continued to flourish in faith. I also recognise that it is all about balance. It should never have my ultimate focus. I also notice that it is necessary for our survival on this planet! It's as much a ministry to manage money wisely as a wife, mother, businesswoman etc. That means God is involved with how it is used. I thank God for the lessons about money and what I continue to learn about money because I get to use them and share them with you!

Finally, find a community of women that you can talk to and develop a healthy financial perspective. Having women that speak the same language, have aspirations, and a joint desire to have a Godly impact on the world through the ministry of money will definitely transform your life in that area.

How Does Money Make You Feel?

This question is a pivotal indicator of whether you are in control of your money or whether your money is in control of you. It doesn't matter whether you can manage the debt and have a certain amount of control over your spending habits; if your financial woes keep you up at night, then it's a problem. Being able to admit that you are ashamed, afraid, uncertain, losing control or even embarrassed about the state of your finances strengthens your ability to deal with it. Take ownership of the financial mistakes you have made; stop burying those mistakes in the hope that they will go away because, in actual fact, those problems will just continue to increase. Your feelings are valid, but they are only half of the story. The other half is your ability to take action and work towards improving your finances. Do you feel like you have already lost control over your finances? Then, how you feel is going to show through your finances. I am not a believer in manifesting (see Chapter 6, *I Had a Dream... Once*), but I am a believer in the power of your mind and that we subconsciously emit the residue of our thoughts into every aspect of our lives.

In Proverbs, we're told, "For as he thinks in his heart, so is he."[53] In other words, what you feel is going to come out somewhere. Your fear of your finances might be the reason that you have been procrastinating in your budgeting and allowing your finances to go wild. When you feel in control, it will show in how you organise your bills, expenses, spending and income. You will have a clearer vision of how you wish to proceed. You will start to execute your financial strategies

---

[53] Proverbs 23:7 (NKJV)

with confidence. In my marriage, we highlight our developments and celebrate each other's wins. We are not in the business of making each other feel inferior or berating each other about the mistakes that we have made. We are constantly celebrating our triumphs and financial achievements. It's crucial that my husband completely believes that he can do anything, that I have his back 1000 per cent (and vice versa).

So, to sum up this chapter: any improvements in your finances depend on the unseen aspects of your relationship. It's not about *looking* financially stable as opposed to actually being wealthy. Make sure that the foundation that your marriage is built on is firm, and it will simply be reflected in how you tackle your finances.

Do Your Research

A financial U-turn doesn't happen by accident. I have learnt that it takes graft to improve the state of finances within marriage. Sometimes sacrifices have to be made. Sometimes all that is required for improvement is knowing where to start. Charitable organisations like Step Change and Christians Against Poverty have free resources (online and in-person) and counsellors who can work with you to get out of financial straits. They also have free downloadable information that you can get from their website. More charities are available to support you and your family as you work towards a better financial situation. Your bank may also offer a free financial advice service.

When we were in the early stages of marriage, we planned out our finances with a financial adviser and, although it was daunting, it was the best thing that we ever did. We realised that we were not sacrificing enough or asking for help. Her advice was not what we wanted to hear but what we *needed* to hear. We could buy a house due to her advice, even though we never dreamt it would be possible for us. So, there you have it! Talking to the right person, doing the research and making informed steps towards your goals can make a world of difference. The school of financing with family is always open, and we are always learning something new every day. The most important thing is that we want to learn and we want to be better at our finances. If you can unify, voice your concerns and be resilient, then there will be no stopping you.

Build on Your United Vision

In every aspect of our marriage, we have talked about what we envision for the future. We look at the whole picture, and then we simplify the steps required to complete the big picture. Our finances are no exception. We have talked about what house we want to live in, where we want to live, where we want to travel, what businesses and ministries we want to establish, what car we want to drive and where we want our kids to go to school. We create a united blueprint to ensure that we are completely on the same page. Then, we work out the financial goals required for us to create those visions. There are many that we have achieved and some that we are still completing. Some visions are so grand that they take time.

The beauty of it all is that we are building together. We agree on the sacrifices that we are willing to make to achieve our visions, and we work through the aspects that we are unwilling to compromise. What is most important is that we are doing it together. It isn't always pretty. Sometimes we have to go away and come back to the difficult topics, but we both are clear that our intentions are focused on what works best for our family. I encourage you to do the same to ensure that you both have the same vision for your financial goals. If it's difficult to agree or find united clarity or direction, I encourage you to write everything down. When you have both written down your thoughts, dreams and expectations, then start numbering them.

Prioritise what works best for your family in terms of time, physical effort and the impact it will have on your marriage and immediate family. I've said it before, and I will say it again. Be patient. The fog will clear, and you will gain the enlightenment you both need to move forward, but first, trust the process. It makes the journey so much easier, and the clarity really strengthens your marriage. As the years go by, you begin to understand so much more about your partner's character, and that includes their finances. You will evolve and become different people when it comes to your financial approach, which will only complement your marriage.

Prayer and Meditation

Let's pray and reflect using the mirror.

Dear Heavenly Father,

You see the pressure points that our finances have induced in our marriage. Bless me with the grit to build a more unified and stable financial situation for my family. I pray for the strategy and innovation to improve our financial circumstances for the sake of our family and ministry. Please give me the strength to implement positive habits that trigger financial breakthroughs.

In Jesus' name, Amen.

ELEVEN

CHEATED AND BROKEN

§

Deep down, she knew the truth.

Her heart was broken into a thousand pieces, and

she was doing everything that she could to keep it all together.

Smiling in every photograph, attending every event,

always in the most stunning outfits that she could find.

She was what most would consider the epitome of the perfect wife.

She was trying to keep it together for the sake of the lifestyle that she wanted to keep on living.

For the children, for her husband and for the sake of her sanity.

She would try to keep the secrets that pierced her soul… those secrets that had her feeling more dead than alive.

It was becoming harder to hide every day.

The pain of being cheated and the feeling of being broken.

It had been weighing heavy on her soul.

The feeling of betraying herself by putting everyone else first.

The neglect of her own desire to heal burned through the armour of her façade.

She seemed to be holding it together, but secretly she was falling apart,

all because she had a broken heart.

Not all cheating happens through infidelity. A betrayal of a friend or breach of trust can leave you feeling cheated. Like you got the short straw or was dealt a bad hand. Deceived. Usurped. Robbed. It can be done in such a way that you wonder if you imagined it: *is it just my imagination?* This question could drive you to a place of insanity. *Maybe, it's just me…* you may think. Allowing your wounds to remain open and at risk of becoming increasingly worse. Knowing that you were completely honest and open. That you trusted them 100 per cent, but they were not equally forthright. Scorched by the reality that they did not know your worth and that you allowed them free rein. They trampled, vandalised and ravaged the sacred places of your heart and left you in ruin. Then, they walked away as if you should be grateful that they even left you alive. It's the kind of pain that can leave you begging to die.

Broken-hearted

A heart that's broken, but the evidence would be impossible to identify by any medical apparatus. Invisible. Deadly. The pain is equally as deadly as it would be if it could be physically identified. It is possible to have a broken heart by the ones that you're not in a marital union with. The feeling of being cheated is not impartial. You can be broken in spirit by a lover or a loved one. The pain can leave you feeling damaged beyond repair. It can have just as much of a negative effect on your marriage as if your husband had cheated. Sometimes it can even affect your ability to be the best wife you can be. The aftermath of the pain could affect your ability to trust your husband. To fully enjoy your marriage without wondering, *when is he going to break my heart? When is he going to give up?* Or even, *when is he going to walk away?*

When you give pieces of yourself in any relationship, it's your way of saying, *I trust you* or *this connection is of high value to me.* When your trust is violated, it could scream, *the love you gave was not reciprocated!* This may or may not be true, but one thing is: you're the one who is left with the broken pieces, like a caged bird whose broken wings have been healed. It has a desire to spread its wings and take to the sky. Nevertheless, if you open the cage and walk away… the bird remains. Why? It lacks the courage to take the risk. Could you, like this bird, need the courage to fly? So accustomed to the prison of loss and brokenness. Healing can feel long and slow. The urge to fast forward this painful season in your life so that you can get to a place of uninhibited joy is yielding nothing but frustration. Stuck. Tired of swimming in the river of tears that you have cried, trying to understand why? *Why did I pull the short straw? Why is it that I lost out when I took the risk? I trusted them enough to give them a chance. I opened up to them, and I let them in. Only to be repaid with pain. Scars. Trauma. Suffering. Now I don't want to feel. I will build the walls higher than I ever built them before,* I hear your heart say. *I will never let them in.*

I Will Never Allow Myself to Be Weak Again…

Does your heart murmur this? If they only knew how broken you were. Playing the tragic scenes in your mind that epitomised the un-ravelling of relationships you thought would never end. If they only knew that your heart couldn't take another hit. You can feel how bro-ken you are deep down. You think that you could never survive the pain of another loss. The pain has you seeing the world through a different lens. A lens that is prone to detecting the pain in life as opposed to joy. Expecting the worst from everyone and always on your guard. Even the ones who love you suffer because you never completely let them in. Suffocating in your own silent prison, drowning in distrust. Days, months and years go by, causing the roots of bitterness to deepen and grip your soul. You could eventually look around and realise that you pushed everyone away. Even if some fight to remain, they will never really get to you because you're holding back the part of you that deserves the abundance of life. You deserve to love unequivocally, to laugh without constraint, to be completely and undeniably happy. Forget the tactics and the games. Forget playing it cool to keep them coming and forget holding back. You deserve relationships that embrace you and empower you to be unreservedly yourself.

Still performing but barely functioning. Conforming to the unspoken pressures that surround you. Be a good wife. Smile. Don't expose your pain. Keep it all together. Shattered by the secret that has vandalised your soul. You limp forward with the hollow places of your heart that remain, hoping that one day it will all fix itself.

If I Am Cheated Out of One More Thing...

Fighting the expectation of being trapped in a lifetime of lies and pain. Never being able to move past the trauma of that pain. Afraid to hope for fear of being let down and trapped in a maze of sorrow. You push the pain to the back of your mind and try to continue to hide in your everyday life's responsibilities, but whenever it is silent, your mind wonders how you will cope.

Will It Ever Get Better?

Will I ever smile and genuinely mean it? Silently praying and waiting for the pain to end. It's easy to look at the broken pieces of your soul and think, *I am beyond repair.* After all, doesn't evidence of the fragments of your heart signify that you are no longer complete? Well, you may feel that way. In reality, what is happening to you is a good thing. You are falling apart to be rebuilt by life's lessons. You are being reconstructed in the way that you were always designed to be. Your pain and your brokenness are just triggers for something beautiful to be birthed. You are now making space for new growth. Growth can be painful, and sometimes it's gradual. Sometimes it won't make sense while you're going through it, but that's the nature of the process. While you're up close and in it, it won't make sense, but when you come out on the other side, at a distance, the potency of its message will be impossible to ignore.

It's a message that God has tailor-made for you. Right now is not the time to become stagnant, build a house or make a bed in your pain. You're not meant to be in this space forever. You're just passing through. Don't try to fight the pain or the journey. Allow yourself to feel. Go through the thick of it so that you can come out on the other side. If you have to cry, then let it out. Work through your pain but don't live your life under false pretences. Don't pretend that you're fine when everything is not; remove the mask. The consequences of pretending are that you will weigh your spirit down. Look ahead. So much beauty awaits you on the other side of your pain. You'll have to journey through the darkest night to get to your brightest days. Adjust your focus. Yes, it hurts, and there are days that you may feel like you're losing your mind. The truth is that your lack of focus is the cause of your demise. You have fuelled the grip of the pain in your life by giving it your focus. Starve your pain by shifting your focus to your growth and healing. Focus on the goodness that you want to see overflow in your life. Beckon to the blessings that await your command. Declare goodness over your mind, health, future and relationships.

"Surely, Goodness and Mercy Shall Follow Me"[54]

Let the words light up your soul until you feel it from the inside out – until it shines through your eyes. Let it radiate from your soul until you become impenetrable, and your power becomes infectious – so much so that you will no longer be identified by the painful experiences that you have been through. All that will be seen is the gold that you are. I speak wisdom from the truth of my own experiences. Whenever I have made a point of deliberately shifting my focus to words of truth, my strength increases. I am comforted by the beauty and the promises of God. His words have ushered me through immensely painful and difficult times. Does every situation improve and get better? Not always. Do I get all the answers that I need for every puzzling situation that occurs? No. What happens then? I get stronger. I consciously expose myself to anything that reminds me that I am gold. I was born to shine. To do and receive everything good in my life. I draw strength from everything that God puts in my path to build me up. Do you ever have times when you feel like you have more than you can handle, but something or someone comes along and uplifts you? That extra push is God's way of holding your hand and giving you rest for the journey. It's a hard road to travel, but the beauty of it all will be revealed when you arrive at your destination. When you reach your destination and look back, you'll realise that God has been with you all along. I can almost hear you saying, "You don't understand,

---

[54] Psalm 23:6 (KJV)

he cheated, and he broke my heart! Someone I trusted broke me, and I can't even trust my husband because of it!"

I Can't Trust Anyone

I hear you; your pain is valid, but it isn't the whole truth. The lessons that you learn will catapult you into the greatness hidden within you all along. They were meant to fail you. They were meant to let you down. They were meant to walk away. You were meant to go this way. It may hurt you to hear these words, but they will take on new meaning as you journey through the course of your life. You were being educated by God and life to bring out the jewels in your soul. Our knee-jerk reaction to show our ugly in response to pain is instinctive. To put walls up. To close out everything that we see as a potential threat. You have to push past the ugly to get to the jewels – greatness.

The diamonds of a new nature are buried deep within you. This may not feel like wife-related wisdom, but the truth is that being the best wife that you can be depends on how you are nurtured as a whole. You can't give your best as a wife if you are not cared for as *the whole person*. The way that you tend to your mind, your soul, your spirit and your body all affect how much you can give to your family. If you are not connected to God, unhealthy, frazzled with no purpose, weighed down by secrets and trapped in the humdrum of life, then guess what? You're not going to put out your best. You also won't be receiving the best of everything around you. Even the sound of God's voice will sound different through the fog of your confusion.

Every word I share is focused on your growth in all these areas. You will see the deliberate transformation in yourself and your circumstances as you tend to the areas of your life that are broken. It takes solitude, reflection, prayer, sincerity and total dependence on the word and truth of God to work through the pain. You have to be willing to rid yourself of the secrets that weigh you down. There's nothing more beautiful than knowing that you have lived your life to the full in every single way. Even though you have made mistakes and have been through so much hardship, you have fought your way through it all. The fact that you are reading this book shows that you are still determined to push forward until you see all the beautiful things God has in store for you.

"We Shall Reap if We Faint Not"[55]

Your evolution is a winding journey. There are so many avenues of your healing to explore. Give yourself another chance to push through to the reward you deserve – the recovery of your soul. You just need time and the right resources to aid your growth and restoration. When you are ready to receive it, and when you least expect it, God will unleash an outpouring of blessing upon your life that shows that He remembers you. I understand how easy it is to feel like your life is being drained, but give yourself time to make sense of it all. It will come to you. God will bring you the answers you need, and you will understand why you had to go through this journey.

Over time you will become better at forgiving others and letting go. You will magnetise to the things that will aid your transformation. You will laugh again – that deep-throated laugh that says, "I remember that girl; she *used* to be me." You won't share her secret anymore. The only secrets that you will be keeping are the weapons of resilience, strength and grit that have kept you standing today. I guarantee that it will be your worst-kept secret because it's the kind of secret that you will want to share with everyone. You will be telling them how glad you are that you no longer have to wear a façade. The mask that you

---

[55] Galatians 6:9 (KJV)

used to wear is now gathering dust. You have revealed the beauty of who you are without the restraint that comes with holding on to your pain and trust once again. The vibrancy that radiates from you as you step into the new. Rebirth. Regenerated. Reinvigorated. Revitalised.

He Cheated, but I Still Bleed...

The tragedy of it all is that you can look very much happily married and alive while you're quite the opposite. Knowing so absolutely that the trust is gone and that you have been broken by him, you may also be afraid to leave him. Publicly, you have made all these promises, and you've become tied to this man. In so many ways, he feels like a stranger. You are uncertain of the difference between the truth and the lies he tells. Resentful. In pain and paralysed by it all. Broken into so many pieces that there's nothing left to break. Cheated. He promised that he would be your protector. Provider. Your eternal friend. Instead, his betrayal has cut deeper than any knife, twisting and tearing every inch of you as it burrows deep into your soul. Hope has been broken. Trust has been broken. You're trying to fix what you feel cannot be fixed. Losing strength, resilience and yourself in the process and wanting out. Nothing is more painful than looking alive but feeling dead inside. Pretending to the world that you are strong when, in fact, you're weaker than you've ever been.

There's Only So Much I Can Take

I can almost hear your heart say, *what was his betrayal?* Did he replace his love for you with something or someone else? That feeling overwhelms you when he is away from home longer than he says that he will be. Changing plans. Unenthusiastic about being intimate on multiple levels. Knowing for certain that he is hiding. He's crushing your soul, and you're doing your best to carry on. You know for sure that he's hiding a piece of himself that he once shared with you, and now you're wondering if he is sharing it with someone or something else. It's too much to carry this alone. Over time the weight of it all increases until it takes its toll. You crave wholeness, but you've forgotten how. If you could just have time to gather up the broken pieces of your soul, to find rest, to get strength, then you could fight. But every time you try to pick yourself up to piece it all together, he hands you another blow. Then you're down again. Broken again. Weak again. You're failing because you are fighting alone. Let someone stronger take the wheel: "The Lord is close to the broken-hearted; he rescues those whose spirits are crushed."[56]

***

You may be so broken-hearted that you literally can almost feel your heart break. Death seems more appealing than having a heart that just refuses to mend. It's ten times worse when you are in a situation that continues to break your heart over and over again. It gets difficult to smile and wear the mask when the pain is so intense. How do you carry on when it feels like you're losing your heart and mind? Desperate to find something to hold onto. Desperate to put it all back together but completely losing control. Broken hearts are God's speciality. God says, "I am with you."

> *... for I am with you. Don't be discouraged, for I am your God.*
> *I will strengthen you and help you;*
> *I will hold you up with my victorious right hand.*
> **—Isaiah 41:10 (NLT)**

---

[56] Psalm 34:18 (NLT)

It will break you, and it's going to hurt, but whatever breaks you... will eventually build you. Those broken pieces are invaluable lessons that are going to heal and reshape you. Those broken pieces will give birth to the most invaluable lessons that you've ever had in your life. Don't despise your fragility or the fact that you were susceptible to the deception of his ways. Wise woman, your class is in session. The beauty of your brokenness is about to reveal itself, and you are about to understand why it has all been so tough.

When the pain is raw and unbearable, one of the most effective ways to start your healing journey is to find someone to cry with. Your heart needs release. Find someone who will pray with you and support you by listening to the pain that you have been holding in for so long. There is such a release that comes with dropping the façade and opening up to your situation's truth. Don't worry about who will think negatively about the situation and start thinking about your wholeness journey. Healing takes time, and it won't happen overnight, especially with so much to consider. Someone who knows how to listen, pray and love on you is essential right now. The answers are within you.

Maybe He Will Change...

Sometimes we hope for the things that we have no control over. I believe that it's great to be optimistic but wise enough to understand that we cannot control the narrative. You have no power to reach into the depths of your husband's soul and make him loyal. You can't guarantee that he will change. You can, however, depend upon the King of Hearts, God, to change your husband's heart. That may not happen within your time frame. It could take weeks, months or even years before the buds of change start to appear. Sometimes it takes life circumstances to reveal to your husband that his actions have consequences. Once again, you have no control over when or how this will happen.

What you do have control over is yourself. What value do you place on *YOU?* Do you value yourself enough to make decisions that will fuel your growth and healing? Or will you continue to focus on his decisions and whether or not you have the ability to change him?

The truth is, you can't force him into a space that he isn't spiritually ready to move into. Even if you cry out to God, He will not force your husband into *your* agenda. Why? Because your husband has the gift of free will. He will continue to make the decisions that he chooses to make. You have the power to cultivate an environment and lifestyle that will facilitate your growth and healing. You can do this with or without your husband. You are in complete control of yourself. You can control how much access you allow him to have and whether he can violate your boundaries. You are in control of whether or not you are going to remain in an environment that allows him to mistreat you and the blessings that surround you. You can choose to be an earthly example of what genuine love looks like regardless of whether or not he understands what love truly is. Does it mean that you allow him to treat you like a doormat? Not at all. Does that mean that you don't love him? Of course not. It means that you protect your mind, heart and emotions with boundaries. Nurture what you have. You have your dignity, heart, mind, spirit, emotions, faith, talents, dreams, aspirations, finances, even your career – those are your resources.

Replenish and nurture what you have at all costs. This will cushion the fall of your marriage if you ever have to face that situation. You can be hopeful that things will get better, but you can also be prepared if things get worse at the same time. Be a woman of abundant wisdom. Wisdom overrides emotions. The rage, the angst, the resentment and the frustration are natural and valid emotions. However, they are ultimately counterproductive. Switch gears.

- What can the wise woman within you find to pre-serve?
- What life is left within your marriage?
- What things can be nursed back to life? What is beyond repair?

Wait for the answers to reveal themselves. Give yourself over to seeking the answer from the only One who knows. God will guide you into all truth about the nature of your circumstances. There have been many relationships that I have had to pray into fruition and growth. Many times, the person I am praying for is not aware that I talk to God about them. I genuinely show God my care for their wellbeing and growth. Sometimes the change is slow. Sometimes it looks like nothing is happening. Have you ever stared at the clouds? It seems like nothing is happening, but if you stop looking at them for a long period and then return to them, then you realise that they have been moving all this time. They change shape and position. All you need to do is watch and wait. See how God moves things around you. Don't try to make things happen ahead of their time. Just trust the process. "At the right time, I, The Lord, will make it happen."[57]

---

[57] Isaiah 60:22 (NLT)

Preservation Mode

Waiting isn't inactively hoping and doing nothing. Waiting is active in stillness. It's working on building your inner being and looking at your circumstance. Is it the marriage itself? Is it the principles and legacy that you are building for your children?

Have you ever seen a building sound alarms and then go into an emergency or alert mode when it recognises that there is an intruder? If there is a sense that there is an intruder in your marriage, then you too will have to go into alert mode. I actually prefer to call this "preservation mode". What your husband may not recognise is that going into preservation mode is also for his benefit as well as everyone else's. It takes wisdom to know that you have to protect the little bit of strength that you have to preserve the life left in your family and home. If he has betrayed the marriage or is willing to leave, you first need to protect your inner person. Protect the spiritual, emotional, mental and physical resources that you have left so that you have the strength to build.

Preserving the Mind

Post-traumatic stress is a real thing. I have no authority to diagnose whether or not it is classified as a disorder in your life. However, there is real trauma in knowing that an event has, or is about to cause a threat to your whole being and way of life. It can easily cause anxiety, despair, depression and stress. You can't control what he does, but you can control the walls of your own mind. As the Bible tells us, "So prepare your minds for action and exercise self-control."[58]

---

[58] 1 Peter 1:13 (NLT)

Another version (of the same scripture) I love says, "Therefore gird up the loins of your mind."[59]

It is so easy to get worn down by betrayal. Your mind can become a maze that is difficult to navigate through. Hazy and indistinct. Lacking in direction. Now more than ever, the Bible carries value. Let the words of truth and life be your anchor. It is the word that unlocks the revelation of our true selves. Just the way that God has created us to be. The true power that lies within. The word of God shows us how to heal from festering wounds and move from a place of pain to power. To be invigorated with life and vibrancy when we rightly unpack it and apply it to our lives. To have a full life. To have a life that overflows and shows. To transform. You won't have to tell anyone about the transformation you have experienced. They will see it ooze from your soul. Your face will be rested and undeniably resemble the life that flows from within. Be determined to be that person. Free of bitterness and resentment. Determined to heal those open wounds.

There is a real danger in not dealing with or acknowledging the broken pieces of your soul. When wounds are left open, accessible and available, predators can take advantage, knowingly or unknowingly. Sometimes your vulnerability can be heard in how you speak about the person(s) or experiences that hurt you. Maybe your tone sounded so bitter that it left an impression on the person that was listening. Or was it your facial expression when their name was mentioned that gave away the angst that you feel about the way you have been wronged? A wound is a potential button that can be pressed. What happens if someone presses that button or tries to use your pain against you? Who knows how you will handle the pain of being broken once more? There is something so powerful about partnering with God to allow

---

[59] 1 Peter 1:13 (NKJV)

healing to transform our lives. When wounds occur, we have to be willing to nurse them to heal. The difficulty lies with the fact that you continue to allow the wrong things to arrest you. It's a kind of torture that you really do not deserve. To be weighed down by pain that you did not instigate. To be poisoned by the brokenness that you carry but did not cause. When you're broken, you have to be bold enough to look at the broken places in your soul… the places that you have been avoiding for so long. Behind your smiles and your composure, you have been trying to overcome the trauma of being cheated. Cheated of expectations, broken promises and unfulfilled actions. What they did and didn't do. What they should and shouldn't have said. The death and bereavement of all the things that you hoped for. Everything that you have loved and lost.

No one has scars without once feeling the pain of them being open wounds. The truth is that it's easier and feels safer to wear a mask, to pretend that everything is okay. But deep down, everybody hurts at some point in their lives. No matter how much they may deny it, everybody experiences heartbreak in one shape or another. It may not be from a spouse or a lover; it could be from a friend or a loved one. We all have to navigate our way to healing. Some never find their way; others still don't recognise that the pain was so vicious and deep that they haven't recovered. Spiritually disfigured but unable to recognise it. Lying beneath the surface, hidden but simmering, always and almost ready to erupt. I can almost hear your heart's cry.

When Will the Pain End?

The pain can feel so intense that it almost feels impossible to breathe. Some days it can be so overwhelming. Some nights the tears don't seem to stop. God sees your pain. Guess what? He's smiling. How can He be smiling at your pain and at your brokenness? The process is a sign that there is progress. Your destination brings God so much joy. He smiles because the painful route is giving way to a destination that is so powerful that the pain of your past will pale in comparison. You are becoming someone so brilliant that you, too, will look back and laugh at the person you once were before you began this journey.

When I was pregnant, there would be times when my babies would be so still that I would ask myself, *is there even a baby in my tummy?* I would lightly graze my hand across my belly, and there would be the occasional movements. However, it wasn't until the babies had finally arrived that I realised the weight of my experience. I remember looking into their faces and being amazed that I had carried these little miracles into the world.

In another sense, you are spiritually on a journey to giving birth – the birth of a version of you that not even you will recognise. Your story will be the awakening of so many women slumbering in the same places as you have been. Your fight is for yourself and for a whole village of women coming behind you. Deep down within you, there's a strong awareness that you are *pregnant* with a miracle. Something so special that it will free you and everyone that surrounds you. The wisdom, growth and strength that you are about to give birth to will eclipse all the pain that you have been struggling with. You will overcome it all when you recognise that you will never be strong enough to heal independently. An apt and poignant scripture that I love says:

> *And He said to me, "My grace is sufficient for you, for My strength is made perfect in weakness."*
> **—2 Corinthians 12:9 (NKJV)**

All you have to do is depend on Christ to be your strength. His strength surpasses our weaknesses. You will be surprised at what you have the strength to overcome when you are truly dependent on God. I understand what it feels like to want to give up on relationships, life, hopes and dreams because of the pressure of it all. If you could only *graze your stomach* and feel the hope stirring within you. Allow your heart to be expectant of the beauty that your pain will give birth to. It's already happening. You already have so much wisdom and have learnt so much about God, yourself and others on your journey. Don't despise the process but learn the lessons that the process is trying to teach you. Pay attention because God is speaking to you through the journey, the pain and the pressure.

Years ago, I received an email with a story that was so poignant that I never forgot it. It was a story about a missionary who took some children to visit a goldsmith. They watched as he refined the gold using an ancient method. The goldsmith would repeatedly embed the gold in a special chemical which would subsequently burn away in the fire. Once the gold was removed and cooled, he would manipulate it in his hands. Each time he would raise the temperature and repeat the process until he was satisfied with the state of the gold. The final time he raised the temperature, he explained how, initially, the gold couldn't tolerate this heat level, but now it could handle it. What would've once caused it to perish now benefits it. Then, one of the children raised a question: "When will the gold be ready?" His response had me floored. "It is ready when I can see my reflection in it."[60]

In the same way, there are painful experiences that will be the making of us. A warrior is being forged through the fire and the pain. You're focused on the pressure, but God is focused on the fact that He is making an ironwoman out of you. Unbreakable. He knows that you

---

[60] *Gold Cord*, Amy Carmichael, CLC Publications, 1st October 1982

can handle the heat. He knows that when the temperature is just right, He will see His reflection in you. His reflection in your marriage. His reflection in your environment and legacy. There will be many times when you are built and broken to be built again. Every single time you will be transformed into someone more beautiful and more powerful than you ever imagined.

> But as it is written, Eye hath not seen, nor ear heard, neither have entered into the heart of man, the things which God hath prepared for them that love him.
> **—1 Corinthians 2:9 (KJV)**

God will heal you, and life's situations will challenge and even break you. Each time will reveal a more resilient version of you. Each time will be the making of you. When you learn to yield to the Divine process and journey, your shaping will always be your making. Your enemies will always wonder how you keep coming back ten times better than when you left. Your secret and your weapon are Him. God. His strength over your weakness.

Find Your Midwives

Those people will hold your hand as you push through the pain. They will support you while giving birth to the resilience you need for the next phase of your life. Those friends you can confide in, who will celebrate you and encourage you. They will tell you the truth when you neglect to nurture the hope that God has released within you. Most importantly, they will pray with and for you. There is nothing more valuable than friends who know God and who will remind you of your value in Him. Cling to those kinds of people.

If you cannot find friends like that at this point in your life, then make yourself available to good communities. You can take your time and find the friends and environment that are conducive to your growth. Your village is waiting to meet you. There are nearly eight billion people on the planet. You can find the right community a thousand times over in that bunch! You have to let your heart be open to trusting, and allow people to have the space to support you. When they fail, you give them a chance to make it right because you have to fight the pain filter that brokenness induces. You may be afraid to let people in after experiencing so much trauma and pain. It's understandable to want to protect your heart, but your heart is more resilient than you realise. Trust yourself to make better decisions in your friendships and relationships: "In all your ways acknowledge Him, And He shall direct your paths."[61]

You're part of a team now. Trust your Divine team player to reveal and draw the right people to trigger your healing. You will know who they are when you listen to their words and observe their actions. Take the healing that those relationships bring. Don't force people to overstay in positions that have expired. Some may be available to bless you for a season. Others may enrich your life for a lot longer. Receive and embrace what you are given. Let it fuel your journey. I could spend the whole chapter focusing on the trauma, bitterness and unforgiveness that can come with being cheated and broken. I could tell you each and every step to take for your unique situation. Maybe you should leave him, or maybe you should not. Maybe those friends should be punished for what they did, or maybe they should not. I don't want to go there. I want to see the fragments of your soul come together so much better than they were before. I believe that, as you

---

[61] Proverbs 3:6 (NKJV)

heal, the clarity and direction will come from God. You will learn to leave the fighting in His hands and focus on healing, winning, laughing and being complete. You will live life to the full. What's the point in being bitter and broken when your offender is walking free, maybe even oblivious to the aftermath that they have left behind? All that energy and effort wasted on wishing that they are suffering or hoping that they care when you could be focused on the *better things* that await you.

Go Where Growth Is

One summer I decided to teach my son about plants. Needless to say, I have never been a fan of plants, but I wanted him to learn about the value of being a nurturer. We planted some seeds, and they started to grow beautifully. Then, one day, he decided to drown one of the plants. He didn't realise that giving them too much water would kill them. We couldn't plant in that soil for weeks. We had to wait for the water to drain out because nothing was growing. It made me think about the environment's value and the importance of surrounding yourself with the right people: people who bring out the best in you and remind you of what matters. Their language is different. Their perspective will challenge and provoke your growth. The seeds buried deep within the soil of your spirit need fertile soil. Only defunct seeds are barren in fertile soil. It is a tragedy to be surrounded by the potential for growth but not to be receptive to it.

Stained by the trauma of past events. Punishing yourself by replaying the scenes over and over again in your mind. Trapped in the space of dysfunction so that you are unable to recognise the potential that surrounds you. They're waiting for you. Make yourself available to life and unavailable to dead things. You will see the impact that this transformational mentality has on your marriage, your children, your family and everything that surrounds you. Everything around you will come to life. You will be a woman and a wife of incredible impact. Nurture your soul by protecting what you expose yourself to and who you allow into your space.

This Is Growth Territory

Sometimes you just need to coach yourself: *hey girl, we only thrive, heal and grow here.* Get used to being your own best friend before you try to make new ones or force your husband into that space. Love yourself and cheer for yourself. Nurse your own soul and be your own superhero. That's the space where you start to protect your value and understand the magnitude of your worth. I understand how hard it is to move forward when you're cheated or cheated upon. I have been cheated with many relationships in my past. Some that I thought would last a lifetime.

Did I go and blast them on social media? No. Did I cry? Yes. Did I hurt? Of course. Even in the broken places, I found the strength to shift my focus. I surrounded myself with and focused on my blessings. Some days were harder than others. When it all got too much, I would confide in and ask for support from those closest to me. I am proof that it gets better. Sometimes relationships and friendships leave scars to remind us to learn and grow from the pain that we have been through. It's okay for it to take a little more time to grow past your pain as long as you put yourself in an environment that will give you the space to do so.

"As iron sharpens iron, so a friend sharpens a friend."[62] The right company will bring out the best in you. In your weakest moments, seek friendship and companionship that will strengthen you. When

---

[62] Proverbs 27:17 (NLT)

surrounded by the right company, they will light up your soul – they will *not* pick at your wounds. They will give your heart reassurance that there are angels literally living on this earth that are sent to aid your healing and growth. Protect and nurture those relationships because they will be the making of you.

Nurturing Your Healing

I would love to tell you that every single wound that we receive in life can be completely healed. Almost as if the infliction of the pain never happened. Sometimes this is true, but some situations change you forever. We never leave them the same way we entered them. You may look, seem or even sound the same, but some experiences draw a new version of ourselves into fruition. We have no choice but to become a new version of a person that we never knew was dormant within us. Stirred up as a product of the pain, growth and lessons that our experiences have handed us. The question is, are you paying attention?

Are you learning from those experiences, or will you need a retake of those lessons again? The cuts leave scars to remind us that we have survived what was supposed to kill us. They also remind us of what we had to go through to become who we are today. You were never meant to forget or even push it to the back of your mind as a coping mechanism. You need to dig up the secrets that you've buried deep under the surface of your soul. Examine yourself. Embrace the wisdom that your circumstances are trying to reveal to you. It is only then that you will find true healing and growth. You've spent too long wishing away the very thing that is going to catapult you into the greatest freedom, self-revelation and exuberant life that you have ever experienced. It will take you from just existing to living fiercely and unapologetically.

Only you can choose to push for this extraordinary version of your-self. Even God is waiting for you to take up the power that He has given to you; use it to walk through the pain of your difficult experi-ences. Be bold enough to push through until you ignite a fire within you that burns away the potency and grip of your circumstances. You will get to the place where you are thankful for what was built out of the pain. You will know that those situations (the betrayal, the feeling of being cheated) have lost their grip when you can revisit those situa-tions through new lenses and see those situations through God's eyes. It's when you can think thoughts like: *yes, that used to hurt, but that was me – then! Now, I have other battles to fight and greater lessons to learn.*

You're not shying away from the pain of the past, and you're ex-pectant about the treasures of wisdom that your future holds. It won't always be easy to work past the pain. Sometimes the healing may be slower than you would like. Honestly, you may have to fight harder than you've ever fought before. The challenge may be that the situa-tion keeps recurring. Maybe your husband keeps cheating or won't leave. Maybe your loved ones continue to cheat you over and over again, and you find it difficult to work out where the boundaries should be. Take your time with yourself. Pay close attention to the situation. Work out what you are meant to be fighting for or against. Once you know, then you must fight with a veracity that you have never fought with before. Take your liberty by force. Do I mean being physically forceful or aggressive? Nope. Do I mean being vindictive or malicious? Absolutely not. I mean having the determination required for closure and healing. I mean being strong in spirit. Assertive. Estab-lishing boundaries. Speaking more firmly and resolutely. Drawing upon your earthly assignment from God and boldly walking in it. Your purpose is tied to the Christlike woman you are becoming: that un-breakable woman of steel. Fight for her!

Finding Clarity

You need clarity on the woman that you want to become. You have to be intentional about the steps that you are going to take to become her. What do you need? The right circle of friends? The right resources? Spiritual growth? Be intentional. I, too, had to take this journey years ago, and this journey led me to you. At the time, I wrote a series of letters to myself, and I described the kind of woman I wanted to be. I want to share an excerpt of those letters in the hope that you will start to visualise and work towards the woman that you need to be.

- I am focused.
- I do not gossip.
- I do not waste time.
- I inspire and bring out the best in others.
- I do not quit.
- I mean what I say.
- I reflect Jesus CHRIST in everything that I do.
- I am a blessing and encouragement to everyone around me.
- My enemies and haters do not deter me from my Divine cause.
- I love others, regardless.
- I am giving, innovative, strategic, discerning, insightful, wise, confident, aware of my worth.
- I am not afraid to be alone.
- I do not suck up to people.
- I do not use people for what they have – my priority is caring for who they actually are.
- I am a catalyst for Divine change, a Glory carrier and a wonder to the whole world [of the power of God].

Today, I have deliberately become the woman that I have described, to the letter. Who I have become has attracted people of my kind, mind and likeness – like the version of me given above. I killed the old version of me by embracing the true person that I have been destined to become all along. I am deliberate about protecting her (or should I say "me"). I put myself in spaces that feed and nurture me, and I am unapologetic about it. In the same sense, I encourage you to nurture and protect your growth and healing. Be unapologetic about it because it will transform so many other lives around you also. There will be so many things and people from your past who will fight you to stay as you are.

Only dead things remain in the space you're in right now. Stagnancy. Spiritual diseases. Infections. Poison. You have to push yourself to fertile spaces. Healing. Growth. Progressive. You will feel renewal ripple through the core of your innermost being. It will shatter you with revelations and rebuild you with God's Divine light. The world will see the change, and your husband will also see the transformation.

Most importantly, you will finally feel the pieces come together. Trust, hope and healing will fall into place. It will be so much clearer why you had to journey this way.

Prayer and Meditation

Let's pray and reflect using the mirror.

Dear Heavenly Father,

Thank you for being so close to my broken-ness. You see all of the things that I mourn and feel an immense sense of loss for. Please be my anchor when I feel like I have nothing more to give. Shine your light of hope on the dark, broken places of my spirit. Please guide me to my healing, my hope and my bright future. Show me how to truly let go, forgive and be free from the pain that I have endured in my marriage and friendships. I ask that you make me an embodiment of love to those who have hurt me.

In Jesus' name, Amen.

TWELVE

WHEN MARRIAGE IS KILLING YOU

§

Parasites are everywhere. He may call himself "Christian" and know the Bible off by heart. You may be unfortunate enough to be married to one. Deep down, you know what I'm talking about – bloodsuckers. Draining every ounce of life from anything that it touches. Such is the silver-tongued vampire's deception that they will even deceive you into thinking that it is your fault that you have been abused. They will manipulate you, misuse and abuse you until you are a shadow of your former self. Mentally, emotionally, spiritually and even physically destitute. A desert empty of all the life that once overflowed from within you.

It doesn't matter what you do to appease or please him; his attacks intensify. You've been hoping for change for such a long time, and change has never come. *Maybe it's my fault*, you've said to yourself over and over again, and you've been determined to make it work. He is a broken man with pieces missing that only God can find. Nothing that you could possibly do will make him complete. He has to choose to allow God to do that for him, and he has to *want* to change. The change must be seen in his actions and not just come from his mouth. It takes time to observe those changes, and it may take a long time to see the fruits of his penitent heart. Don't risk losing the last pieces of your heart in a game that you lost a long time ago. You know the truth. Maybe you made a bad call from the moment that you said: "I do." Maybe he was so brilliant at hiding his ugly behind his silver tongue, and as the years went by, it became clear who he really was.

All you know is that staying in your marital home is a bad idea because you literally may not survive if you do. Maybe it will be his hands that make the final blow, or maybe, it will be yours. Maybe you feel like you are close to a mental break, and if he says another word, then you will *crack*. Maybe the abuse is not about what he does but what he doesn't do. It's all dangerous and shaky ground. It's a foundation that cannot stand the test of time.

I remember the pain in my mother's eyes as my father tightened his grip around her neck. "Daddy!" I shouted as a wave of fear washed over me. I was confused, scared and in immense distress. My mum had rushed us into the church kitchen for a quick snack before heading to the church service. I can't remember what I said, but I remember Mum being preoccupied as she pulled me into the kitchen. I hit the doorpost and yelped in response. My dad came rushing towards her and threw her against the wall, hands around her neck.

The previous incident was long forgotten and, in its place, something I will never forget: the rage in his eyes. His justification was his protection of his daughter, but that moment made me aware of how dysfunctional their marriage had been.

I was petrified that he would kill my mother, and I was also powerless in preventing that from happening. At the sound of my distress, he jumped away from my mother, who was visibly shaken. I don't remember much more about the situation, but I do remember how well my mother did in hiding the abuse she suffered within her marriage up until that day. Even though my parents were separated for most of my life, that was the first time I had seen my dad put his hands on my mum. From then onwards, I noticed how she would shuffle reverently to her house's front door at his abrupt call, "Woman!" He never called her by her name. She never challenged him for it. I despised the fact that she was intimidated by him. There was always an air of predator and prey whenever they were in a room together. She seemed broken by him. It confused and frustrated me. I loved him because he was my dad, which was the confusing aspect, but I resented how he treated my mother. I took on so much of her pain, but I didn't want to burn bridges with Dad.

Children are more aware than we think. They also take on more than we think they do. I know that I took the weight of it all on my shoulders, because from then onwards... I grew up. Fast. No man would treat me like that. I would be fierce and independent like a lioness. I would never shrink back. Ultimately, what impresses me to this day is my mother's resilience. She was so broken in spirit for many years. She spent a lot of time trying to get away from my dad. Living in hostels with three children. Out of a job, not sure about her future but determined to change the narrative from surviving to thriving. She stands taller and bolder. Her prayers light every soul on fire. Although I still love my dad, I am incredibly inspired by how my mother fought to triumph today. Not concerned about being in relationships with any men but in love with Jesus. A giver. A loving soul. "She laughs without fear of the future."[63]

---

[63] Proverbs 31:25 (NLT)

We all deserve to be that woman. Like my mother and this proverb, we should all laugh without fear. No more looking over your shoulder. No more sleepless nights. No more worry – just joy and expectancy. Your best days are ahead of you. All you have to do is raise your expectancy level.

Victim to Victor

In my mother's words…

When I met my ex-husband, I was very young and vulnerable. It was all new. I felt that I needed to be taken care of. I came from a big family, and the attention of my ex-husband was liberating. The thought of someone wanting me to be theirs, taking an interest in me and being overwhelmed by what I thought was his love was an emotion that I couldn't resist. I was charmed by him. I was eager to leave home. Yearning for attention. Overlooked. Drowned out. My mistake was that I got married so quickly that I could not see the red flags in our relationship. We then went on to have three children, and during that time, our relationship was extremely turbulent. I felt alone in my marriage. There were so many hard days where I couldn't see the end in sight. My fuel to survive was prayer. Connecting with my community and other victims of abuse carried me through. I never knew that my daughter observed so much about my marriage, and I thought that my daughter was unaware due to her being so young and innocent. The situation that she has described above was the first time that my ex-husband had been physical towards me, but the verbal abuse was constant from the beginning of our marriage.

Over time, I began to see a pattern of abusive behaviour that was not improving or changing. A lack of care or concern for my

*pain. I knew that I shouldn't be in this relationship when I rec-
ognised that the behaviour pattern weakened me. I was afraid of
what he would do, but I was also afraid of what I would do to
survive. I knew that I had to leave for the sake of us both. After I
had my youngest child in the hospital, I remember promising myself that I would never go back. I concluded that this was not good
for me and that this was going to destroy me. After I had decided
that my marriage was finally over, I was fearful that he would
come after me. I knew that it would be difficult because we had
three children together. We had already started to build a life as
a family, but I decided that I would rather die trying to escape
than die staying in the marriage. Living in fear for my life, happiness and being permanently lost was no way to live. When
you're (verbally) beaten without a bruise and when every word
that comes from his mouth breaks you, you know that you cannot
stay in the marriage. It's a tough and painful decision to make,
but I chose to make the decision to live.*

*Looking back, I realise that I was in a desperate and broken
state when I left the marriage. I was relieved to close that chapter
of my life, and I felt that I had finally broken free from the pain
of my marriage. There were so many highs and lows during that
period. I didn't realise that when I married him, I would be united
with his world of chaos. However, when we separated, I was able
to break away from all the oppression and pain.*

*I cannot describe the weightlessness that I felt when my mar-
riage was over. When I began to ask myself, how was this serving
me? The answers gave me the courage to leave the relationship.
Over time my relationship with God was rebuilt. I found the
strength to leave because I had no other choice but to throw the
whole of my emotional weight on someone stronger than myself —*

God. Instead of wallowing in self-pity, I shifted my focus to help-
ing others. I helped the helpless, I supported other members of my
family, I spent a lot of time with God. I literally took the focus
off of me. I had great support from my church community and my
family. I found joy in seeing others find happiness. I transformed
my home from a place of abuse to a sanctuary for others who were
abused (in the same or similar predicament). I became aware of
my own strength. I felt empowered by standing my ground. With
every day that I resisted his plight, I was strengthened and believed
I could do this. I began to have structure; the sense of drifting
lifted. My direction became clearer, my finances improved. I came
from a council flat (and benefits) to owning properties. I travelled
more, I got a great job, but more than that, I found peace. I found
me. I stepped out of just existing, into purpose.

There Are So Many Ways That He Can Break You...

It was difficult to know that the man that you opened up the depths of
your soul to would be the same person that broke you. It could happen
in a moment or over a long period. Maybe you saw it on the horizon
or were blindsided by it. Maybe the signs were always there, or he just
changed overnight. Abuse takes so many forms. Maybe it was subtle.
Was he deceitful enough to stop you from realising that you were the
victim?

You will know that you have been the victim based upon the effect
that it is having on you. It could be as a result of the look he gives you,
the words he says or the way that he touches you. The way he makes
you feel ashamed, but no matter how much you try, you just can't
understand how his rage is somehow your fault. He can be so charm-
ing in one moment, and in the next, he's your worst nightmare. How
about the information that he chooses to withhold? It's *his* money, so

you have no right asking about it, right? Or is it in the way that he controls your money or identification? Did he say that he's helping you manage it all properly because you're not responsible enough? Or was it in other words? How about the way that he tries to alienate you from your friends and family? For some reason, he doesn't like any of your friends and family. Or even how he controls the management of your medication?

The red flags are everywhere, and you have ignored them for so long. Your loyalty and love for him have blinded you from what is right in front of you. You're not going crazy, and it's not your fault. The nature of your marriage is toxic, and it is not loving or biblical. It's a myth to believe that God wants you to stay in a marriage that is *literally* killing you. You are God's child first. A rare and precious gem and of great value to Him. Whatever issues your husband has should not take away every ounce of the life that God has placed within you.

Love in its very nature is kind. When you stand before God and man, you make a vow that promises that your marriage will be filled with love and that you will be cherished. Any abuse of that vow is an abuse of the covenant that you both have made to one another. See your value through God's eyes. You are a lioness, and like my mother said (as a woman who has triumphed over tremendous pain in her life), you will die if you stay where you are. You have so much life, wisdom and strength to give. God will clear your path, give you the strength to get past this and heal your pain if you just make the first step.

To abuse something means to go against the proper function of something. For something to be misused, it must first, have had an original use. In Chapter 3, *Who Am I… Again?*, we talked about purpose, worth and boundaries. I believe that everything that you have received on these issues will have a great impact on your journey out of abuse. Recognise your value and walk in it. You are worth more than diamonds. However, I can tell you that until the year 3000, but if you don't walk, talk and act like you know your function, you will die misused, abused, ill-functioning and completely unaware of the treasures that God has given you.

You have to fight for your value. Push through the dirt of your situation and allow the rays of Divine purpose to cascade over you. Maybe you've never known what your purpose was. I've been there. It's scary and alienating to live a life floating, like a ship without direction. Ask the question that you seek. *Why am I alive? What is my purpose?* Ask God questions, and you will receive answers to questions that you never realised that your heart was asking. Be completely open to receiving answers and do not worry about the answers not being what you expected: "Seek and ye shall find."[64] Position your heart to receive the answers that you need. God says, "You will seek Me and find Me when you search for Me with all your heart."[65] His presence is the space where healing begins and is completed. He is where you draw strength to war for everything that He has invested in you. Partner with God, and you will find the strength because, in our weakness, His strength is perfected.

Healing

How do you heal from scars that you cannot see? When words are spoken, where is the evidence of the damage that they have caused? The slamming of a fist is not the only thing that can kill. A broken soul is just as deadly. Hearts that refuse to heal can, in so many ways, kill quicker than a knife. Could it be that his deadly influence has coiled

---

[64] Matthew 7:7-8 (KJV)
[65] Jeremiah 29:13 (NKJV)

around your soul? Is your silence fuelling his strength? Your inability to cry for help has kept you in a state of spiritual paralysis. You may not realise it, but there are weights and secrets you have been carrying that do not belong to you. The torment, suffering and agony may actually belong to your husband. Maybe he has managed to make you feel that you deserve the abuse? Has your marriage taken a slow descent into chaos? Or was your relationship toxic from the beginning? The power plays, games, isolation and pain just rotated and left you feeling like you were stuck on a not-so-merry go round. You just want to get off, break free and be stronger, but you don't know how. Craving clarity but stuck in your own personal and mental chaos. A maze inside your mind that leaves you without an exit. It's hard to know where to start and when to let go.

Start with yourself…

The confusion intensified over time, coiling a crippling web around your mind. The spiritual concoction of fear, confusion and dependency lulled you into a paralytic slumber that has held you in the most dangerous position awaiting your end. Could there be a part of you secretly hoping that one day that final blow would erase everything? The fight, the ride and especially the pain. Then, most strangely, you feel like you would be free: no more struggle, no more fear, just an end. The truth is that you just want the pain to stop. You crave clarity and peace. Maybe his words have been so intensely damaging that you wished that he would hit you. You feel like the aggressive and violent touch of his hand would be kinder than the vitriol that comes from his mouth. Or does he make you feel guilty when you don't hand over the cash, gifts or when you don't want to be intimate with him? Are you in constant fear, and you just don't know how, when or if he will explode one day? What will you do if he does lash out and there is nowhere for you to go?

Abuse comes in so many forms, and sometimes you can be completely unaware that it is happening. One of the biggest signs is the strong sense of bewilderment. Someone who has been abused once told me, "He can be an angel one minute and then a demon the next." His ability to change can leave you with a strong sense of confusion. Maybe deep down, you're hoping that he will be as radiant, doting and loving as he was in the beginning. Maybe there are days where you see glimpses of the man that you fell in love with. Every time he touches you, kisses you or is intimate with you. The confusion has mounted. I can almost hear you thinking, *weren't these the same hands that just tried to break me? Wasn't this the same mouth that violated the broken places of my soul? He loves me?* I can almost hear you saying to yourself, *it will change.* Or, *today, he seems better, calmer, nicer. If I can just hold out for the "good" days.*

You mean the days when he's a little less frog – the days when he's a little more prince?! What will the price be? How many hits do you have to take before you get past the painful, hard days? Will you survive the dark days until you get to the brighter days? It just takes a harder blow, a darker mood, a more menacing glare to take you over the edge. Maybe there will be repercussions when you leave.

Maybe your freedom will come at a price. Maybe your finances, children, career, extended family or even quality of life will suffer. You are not alone, and you can rebuild again. God is with you every step of the way. Every single day that you stay, you are subconsciously telling yourself that you deserve the abuse. Maybe you even tell yourself that you deserve to die. You have missed out on one invaluable factor… that God took great detail in moulding and sculpting every aspect of your beauty. He gave you dormant strength, incredible gifts. He gave you a unique map of greatness. His Divine plan for your life has always been bigger than you could ever conceive in your mind, heart and soul. If you could see all the amazing things that were waiting for you on the other side of this painful situation, then you would not hesitate to break away and begin the journey to a future so bright that it would eclipse the pain of the life that you're living right now.

Somehow, you've allowed your husband to distract you from a greater Divine purpose in life and to bring you to a halt in every possible way. He's caused you to be alienated from the abundant life that God so carefully and lovingly planned for you. You are a Queen that has been drawn into the mire of someone else's mess. No matter how many times he tries to convince you that it's *your* mess, that's an absolute lie. Nothing that you could ever do is deserving of abuse. His hand pounding your face is not your fault. His abusive words are not your fault. This kind of deceit is designed to take you away from all the mind-blowing things that God has prepared for your future.

> *No eye has seen, no ear has heard,*
> *and no mind has imagined*
> *what God has prepared*
> *for those who love him.*
> **—1 Corinthians 2:9 (NLT)**

Finding Joy

God literally wants to BLOW. YOUR. MIND with the level of joy that He is waiting for you to tap into. Only you can take steps to complete freedom. No one else will make that call for you. I am not saying that this is defined by getting a new husband or lots of fancy things but definitely with the freedom, joy and contentment that you will feel once you are completely (mentally, emotionally, spiritually and physically) healed from the pain of this situation. Realign your focus to the eventuality that you will be better – so much better than the position that you are in right now. Begin to believe that you have the power to get unstuck. This mentality has kept you in a situation that is sucking every ounce of life out of you. Stuck in your mind. Stuck in his grasp. Stuck in your pain. Stuck in your secrets, his secrets and your silence. His mistreatment of your property, person, life, values, faith and kindness shows that he is blinded to the wonder of what is in front of him. You are a wonder, but you have to accept that it is not up to you to reveal it to him. You have to take ownership of your value and establish the boundaries.

Abuse tarnishes and stains the mind. It can even leave devastation that is almost impossible to remove. I said *almost*. That's why it takes all the fight you have within you to claw your way out from under the clutches of abuse. Many people don't have the strength to make it out, but you certainly do. I believe in you. I know that you have what it takes with God on your side. The odds will always be in your favour. You are ROYAL. GOLD. SPLENDID. I know that there are lives that will be greatly and positively impacted by the lessons you have learnt from this experience. You just have to get out of the dirt first.

JOURNAL

- How did I get here?
- Do I have a history of being in abusive relationships?
- Think back to your childhood: were you brought up in an abusive family or home?

How you were brought up has an influence on your lifestyle in this present day. Our childhood environment, lessons and company can profoundly impact us subconsciously and consciously. So, what are you consciously aware of? What habits and inaccurate lessons have guided you down the path that has led you into this abusive relationship? Was there something in your past that broke and blindsided you, causing you to blindly believe that this relationship would save you?

Sometimes the answers to the decisions lie in our past experiences, our character and reverberate in the present day. They're all pieces to a greater puzzle. The only way to get clarity is to be brutally honest about the journey – about the things that were your fault and the things that you had no control over. You had no control over the abuse that happened to you all those years ago. You had no control over the lessons that taught you to value yourself a little less when you were a child. You have complete control over who you surround yourself with and what happens to you now. Regardless of how much others may want you to believe that you don't. You have a right to decide to leave the table when you are no longer served the things you need. It's up to you to say, "No. No, thank you," and head for the first exit.

Brokenness is another factor that can mean you enter a relationship too soon or without really considering the costs of the decision. Have you been so broken that you felt like this relationship was going to be the perfect antidote? Did it turn out to be a more vicious poison than the relationship that you left behind? What could you have done differently to protect yourself from such a deadly situation? What was it about him that appealed to you in the first place? (Have a look at my mum's example earlier in this chapter; like her, were you attracted to the care and love that your husband initially showed you?) Take your time and reflect. Write in your journal if you have to. Put a bookmark on this page and think back. Think back on the little (or big) indicators that this relationship was not right for you. Believe it or not, there are always signs. People always give away the nature of their character when they open their mouths. Sometimes they reveal their nature before they even open their mouths. The question is, are you paying attention?

> *Out of the abundance of the heart, the mouth speaks.*
> **—Matthew 12:34 (NKJV)**

He told you who he was, but you were not listening. Maybe it was because your pain was screaming so loud that you thought being with him would make it stop. Maybe you simply were not paying attention. Take the time now. Pay attention to the indicators, because this will teach you all the lessons that you need. As you begin your journey to self-discovery and awareness, the biggest revelation about who you are will happen. You can be your own hero or your worst enemy based on the decisions that you make now. It all fundamentally depends on whether you can win the war inside your mind. One of the characteristics that will hold you in a state of paralysis (and suffering) is denial. Not being able to recognise that love doesn't try to put you in harm's way.

Love Is...

Can you honestly say that your relationship is the embodiment of this definition of love?

> *Love is patient and kind. Love is not jealous or boastful or proud or rude.*
> *It does not demand its own way. It is not irritable, and it keeps no record of being wronged.*

> *It does not rejoice about injustice but rejoices whenever the truth wins out.*
>
> *Love never gives up, never loses faith, is always hopeful…*
>
> **—1 Corinthians 13:4-7 (NLT)**

You may offer all of these virtues to him, but if love is one-sided, then your marriage is likely to fail. This scripture highlights that love is not destructive. It's constructive. Love should build and strengthen you. It's okay for you to love him from a distance, especially if it keeps you alive. You are not giving up on him by creating a safe distance. You can pray for him and wish him all the best… from a distance! I think you're getting the importance of distance by this point. You can't help yourself and heal yourself when you're in such close proximity to someone unwilling to do the work. "Bad company corrupts good character."[66] Removing yourself from toxic situations will give you clarity and perspective. It also removes the influence of the people that are having negative effects on you.

JOURNAL

- Can you identify situations where abuse has taken place?
- What was said? What was done?
- How did it make you feel?
- How does it affect you in the day to day?

---

[66] 1 Corinthians 15:33 (NLT)

The aim of answering these questions is to gain clarity. Also, if there are any legal implications, then you also have the opportunity to specify clearly what was done. This is clear evidence of the abuse that you have experienced.

The Many Forms of Abuse

Are you able to recognise when you are being abused? Sometimes abusers operate in the most subtle ways. You may not even recognise it as abuse. Some of the different forms of abuse are: spiritual, physical (also can be recognised as domestic violence), neglect or self-neglect, financial, emotional, mental and material.

Spiritual Abuse

One of the less common aspects of abuse is spiritual abuse. More and more light has been shed on this form of abuse in recent years, but it's important to share how spiritual abuse can affect a marriage.

Spiritual abuse operates under the appearance of religion and spirituality. This also includes the Christian faith. Spiritual abuse includes being humiliated or harassed and can cause psychological trauma. Spirituality and religion for self-centred, non-religious and ideological outcomes can also be classified as abuse. How does this relate to wifehood? The abuser may use spirituality for the benefit or justification of other abusive behaviour; for example, financial abuse, physical, sexual and so on. You can guard against spiritual abuse by understanding the Bible's interpretations in the context of your faith. Develop discernment and awareness by learning and studying the Bible for yourself. Guard against false interpretations.

For example, if you're under pressure to have sex whenever your husband feels like it based on his interpretation of the Bible, then your understanding of the scriptures will help you to refuse his demands.

Remember that rape happens when you have been clear that you don't want sex, whether you're married or not. Also, recognise that rape can happen under the guise of spirituality. Abuse can happen under that same guise. You have a right to say "no". You should not be made to feel guilty if you don't want sex. It is a sad thing when a man wants to satiate his own needs without consideration for the woman that he has promised to nurture and protect.

Sex within marriage should be a beautiful climax to a journey of being wooed. Romance shouldn't be lost because you've been married for 25 years. The care, love and nurture should grow over time. Sexual intimacy is a product of that growth. I love being sexually intimate with my husband, but there may be reasons that I can't or won't do it on occasions. We both have to respect each other's desire not to be intimate on occasions when we cannot be. No scripture pressurises couples to have sex whenever they are unable to. However, many scriptures have been taken out of context. The emphasis within scripture is always on mutual agreement. Marriage is about honour, respect, care, tenderness and love. All of which should be evident whether you're intimate or not. Fundamentally, balance is everything within marriage. Intimacy, in every sense, strengthens marriage. The absence of games (i.e. withholding for punishment or pressure to be intimate) removes power plays. Removing power plays is a sign of humility and genuine respect and will contribute to a flourishing marriage. In other words, if your husband gets upset, you have the conversations and move on. Resentment is a waste of time. Say whatever it is that you need to say and move on. Heal. Be as weightless as you possibly can be.

Physical Abuse

Physical abuse is what it says on the tin, but what does it entail? Did you know that physical abuse includes scolding, misuse of medication, force-feeding, making someone purposefully uncomfortable (i.e. removing duvets and leaving windows open), restraint (i.e. tying someone to a chair)? The category for physical abuse covers a wide scope. Do your research and learn about what is okay and what isn't. Also, ask yourself the question, *how is something making me feel?* Does it make you feel afraid or intimidated? Do you feel like you have to walk on eggshells around the person? Do you feel like you are not allowed to speak your truth?

Sometimes your feelings can be the biggest indicator that there is more going on in your situation than you're actually aware of. Abuse covers a wide area and can have severe repercussions physically and mentally. There are so many different forms of abuse, and it's not possible to cover every single area of abuse without this book turning into something resembling a dictionary! Other than the abuse mentioned here, I talk more about financially abusive behaviours in Chapter 10, *Money Matters*.

Emotional Abuse

Emotional abuse can be quite common in marriage. Belittling, intimidation, gaslighting, patronising, social media shaming, criticism, and even refusing to be pleased is emotional abuse. It's difficult to guard your heart against something when you are unaware that it's happening to you. Emotional abuse is sometimes so subtle that even the abuser may be unaware that they are doing it. That's why it's important to evaluate how someone is making you feel and speak up – whether to them or to someone that can help you address the situation.

Marriage is supposed to be a safe place. Still, if you are experiencing emotional abuse, it can be just as damaging as the other categories of abuse previously mentioned. It can affect your mental health and is extremely tormenting. Especially if you're uncertain that it is happening. To be trapped in an emotionally damaging marriage can have devastating long-term repercussions. It's the kind of secret that is too much to bear. Shame and fear should not hold you in a space that can make you a shadow of your former self. That's too high a price for you to pay for genuinely loving him.

One Thing Leads to Another

Different categories of abuse go hand in hand. One form of abuse could lead to another. For example, your partner may initially force you to isolate yourself from loved ones and eventually escalate to hitting you. It's not always covert. It is also common for abusers to see how far they can go before things escalate. What you allow will continue. Be alert and careful. Remember, it's never too late to establish and enforce boundaries.

It is crucial to shed light on abuse and how easily it can operate within the shadows of your marriage. Especially when everything seems beautiful on the outside, but secretly – it's decaying on the inside. Sometimes the masks hide infectious wounds that continue to grow and fester. No matter how much you try to fix it without getting outside help, it just spreads and becomes out of control. Trying to heal and keep the façade will become increasingly difficult over time. Eventually, the mask will start to slip, and ugly will come out in various ways.

By this point, there will be no strength left for you to recover from the devastation. Why not rip the band-aid off now? Clarity and truth are the standpoint by which a new path to healing can be forged.

I truly believe that you need to recognise that this is not your fault, regardless of what your friends, family and confidantes say, regardless of what the pastors say, regardless of what your neighbour's mama and her dog says. You know the pain that you have had to push through. The truth belongs to you and God. If God is not condemning you for surviving the trauma and grafting your way to healing, then you can be at peace.

Here, I have focused on some of the forms of abuse that relate to marriage and faith to highlight how easy it is to experience abuse so that you will find healing. Do the research. Learn about what is and isn't appropriate. Pay more attention and ask yourself questions – even if you're afraid of the answers. Asking the right questions will give you the clarity you need to find direction out of this crippling situation. The questions must be self-focused to be as helpful to your situation as possible. They shouldn't be centred around your husband if you know for certain that he is abusive, because it will shift your focus to him and his needs/desires. How he would feel about you leaving the abusive relationship is not your priority or focus. Focus on questions like, *what is happening to my mind, spirit, body and emotions?* The questions in this chapter are designed to help you to become more aware of what is happening around and to you.

Stop Nursing His Demons

No scripture in the Bible condones or justifies abuse. In fact, every scripture goes against mistreatment and abuse (within and outside of marriage). In one scripture, it says: "It would be better for him if a millstone were hung around his neck, and he were thrown into the sea, than that he should offend one of these little ones."[67]

---

[67] Luke 17:2 (NKJV)

This scripture says that God values you so much that anyone who hurts you should be concerned about the weight of their decision to cause you harm. It speaks of your value to God and how much it hurts God to see you hurt. Does that mean that you should go and get a millstone and throw it over your husband's neck? No! Please don't even think about harming him. This scripture just emphasises that you are of the highest levels of value to God. You are literally the most valuable jewel on this planet. God wants to see you weightless with a joy that goes far beyond your comprehension.

Awaken to the truth and reality that the greatest love you will ever experience comes from God, who is the abundant life-giver. Let His transformative life pierce through the painful crevices of your soul to such an extent that you will never settle for a lesser love. There is absolutely no greater love than the love of the One who laid down His life so that you could receive His abundant life – Jesus Christ. This kind of love will be the blueprint and show you how to be receptive and open to love that is only of the same kind. Any other counterfeit simply will not be accepted. Why? Because only a love that radical, that true, that potent, will take you out of the ashes of your pain. Only that kind of love will spark a transformation within you that will allow you to outshine the pain.

About Your Mind...

With any form of abuse, the key to your survival starts in the maze of your mind. You have to simplify that maze to find clarity. Clear the fog. Gain direction within the space of your heart before you see it in the world around you. Feed your mind.

> *Finally, brethren, whatever things are true, whatever things are noble, whatever things are just, whatever things are pure, whatever*

things are lovely, whatever things are of good report, if there is any virtue and if there is anything praiseworthy – meditate on these things.

—Philippians 4:8 (NKJV)

Actively and deliberately seek good things in your life from every direction. Think about the things that you want to magnetise to you. Whatever you tell yourself is going to be your truth. Whatever you focus on will grow. Make yourself available to people that will uplift and strengthen you. Journal. Write down all the blessings that you already have or want to have in your life. Streamline your focus. Even when it comes to what you see on TV and the internet. Monitor how things are making you feel and make yourself available to the things that are going to build you.

I cannot emphasise enough the importance of seeking a counsellor, calling a helpline and joining a community that can support you on your journey to healing and recovery. Make time for reflection and meditation. Talk to God about the journey and be honest. If you feel like you hate your husband that day, tell God about it. He can handle and work with you from the space of the truth. If you're angry or scared, it's okay to pour out your pain before God. In fact, He absolutely loves it because that's what friends do. You truly have a friend in God. He loves it when we tell Him what we REALLY feel, not what we *think* we should feel. By letting it out before Him, you're allowing Him to take it.

Personally, I've done this so many times when my heart's been broken (and it has been broken so many times). I love Divine dialogue (prayer) because I know that God is the only one who can fix the mess in me. Because – let's be honest – if you dig deep, we have all been a mess that only God can clean up (on so many different levels and in so many different ways). He said, "all have sinned and fall short of the glory of God."[68]

We've all been a mess in one way or the other. He's always there and always available to help. How beautiful, right?! It just gets me every time that God is *actually* my friend! He's yours, too, if you're up for something greater! Does healing happen overnight? Who can really say how long it's going to take for you to heal? The healing journey is so different for so many people. Be patient with yourself as you nurture yourself to full recovery. Don't try to rush ahead but build yourself carefully. If you are in a life-threatening situation, then – run! Ensure your safety first, then build. God would never promise you abundant life, then force you to stay in a position that is a threat to your life. Gaining clarity on the journey ahead within the space of your mind will help.

JOURNAL

- How did I get here?
- Did I ignore the warning signs?
- Was my desire to be with him louder than the danger signals?
- What do I need to do to heal?
- What do I need to do to exit?
- What do I want/need for the next phase of my life?

---

[68] Romans 3:23 (NKJV)

These questions should have answers heavily centred around self-discovery, identity, knowing your standards and boundaries. I also explore these in Chapter 3, *Who Am I… Again?*

The journey to self-healing and self-discovery isn't an easy one. It takes great awareness of self and even more awareness of who God is and how He impacts your life. When the roots of pain run deep into the crevices of your soul, you're likely to react and operate from those places of pain without knowing it. Anything could trigger a reaction. It would be easy for someone to say or do something that could easily take you back to that place of immense pain. In that space of pain, what action would your reaction give way to? Self-defence? Retreat? Attack? Who would you become when those triggers are set off? Having someone to help you work through deep-rooted pain and the triggers will make an amazing difference to your recovery. Even if it's simply knowing you are not alone. Someone to counsel you through trauma, encourage and uplift you through the word. Prayer journals are great for inspiring dialogue with God. Therapy through hobbies and community also enriches the soul.

About Your Future

What does your future look like? How will you ensure that you are not vulnerable and exposed to the same abuse patterns in the future? (For example, will you change your environment, community, develop self-awareness using more resources like books, courses, networking, seminars etc.?) Maybe you'll make the personal choice of not dating for a dedicated term? Visualise your dream life as a possibility, even if you don't feel like it's possible at the moment. Your heart's desires are prayers to God to do what seems impossible. Even if it doesn't feel like it is possible for you to be happy, whole and free, your prayers are daring God to make it a possibility.

My mother's journey to the life of freedom that she lives now is due to her prayers and belief that there were better days ahead. She was one of the blessed ones who made it out, because so many women don't make it. I literally witnessed her push past dark days to live the life of abundance and freedom that she lives now.

You, too, can have a better and brighter future as a result of the decisions that you make right now. Your choices from the minute that you are aware are completely yours. You can't say that you didn't know or understand the weight of the decision to stay in the place of suffering that you are in now. So many people will be willing to stretch out their hands to support you on your journey. You just have to take it. There are nearly eight billion people on the planet! Somewhere is your tribe – a set of people that will support you when you want to give up on yourself. That will celebrate you when you get your win. They will cry with you when you feel overwhelmed by it all, and they will ride the waves with you. You just need to open your eyes to who they actually are. Some of them are around you already. You may have been shutting some of them out. You may have confided in some of them. You will know who they are and the value that they have in your life and season right now. Embrace them. Ask God to show you how to accommodate them, love them and LET THEM IN.

Queen, in this next season, I really want you to take care of yourself. Focus on your healing, laugh more, value enriching relationships that only build you up, don't feel an ounce of regret for walking away from anything that will hurt you. You've already had enough of that. Spoil yourself. Eat great food. Find yourself. Love yourself. Get to know God in a deep and life-transforming way. Ask God to show you how to be a blessing to others, and find and walk in your purpose. Pour out your pain and struggles before Him. Take in the details as you travel the world. Look for the beauty in everything. Create. Build on your hobbies or learn a new skill. Give birth to new visions, ideas and inventions. Love yourself and be your favourite company. Most of all – heal.

Why This Will Never Happen to You Again

If you have answered the questions within the previous segment honestly and taken in your answers, then the process will awaken the Queen within. When you observe a Queen's nature, you will notice that a Queen does not bow to her subjects, but her subjects bow to her. She sets the standard and the protocol. They roll out the red carpet for her, and when she enters a room, her presence electrifies the atmosphere because all eyes are on her. She is fully aware of her inner lioness. She knows full well that she is royalty and that there is no one else like her. Her tone, her poise and even the way that she distributes her attention speak volumes of her value. She is completely aware of her value and will never allow another to barter for it.

There is a Queen in you. She's waiting for you to tap into her. To live a life free of being controlled, free of fear and free of secrets. Adapt to your new royal ways and do not falter. Be so certain of your value that when your accusers and abusers see you, they will not recognise you. They will be stunned and in awe of you. They will wish that they had known your value and treated you in accordance with your *true* worth. Unfortunately for them, it will be too late because you are accustomed to a new way of thinking, doing and living. You know that where you came from is a place of lack, but where you are going is your eternal destination that overflows with abundant life.

Prayer and Meditation

Let's pray and reflect using the mirror.

Dear Heavenly Father,

Please help me to make the right choices for myself, my marriage and my relationships. Show me when to let go. Show me when the love that I am giving is not enough to keep me alive within my marriage. Give me the courage to face the future without my husband if it means staying alive. Lead me to the right people, resources and environment to receive the help that I need. May the truth of your word, the resources of this book and the choices that I make be the foundation upon which I can begin anew.

In Jesus' name, Amen.

THIRTEEN

LIFE AFTER MARRIAGE

§

I can imagine the feeling of dread that overwhelmed her as she stood at the doorpost of a room filled with a crowd of men. She knew that they would consider her unworthy of even being hundreds of yards within that vicinity, but she didn't care. She knew that she would be considered the lowest of the low, and what she was about to do was highly undignified. What she was about to do was unexpected and unorthodox, but He deserved it. She was once crippled by pain, and it shattered every aspect of her life, but this encounter had freed her in ways that she couldn't possibly imagine. He deserved her act of love, and she was going to pour it all out before Him.

Silently, she proceeded to take steps towards Jesus. The room's silence began to imitate hers as she edged her way closer and closer. She became more and more aware of the ointment in her hand. Holding it gently as she knelt before her King and Lord. Her eyes met His feet as she shook away thoughts of being unworthy and focused on one thing – her tears. They spoke of her pain and her joy. They spoke of her love and her freedom. They began to flow, and her head bowed closer. She dared not to look up as she continued to speak without words. The murmurs began around her, but she did not care. She leant closer and began to wipe her tears with her own hair.

Undignified. Open. Pure. These are the words that describe the nature of her form of worship. It was an act that many couldn't recognise because they had never experienced her pain. Her hair absorbed every tear, and she was almost satisfied with her expression of love. There was one more thing to do. She took the ointment that she had been holding so carefully and lavished it on His feet. Aware that He had not moved but determined to finish her expression of love, she emptied every drop. The men protested, but she honestly would have done it all over again. The level of her gratitude surpassed her shame. Gratitude to be alive, healed, even transformed by her encounter. After all, it only takes a moment to be transformed by the Master whom we call Jesus Christ.

The End of a Chapter

The journey may have been short, or it may have been long, but it was never easy to close this chapter in your life. Marriage was designed to be for a lifetime. However, for you, that wasn't the case. Maybe you were blessed to escape alive, or maybe it was an obvious and joint conclusion. However it ended, it's now out of your control. Like the woman who washed Jesus' feet, maybe you have experienced unspeakable pain from being in an unhappy marriage. A marital experience that has left you feeling worn, drained and broken. Like Mary, there may have been angst and uncertainty about the road ahead. The voices of those who are critical of your journey weigh heavily on your heart. It takes a supernatural level of bravery to step out anyway. To act even when others don't understand. That's exactly what Mary did. She stepped out because she understood that He was the only person who truly understood her. It's the same for you. Jesus is ready to be for you what He has been for Mary. A secret place to dwell. Shade. Protection. The safest place that you can pour your pain because only Jesus can meet you where you're at and take you to a place of complete liberty. Stripped of the mask and free of secrets. Only He has the power to do for us what we are unable to do for ourselves.

How do you move forward? How do you heal from the pain of the past? "When I was a child, I spake as a child, I understood as a child, I thought as a child: but when I became a man, I put away childish things."[69] There are things that children do that adults do not imitate because of their level of understanding. Their thought process is different. Their experiences are different, and their responses to an innumerable variety of situations are different. There's no way that you would see my mother rolling around on the supermarket floor because she didn't get her favourite chocolate. Firstly, that would be extremely unsightly. Secondly, she would probably pull a muscle. Thirdly, and much more importantly, her understanding is more mature than that of a child. She may understand that they just don't have that chocolate in stock or simply that we have to be okay because we can't always get what we want.

Before you were married, your understanding of your marriage was like that of a child. Marriage revealed excruciating and unbearable amounts of pain, but what it also gave you was understanding. Like an adult to your experiences, your power lies in your ability to see beyond your pain to the lessons and how they will equip you for the rest of your life. It is a sad state of affairs when life hands you crucial

---

[69] 1 Corinthians 13:11 (KJV)

lessons, and nothing is actually learnt from those experiences. Thank God for the lessons that you've learnt of yourself, your ex-husband and jointly, because now "you have put away childish things".

Your ability to share the children with your husband, not fight about trivial things and express kindness (wherever you can) speaks volumes of your growth. Your ability to be kind, loving and courteous also speaks highly of your growth. You can keep it together even if you're falling apart inside because better days are coming.

Instead of breaking down, focus all your energy on rebuilding. I have written this out of observing so many women go through the pain of marriage breakdown and wonder, *does God see me?* Does He see how hard you are fighting to stay alive and to move past your pain? It's been a rough road, and you haven't been sure who you could count on to push through the darkest days of your life to the Son. He sees you. He's with you, and He fights for you. Your only part to play is to partner with God. Depend on Him and hold onto your integrity. You will see that it was all worth it in the end.

Finding Healing After Marriage

What's holding you? Is it the fear of moving on? The resentment of all the things that he did that broke you – the regret of getting married in the first place? The pain can be raw and overwhelming, especially when the journey was so hard and rough. There can be so much shame and embarrassment because the breakup was so public. Maybe you've even got the indirect comment, "I told you it wasn't going to work." Or is it when people ask, "How is the family?", not realising that the family dynamics have changed. Shame can be crippling. You can find yourself impulsively wanting to explain to people what he did and why you are no longer together. Feeling yourself become uncontrollably shifty when the topic of your relationship arises in some form or another.

Shame is a weight that you don't have to carry. It's too heavy a load to allow the mistakes you've made to weigh you down for the rest of your life. You have a right to heal. You have a right to grow. Jesus said, "neither do I condemn you",[70] in response to the woman accused of committing adultery. He shut the mouths of those that wanted to throw stones when she was brought before Him. He removed her shame by highlighting that none of her accusers was without sin. Sometimes the person wanting to highlight the flaws in your character has "a plank in their eye".[71] Their mistakes are bigger than yours. I say this not to belittle or condemn them but to highlight that we are all on our own journey through life and with Jesus. Shame will have you stuck in a painful situation. Loathing yourself. Alienated from God. Hiding with festering wounds. He sees your wounds, and He wants you to heal completely and irrevocably. Your marriage didn't work out, but your life certainly will. You just have to gather your strength together. Cry if you must. Get curious about what would happen if you *really* believed, without a doubt, that you would get the best out of your life.

Your healing is dependent on where your focus lies. When a seed is sown, it is buried in the ground and rooted in darkness. Your marriage saw many seasons when you were buried in pain, and even now, you may still feel its residue. It takes the pressure of that darkness and pain for the seed to be transformed.

When the time is right, the seed outgrows the darkness. Even though the dirt and soil still remain, the seed grows tall and strong.

---

[70] John 8:11 (NKJV)
[71] Matthew 7:3-5 (KJV)

The seed becomes a plant that bears fruit and thrives in the light. In the same manner, the pain of your situation may not necessarily change. Your ex-husband may not become the person that you may have wanted him to be. The relationship may not improve, just like the soil that continues to surround the seed. However, *you* will grow. You will outgrow the pain. You will see the situation differently. You will become stronger, and like the plant, you will bear fruit. That means that you will flourish, shine and bless those that surround you. There is so much blessing that you will give birth to as a result of your pain.

That being said, if you are still bitter about what he did or didn't do, then your suffering will intensify. If you still want to make him feel the pain that you are feeling, then you will go round and round in circles endlessly. It will torment you, and you will turn every blessing around you into a curse. You don't have to go down that road. You can choose to allow your healing to transform your future. It will cause a light to radiate from your soul that will shock those who knew the old you. It's okay for the process to take a little time. While you are coming to terms with the transition, find solace in the fact that you have a friend that is more loyal and closer than a brother. Jesus wants to take all the pain, all the fear, all the uncertainty and replace it with complete peace. Embrace and cling to His peace. Will you have times where you struggle, cry or lash out? Maybe.

Transition is different for everyone. Sometimes, you may even feel numb, or possibly, look back and wonder why you bothered to go into that relationship in the first place. Everyone is different. You know how your journey has affected you, and you know the price you will have to pay to get out. I just want you to understand that, regardless of what you have been told or made to feel, you are not alone.

It may take a while, or you may wake up one day and feel like a weight has come off your shoulders. The court battles, adjustments to new living, parenting arrangements, new routines may be overwhelming at times. There may be times where you just don't want to get out of bed. You may want to smash something. You may have to live on pasta and ketchup for a while. You might have to go back to school or college. You may have to take that job that nobody wants. You may be smiling when, deep down, your heart is broken into a thousand pieces. You may want to share how you feel with others, but the words choke in your throat. You may feel crushed and broken. However, if you could just take a minute to see what you have managed to overcome, you would see that you are a fighter. You have gone through your darkest days and come out on the other side. You have amplified your voice and made it matter when it had been silenced for so long. What you don't realise is that you are about to hit your winning streak. Because, for the first time since you can remember, you're steering your own ship.

You are not alone. Just like Mary, God may seem still, but His gaze is focused on you. Your journey may be unorthodox and misunderstood by many, but He understands and is right there on the journey with you. While Mary (at the beginning of this chapter) was washing Jesus' feet, He was still. She was so focused on her adoration and her expression of love for Jesus that she paid no attention to His reaction or observation. In the same sense, it's easy for us to feel like God is ignoring our pain. It's easy to think that while we are doing our best, God hasn't taken any notice. The truth is, God isn't leaving you untethered in this critical time in your life. He is right here working with you through these tough decisions. He will work through it all with you if you just let Him. One thing that I will encourage you to do is to forgive yourself. Forgive yourself for all the wrong decisions that you have made. Forgive yourself for letting it come to this. Don't hold your mind, body or spirit in a state of unforgiveness of any kind. Let yourself go. Let him go. Release it all into God's hands and start making the journey towards a better you. Learn from your mistakes. Love yourself. Build on your relationship with God. Get a journal. Leave dating alone. Teach yourself something new. Make new friends. Travel. Live! Reconnect and discover yourself again. This time is too precious and crucial to be in a paralytic state. I am not saying that you don't feel the pain but work through it.

How are you? If no one has asked you recently, then I am asking you. Here's your opportunity to answer honestly. With all the turbulence you have recently been through, you may not have made yourself and how you feel a priority. You must be self-aware when you go through traumatic life experiences, so that you can gain clarity on how to heal. Honestly write the answer and look at what you've written. You may be surprised at what you discover about yourself.

Check-in with yourself regularly by asking yourself these questions as you journey through the new seasons of your life.

JOURNAL

- How is your mental state?
- How are you feeling emotionally?
- What do you need?

Kill the Cycle

I really believe that to truly heal, you have to uproot the old habits that have been toxic in your life. This could have started before your marriage, during your marriage or now. At some point, you have to be brutal when reflecting on yourself and the part that you played in the marriage. It could be how the marriage began or ended or what happened during the marriage. Look at your actions:

+ What were the triggers and causes of your actions?
+ Is there pain buried deep within you that has caused you to suffocate the blessings in your life?
+ Is separation a potential barrier to the blessings that will come into your life because of the pain that it has inflicted?

Kill the cycle. You don't want the pain of the past to spill onto your children and their children. You don't want someone to pay for the pain that they didn't cause. I am certain that you don't want to go into marriage after marriage with the same pain, the same triggers and find that there is no healing, no trust. All that's added is more pain. The cycle needs to stop with you. You have the strength to break it because God is with you in this. The fact that you are reading this is because He wants access. He wants to be the solution to the situation. He says, "For My yoke is easy [to bear], and My burden is light."[72]

It's no longer an unbearable weight when you hand it over to God. The weight was never designed for you to carry. When you surrender that heavy load over to God, the journey becomes more bearable, even though you may not be able to see the outcome right now. You're moving forward in faith and trusting that God can see the things that you cannot. Only God can see the destination, but He wants to guide

---

[72] Matthew 11:30 (AMP)

you to it. This is the stage in your life where you have the opportunity to learn to truly partner with God and allow Him to clear the path that you're taking.

Will You Ever Find Love Again?

This question may have crossed your mind from time to time, or maybe this question is too early to think about. I have one question for you. Do you have to *find* love? The mentality of taking things into your own hands can be a dangerous thing. Focus on your growth, self-nurture and development. Whether you feel like it or not, you're in the most vulnerable space that you could possibly be in right now. Being vulnerable blurs vision. You could make severely detrimental mistakes when your vision is blurred. New love should not be your focus right now but taking care of your mental, spiritual, emotional and physical needs.

Take time out for yourself and trust that the future is in God's hands. Are you lonely? Being alone can be scary. It's like the sound of your own mental voice is amplified. Sometimes, when you come face to face with yourself, it may seem daunting, but it's a great time to say, *hello self, let me get to know you again.* What's going on in your heart and your mind? What do you want to do more of? What new structures are you going to put in place to facilitate your own growth? You have a great opportunity to build on yourself again. That means saying no to that guy who keeps bugging you for a date, and meaning it. Stop stalking him online, reading his texts and fantasising about what your future could look like with him. Be okay with the fact your sex life no longer exists. Trust God with the bigger picture and the details of the bigger picture. Believe that God's promise stands when He says, "I know the plans I have for you says the LORD. They are plans for good and not for disaster, to give you a future and a hope."[73]

God always has and will always have you in mind. Whatever your future holds is completely in God's hands. It's great to know that we are taken care of by someone who has the best intentions for us in every aspect of our lives. When you absolutely embrace this truth, your life will become less lumbered with the weight of past hurt. Whoever is meant to be in your life will gravitate to you without effort, and they will bring only light and laughter. It won't be a fight, but it will be absolutely effortless. All because you're trusting the Author of your life to work it all out on your behalf. Notice that the focus here isn't on your ex. It's never about revenge, proving that you were better without him, replacing him or anything like that. The goal is your healing, a pure and sincere heart and growth. A life that brings honour to God and joy into your whole being. This all comes as a result of a focus shift. Be determined to love your ex-husband regardless of whatever broke you. He can't break you any further than he has, because your separation has removed his power from the situation. That being said, you can give him that power if you choose to go to war with him. Let it go. Heal.

About Your Wrongs

At some point, you will have to take ownership of the mistakes that you contributed to the relationship. You will need to exercise humility and the art of being contrite by saying, "I'm sorry." Have you ever thought that the reason that it keeps getting worse is simply due to not saying the words that your ex so desperately needs to hear? Do what needs to be done so that you can close this chapter of your life.

---

[73] Jeremiah 29:11 (NLT)

I say this because, regardless of the part that he played in the break-down of your marriage, he's human, and his pain matters. Just because he *might* have become your enemy doesn't mean that he is an enemy of God. We are all God's children, and we should always operate out of kindness and the spirit of love towards all His children. Plus, the words "I'm so sorry" are free! Interestingly enough, they can be so hard to say because they mean so much. You may not want to look weak, or you may not think that he deserves to hear it. I believe that it reflects how much of God's Divine DNA is in us when we don't try to give others what we think that they deserve. Of a truth, they actually might deserve punishment, but saying "I'm sorry" speaks so much about the beauty of your own heart. It speaks of your good intentions and the sincerity of your love. It speaks of wanting to see them be their best selves and receive everything good. Most importantly, it frees you of any obligation and any wrongdoing. It's telling of the new chapter that you are about to begin. He can't hold you in that place of pain any longer. You're opening a new door to a new season of your life. *I'm sorry* is also *goodbye. Goodbye pain. Goodbye, blame. Goodbye, shame. Hello, joy. Hello, strength. Hello, new growth.*

Do You Have a Place to Put Your Pain?

There is a fundamental difference between those who thrive and those who fall apart, and it's simply this: having a place to put your pain. You could give two people exactly the same situation to handle, and one will fall apart. Why? Because one was consumed by their pain, and the other knew how to let it go. I believe that pain has a physical effect on our wellbeing and longevity. Bitterness, resentment, anguish, depression, anxiety and fear are all intense emotions that can hold your whole being captive to silent suffering. It's like you're literally beating yourself up from the inside.

These emotions can naturally occur instantaneously. We're human and so will instinctively feel these emotions as trigger responses to situations. For example, if someone you love died, you would immediately feel anguish, but how is that emotional tension released in the years to come? If it's trapped in your body, mind and spirit, it becomes heavy. It shows in the lines on your forehead or the crow's feet etched in the corner of your eyes. Pain is inevitable but should not set up house in your being. You have to give it an exit to be weightless. Get into the habit of catching and releasing those emotions. By this, I mean that if you have a negative thought about your ex, those feelings will immediately come flooding in. That's where you take a deep breath and speak the complete opposite out loud, until your focus begins to shift to the truth of your words.

It doesn't end there. Be conscious and deliberate about how you think and feel. If you can master how you feel and if you can control whatever emotions have been controlling you, then you will be able to move from pain to power. The situation may not change, but you can get stronger because of the wisdom you apply to the situation. It's so important to learn how to put your fight in the right place. Fight for yourself. Fight for your dignity and for all the good that awaits you beyond this difficult season. It always helps to find a friend who can be vulnerable and bear the pain in your soul.

For those who don't find it easy to pray or just aren't used to it, I would say that a prayer journal will be the best first step. It helps to share what's on your heart with the only person that you need to become more intimately acquainted with to thrive. God is waiting for you, Queen. This is the place to release your pain. This is where you become weightless, and this is where you gain strength. Conquerors are built through an intensified prayer life. Not the kind that you do repetitiously or religiously, but deep, enriching dialogue kind of prayer. The kind of prayer that increases your sensitivity to the Holy Spirit. The kind where you listen as much as you speak. The kind where you pour out your pain through tears, groans or in whatever way that you need to express it. Whether by writing words, talking to a confidante, worshiping and praying – these are all great places to release your pain. It's okay not to have the words. It's okay to play an instrument, write a poem or paint. You may not have all the hours of the day to spend isolated and in your bedroom with God. You may have children screaming in your ear for most of the day or a demanding job that seems to take you away for all the hours that exist. That doesn't have to stop your chances of having an *intensified connection* with God. Turn on your worship music, sing a song of worship, go hide in the toilet if you can. He will make His presence known, and you will be so invigorated and enriched by every encounter.

We all have unique and innate ways to release our pain, but find the expression that works best for you to connect with God. This expression will also draw you closer to our Father. There's a place that your pain belongs, but it's never within you: "casting all your cares [all your anxieties, all your worries, and all your concerns, once and for all] on Him, for He cares about you [with deepest affection, and watches over you very carefully]."[74] He can handle it. He can handle your pain, hurt, hate, resentment, fear, anxiety and depression. Unleash all of it to Him. He is not deceived by your façade. He can see it all there. He wants your confidence in His ability to heal and transform the situation.

You have to be the one to let go. When you hold onto all these heavy loads, the only person who suffers is you. When you tell yourself, *I'm strong* or *I've got this*, then you only deceive yourself. The strongest

---

[74] 1 Peter 5:7 (AMP)

of us understands that to thrive in life, we have to be weightless. Weightlessness comes from knowing that there is a place to put all heavy weights. People that win battle after battle know that they must *catch and release* so that they can run light.

Catch

I see so many people refuse to acknowledge how they are feeling. "I'm fine," they say as their eyes well up. "I'm fine," as their bodies begin to convulse at the pressure of suppressing their emotions. "Honestly, I can handle it," they say up until the point that they collapse as a result of a nervous breakdown. The emotions, the pain and the weight are all there, but they're afraid to do what's necessary to get rid of it.

Firstly, acknowledge what you feel! *I'm angry. I'm in pain. I'm hurt.* Say what you feel, listen and see what you said. Feel the pain and acknowledge it. Stop hiding it somewhere deep within you. You will end up carrying it for years. It will come out on some poor soul that you absolutely don't mean to harm. You won't understand why but you won't be able to help it, because that emotion has lost its proper function. That emotion was there to help you come to terms with the change in the situation. If your hand is too close to the fire, then the pain will tell you that the heat is about to consume you. That is the proper function of the pain. It's the same with your emotions. They tell you how close you are to fire, but their purpose is never to consume you.

Your life should not revolve around the painful situation that you have experienced. You shouldn't still be talking about what Johnny did 20 years from now with the same angst in your tone. Your eyes should be void of tears 20 years from that circumstance. There's no way that you should allow resentment to rob you of years of your life. Learn from that situation. Don't let it take you out. Journey through the process of your pain. Let those feelings tell you what you need to know. You've been stung. Badly. It hurts. It's okay because it's only a *part* of the process.

Release

How are you going to deal with the pain? The worst thing that you could do is nurse the torment that has weighed down your soul. You know what's there. Now you need to talk to the right people, spend time reflecting and building on yourself. Find as many places and opportunities to release the pain as possible. This is very personal. There have been so many of my own secrets written in this section that you would be astonished. I have been (and am sure will continue to be) that girl who has gone through painful situation after painful situation but always comes out of the fire unscathed.

My heart has been broken and put back together over and over again. There have been so many situations that I *should not* have come back from. I understand the importance of letting go of the pain. I understand that it is crucial to my survival to partner with God. That is determined by my trusting in Him and His removal of my weight. It defines a strategy that wins battles and obliterates wars. I know that I am on the winning side, so even in the event of death, I'm still going to be winning on the other side of this life. Not everyone gets to the point where they can say that they release and let go of the weight of pain that separation or divorce can induce. Letting go is not easy, but it is necessary for your survival. You were made to soar to unknown heights, but you need to be weightless to soar. Now you have an opportunity to do things better than you did when your marriage took a turn for the worst. Identify and shift negative patterns in behaviour, speech and mentality. I know you can do it! Deep down within you is the ability to kill your past cycle for the betterment of your future. Do it for you, your family and everyone that is connected to you. Only you can impact them in a great and long-lasting way for a thousand lifetimes.

Grow

Always be determined to have a growth mindset. We females are overly emotional creatures (that doesn't mean that men aren't, for argument's sake), so it's easy to get caught up in vindictive antics where separation and disputes are concerned. One thing that I firmly believe and have observed is that when you put your mindset in the right place, then you will position yourself to receive ten times more than what you lost. I've seen it happen so many times. God honours integrity. When you do the right thing when no one else is watching. When you don't cut corners. When you say what you mean. When you do what you say. There are power and strength in that. Flourish in your mind and spirit, and watch it permeate every area of your life.

You don't have to respond to every negative word, do tit-for-tat and get everyone on your side. Instead, go on a retreat and get some alone time. Nurse yourself. Take your time with God. It's what He wants for you. Take the focus off of the people who are disapproving. Maybe it's the family of your ex-husband. Maybe it's the church community that you were both connected with. Their opinions of you don't matter if they couldn't walk a mile in your shoes. It's okay for them to have an opinion, but only you have to make the journey. Be silent. Be focused on cultivating a future that is filled with greatness. Don't give your peace away. *Grow!*

Prayer and Meditation

Let's pray and reflect using the mirror.

Dear Heavenly Father,

Please make me brave enough to walk a new path, free of shame. Take away the fear and anxiety of the things to come. Show me how to break the toxic cycles that I have perpetuated in my past. Give me the strength and confidence to leave the mask behind as I completely embrace your liberty from all of the weight and pain of my past. I look to you for guidance as you take me on a journey that I have never travelled, and I trust that it will all work together for my good.

In Jesus' name, Amen.

FOURTEEN

SECRETS THAT SAVE

§

I've always been outspoken and vocal, but I've learnt (as a wife) not every secret is a bad one. Knowing when to *shhhhh* is an invaluable skill. It could save your marriage. It could unite your family. It could uphold peace. If you are a wild woman, like me, holding your tongue could take incredible discipline. Especially if emotions are involved or tensions are running high. That time when your husband says something that hurts you and all you want to do is hurt him back. Doing so could be the first step in the breakdown of your marriage. Honestly, there is value in the virtue of wisdom.

What to Share and What Not To

Maybe you're inclined to speak too soon? Or maybe you hesitate for so long that you are misunderstood? Timing can be just as important as what has been said or not. Learning how, when and what to say, sometimes, is half the problem solved. On our journey to learning, discovering more about our husbands (which, might I add, is a lifelong one) clarifies your actions crucial to collective growth.

For example, "Babe, sometimes I get a little anxious, and it's the reason why I blurt out whatever comes to my head," is a sentence that I have used in my relationship from time to time. It has helped my husband to understand me better. Having the necessary conversations will make a massive difference in how patient you are with one another's growth and help you to better understand why they respond to things the way that they do. It's always more helpful to have these discussions when you're relaxed. No one thinks straight when they are furious. Timing is everything.

What is sacred in your marriage? Do you consciously discuss what you would like to be kept between you both? It's important to make sure certain aspects of your husband's character, journey and soul are protected by your silence (and obviously vice versa). Guessing what's sacred is risky. I always emphasise having the necessary conversations to avoid breaking trust later on. What you may consider trivial may be something of great importance to him and the same for you. When you are clear about what you both value, then you prevent turmoil in your relationship. Protect your marriage. Not everyone will have the best intentions for you and your husband. Some people may deliberately want to sabotage your relationship, and for others it may be an accidental lack of foresight. It could be their perspective based on their status in life (i.e. single, in a complicated relationship etc.). Whatever their reasoning, wisdom lies in your ability to test the spirit of the advice that they are sharing.

The Power of the Tongue

It's a little organ, but it can bring down kings and destroy nations; in the same sense, it can also do the opposite: "Death and life are in the power of the tongue, And those who love it will eat its fruit."[75] When you know the power of words, then you can know how to use that powerful weapon, that is, the tongue. Will you use it to build? Will you use it to break? When pain erodes your soul, it starts to become evident in the things that you say. Healing has to take place deep within. Be deliberate with how you use your tongue. Use it to inspire, uplift, sustain and preserve life.

What's Your Language?

When you don't understand who you are, it is apparent in your language. How you speak about yourself, others, circumstances and God reflects strongly on how you value yourself.

> **JOURNAL**
>
> - Are you inspiring or negative?
> - What inspires you?
> - Do you talk a lot?
> - Do you journal?
> - Who are your closest friends? Why?
> - Can you trust them to keep your secrets?
> - Have you shared secrets that should not have been shared? What were the repercussions?
> - What have you learnt from the outcome of sharing the secrets that you should have kept?

---

[75] Proverbs 18:21 (NKJV)

What do you expose yourself to? (see Chapter 3, *Who Am I… Again?*) It is all there on your tongue. It starts in the heart and mind, then it flows to the tongue: "For as he thinketh in his heart, so is he…[76]"

I always say that whatever you tell yourself is true. There are so many suffering unnecessarily because of their perspective of their value. They tell themselves, *I'm a failure,* in the way that they speak. They tell themselves, *my marriage is doomed. This is irreparable,* or even, *I'm not going to survive this.* They say this in so many ways… without even saying the actual words. They restrict or cancel opportunities with their perspectives and approach. Lacking foresight, they suffocate relationships because they don't recognise their value. You need to understand this if you don't get anything else from the words written in this book. The most powerful secret that will save you is knowing your value in Christ and operating from that place. Speak to your storms like you know that God is the controller of the storms. Let faith ooze from your pores. Don't shrink back. You are a winner. Whatever valleys and mountains you go through are nothing compared to the prize you are about to gain. Focus on the prize.

Who Are You Talking To?

Marriage is fragile. When trust is broken, it is incredibly hard to restore. Speaking about marital issues to anyone who will listen is dangerous. One of the most invaluable principles that still strengthens marriage is knowing who to share information with.

When your husband does something that angers or irritates you, it is wise not to share it with your whole family, friends etc. Why? Because long after you've jointly overcome the issue, it could still tarnish their perspective of him. It's always wiser to find someone removed

---

[76] Proverbs 23:7 (KJV)

emotionally from your relationship and have discussions with them. Always make it a point to *agree* on who you would like to support and advise you, because they could strengthen or weaken the marriage.

People that speak into your marriage have a lot of power through influence, consciously or subconsciously. Be a wise woman who understands that your role as a wife is crucial and pivotal to your marriage's success as a whole. You give birth to so many things that can bless your marriage (if you let them). Now, as we've come to the end of the book, I pray that you leave the masks behind and embrace the beauty of your true reflection. Embrace your true reflection and do it without shame. See the brilliance and beauty in every aspect of your journey – including the painful aspects. Embrace your newfound freedom, and don't allow anything to pull you back into a place of obscurity or confusion again. Always hold onto the truth that if God sets you free, then you are free unreservedly and indefinitely (without clauses or debate). No more prisons. No more shame and no more shadows. Shine!

Prayer and Meditation

Let's pray and reflect using the mirror.

Dear Heavenly Father,

May my tongue be life-giving, uplifting and wise. Show me how to use my tongue to produce fruitfulness, sincerity and clarity. Teach me how to be deliberate about rejecting gossiping, slanderous and malicious talk. Please provide me with opportunities to connect with others who are willing to do the same. Show me uplifting ways to protect, build and edify others with the words that I speak.

In Jesus' name, Amen.

CONCLUSION

§

All the principles, guidance, inspiration and support within this book are based on teachings from the Bible. I have experienced proven and impactful transformation in my life due to everything that has been imparted in this prolific, life-changing book. If you have felt like you want to become more acquainted with God on a deeper level, you have an opportunity to do so by inviting Him into your life on a more intimate level. Let's start with prayer…

> *Dear Heavenly Father,*
> *I admit that I need you and that I need a deeper relationship with you. Reveal yourself to me in an enriching and life-changing way. Show me the power, impact and value of knowing you. Please allow Jesus to become personal and real in my life. I believe and declare that Jesus is the Son of God, and I believe that through Him, abundant life overflows to me. Thank you for hearing my prayer – from my heart. I receive everything that you are.*
> *In Jesus' name, Amen.*

You can grow deeper in your faith and get support from a community of other Christians at your local church, online church communities or get in touch via www.thetwirlhub.com, and we will be happy to support you.

ABOUT THE AUTHOR

Salomé is the founder of a women's movement, TWIRL (Thriving Women In Real Life), a businesswoman, motivational speaker and author of *A Whole New Bundle of Love*. A true Renaissance woman, Salomé balances her passions and work with the demands of mother and wifehood, sharing tools, resources and opportunities with other women to help them thrive. Drawing heavily on candid conversations with prolific and unconventional women of faith and her own wealth of experience, Salomé helps women pinpoint and broaden their own success in all aspects of their lives. She is determined to inspire women to find their voice and live, liberated from their past pain. She is passionate about God and seeing people thrive in every area of their lives. It is her hope that this book will transform lives and relationships for years to come. Salomé lives in Essex with husband, Paul, and their two boys, Ezra and Boaz.

Printed in Great Britain
by Amazon

68064982R00210